THE

SECRET WARFARE

OF

FREEMASONRY

AGAINST

CHURCH AND STATE.

𝔗𝔯𝔞𝔫𝔰𝔩𝔞𝔱𝔢𝔡 𝔣𝔯𝔬𝔪 𝔱𝔥𝔢 𝔊𝔢𝔯𝔪𝔞𝔫.

WITH AN INTRODUCTION

Catholic Authors Press
www.CatholicAuthors.com

PREFACE.

———o———

ANY one who studies carefully the phenomena of
modern, and especially of more recent times, and
endeavours to discover the hidden spring which
directs the sequence of events, will always find his
researches lead him back to one and the same
central motive power, producing the state of mind
through which the evil spirit of the age contrives
to distort truth, history, and justice. The radical
perversion of men's minds going on around us is
indeed terribly systematic. Comparing the onward
progress of the social, political, and religious world
to that of a river, we shall find that the poison
which taints the water comes in each case from
the same source. There are, it is true, some tribu-
tary rivulets which add their quota of infection to
the main stream, but these are of secondary importance.

Human errors and passions, organised as they are
by the secret Society of Freemasonry, constitute the
chief power of this evil.

The Christian world has for many years past lulled

itself to sleep in the pleasing thought that this sinister conspiracy is, after all, not so very formidable, and is gradually becoming a mere matter of ridicule. A great mistake has been made on this subject. Even before the outbreak of the first French Revolution, Freemasonry had not so vast a power, so much internal unity, so firm a footing in influential circles, so world-wide a command of the press, as it has in our own day. It is high time to awake from sleep, and carefully to reconnoitre the forces of the enemy.

This we have attempted to do, and have drawn our information from most trustworthy sources, principally from the records of the Lodges. Furthermore, every assertion is supported by proof. Amongst these proofs, some may be found hitherto unknown, or at least unpublished in Germany; for it was during our sojourn in a foreign land that, thanks to an exceptionally fortunate chain of circumstances, we were enabled finally to unravel the mystery of this dark Association.

As we are attacking things, and not individuals, we have carefully avoided any mention of the names of persons yet living; and this reticence, dictated by Christian principle, has often obliged us merely to hint at what we would fain have expressed more definitely.

We here wish distinctly to assert, as we shall have occasion repeatedly to do in the course of this work, that we do not impute to *all* Freemasons the ultimate aims of their Secret Society. Few only are completely initiated; the greater number of the Brethren sin in ignorance. It is to be hoped, therefore, that these too may read this little book, and be enlightened as to their real position.

We will conclude, in the words of Barruel ("Mémoires pour servir à l'Histoire du Jacobinisme," vol. i. p. 20. Hamburg, 1803.):—"To whatever creed, to whatever government, to whatever class of society you belong, as soon as Jacobinism gains the ascendant, and the plans and sworn designs of the Secret Society come into operation, there is an end to your religion, your clergy, your government, and your laws, your property and your authority. All your possessions, your lands and houses, your very families and firesides, all these from that day forth you can no longer call your own."

January 4, 1873

CONTENTS.

———o———

APPENDIX.

DOCUMENTARY EVIDENCE.

b

Contents.

INTRODUCTION.

——o——

THE recent resignation by the Marquis of Ripon of the Grand Mastership, and the consequent acceptance of that office by the Prince of Wales, have drawn public attention in this country to the proceedings of Freemasonry, and have awakened a not unreasonable curiosity touching its constitution and aims. Not that the subject stands in need of such adventitious and transitory motives in order to win for itself a claim on our notice, for, considered merely as a *fact* of contemporaneous history, it merits the most serious and most careful inquiry. That a society should exist in the midst of us, which has already extended its ramifications in all quarters of the world, and embraces at this time, as we have been told, above seventeen millions of members,— that it should be compacted in visible unity by virtue of a secret oath, binding under the most terrible sanctions on each and all of its members,—that it should claim exclusive possession of an esoteric doctrine, unknown to the profane, by which the world is eventually to be freed from all its moral, social, and poli-

tical diseases, and the universal brotherhood of man
is to be regenerated into light,—that it should, while
professing to tolerate all forms of religion, yet preserve a sort of theology and a grotesque ritualism
exclusively its own,—that it should exact from all its
adherents a blind obedience to orders mysteriously
issued and secretly conveyed,—is a phenomenon so
startling, so pregnant with probable results in the
future, as to demand the closest examination.

No apology, therefore, is necessary for presenting
to the public in an English dress an account of Freemasonry which has been recently published in Germany. The reader will not fail to notice, while
perusing its pages, that the information contained
therein is principally obtained from official documents
of the body, and from the speeches of its more prominent officials in different parts of Europe. This, of
course, greatly enhances its value, and gives increased
weight to the conclusions at which the author has
arrived. Indeed, it can scarcely now be doubted
that the covert aims of this remarkable body are
directed to the ultimate subversion of all altars and
thrones, and to a complete revolution in the moral
and social life, as at present established. It is true
that the main efforts of Freemasonry are directed to
the extirpation of the Catholic Church, if possible ;
and, failing this, to the greatest practical diminution
of her influence over the souls of men, by restricting
her liberty of action, undermining her supremacy
over the consciences of her children, and most

especially by depriving her of her divinely appointed office as schoolmistress of youth. But one
very sufficient reason for this policy is to be discovered in the fact that the Catholic Church is the
mainstay of constituted authority, and that to her
authority it is, even in non-Catholic states, principally
owing that the moral laws and social as well as
political life which were originally the products of the
Christian faith, still retain their hold on the public
conscience, and continue to mould and animate
modern society. Freemasonry, therefore, is clear-
headed enough to perceive that the Catholic Church
is the greatest existing hindrance to the success of its
projects, and that, if once it could remove her out of
the way, its eventual triumph would only be a question of time. But it does not essay a wrestling-
match with that Church alone ; Christianity itself, as
a system of revealed truths, must be uprooted, in
order that the new gospel may be planted in its
place, and the supposed dupes of an effete superstition may be transformed into veritable Gnostics—into
children of the new light.

It is not for one moment to be supposed that all
the seventeen million members of this secret association are aware of the ultimate issues contemplated
by the more thoroughly initiated. There is a vast
majority, doubtless, which lives and dies in those
inferior grades in which nothing is presented to the
mind that might cause too rude a shock to religious
prejudice, and to a loyalty as yet unweaned. Many,

ıt may be well imagined, are kept in this state of
Gnostic infancy, because they are by nature deprived
of that eagle eye which can bear unflinching the full
light of the new revelation. For such there is provided a *disciplina arcani,* by which they are hood-
winked to the end ; and Freemasonry, to these
apprentices in the Craft, is little else than a friendly
confederation occupied in offices of mutual help and
charity. Very much the same may be said of those
exalted personages who are induced to assume the
apron. There are honorary degrees astutely provided for them, and their knowledge of the esoteric
teaching is in inverse proportion to their dignity of
order. They are, nevertheless, eminently useful, for
they serve at once as pledges of respectability, and
as decoys for the association to which they are thus
affiliated. They at once attract others to follow
in their footsteps by their powerful example, and
they themselves, as well as others outside, are lulled
into a false security by the simple fact of their initiation. It is to be feared that there are some among
this class who are more or less aware of the dangers
by which they are environed, and join the Society
either with the cowardly and fallacious hope of being
able to direct what they dare not confront, or perhaps, in some cases, with the baser motive of eventually securing themselves at the expense of their
country and of the stability of modern society.

Comparatively small, however, is the number of
those before whose eyes the veil of symbol and fan-

tastic rite is raised, and the real object to which they have dedicated themselves blindfold is openly revealed. Even these must submit to a long course of patient preparation, during which the first principles of religion and loyalty are gradually and dexterously eradicated, ere they are deemed worthy of admission to that grade of Manichean sanctity (Kadosh), which supposes the votary to be prepared for unshrinking obedience to the commandments of this new gospel of darkness.

But here we are met with a difficulty which must be fairly confronted, at least if the present translation from the German is to answer the purpose for which it is now presented to the English public. It is generally supposed amongst us that English Freemasonry is totally distinct and different from that which has already done so much mischief on the Continent, and is preparing yet more gigantic evils for a future time. Let it be as evil abroad as its most uncompromising enemies have described it, here in England, at least, men may say, it is quite innocuous, and, however fantastic may be its outer forms, and however unnecessarily secret may be its bond of union, it is really little else than a charitable institution. There is, doubtless, an element of truth in this general belief. The English character could not easily be shaped to ends such as are contemplated in the occult philosophy of the higher grades. It is loyal and naturally religious, and would not brook an unveiled conspiracy against the altar and the throne.

Moreover it is eminently practical, and could not easily be brought to sanction a proclamation of war against property and the recognised principles of social and political life. Would it then be matter of surprise if it should turn out that the number of those who have been admitted in our country into that thirtieth degree of full enlightenment is very small indeed? It may be that by far the majority of English Freemasons do not get beyond the degree of mere apprenticeship, and are utterly unsuspicious of the revolutionary and atheistic schemes that are being insidiously pushed on to their final issues by more knowing associates, while they give the prestige of respectability and their collective weight to a body that trades upon their ignorance and simplicity. Nevertheless, after all that may be pleaded in favour of the exceptional character commonly attributed to English Freemasonry, there is, it must be owned, another side of the question which is deserving of the gravest consideration.

So far as Catholics are concerned, the question has been already settled. No Catholic can enroll himself in a secret society without incurring excommunication ; and no Freemason can be received into the fold of Christ, unless he has previously made up his mind to withdraw altogether from such an association. The course of ecclesiastical legislation is sufficiently plain, and every true child of the Church would be prepared to yield unconditional submission to its provisions. But there are many, nevertheless, who, while ready to accept on faith the judgment of the Church, are puzzled to discover a sufficient reason for such prohibition. It may be that they are personally acquainted with members of the Craft whose loyalty is undoubted, whose moral and social character are exemplary. The persons in question appear, moreover, to be faithful and conscientious members of the religious communion to which they have attached themselves, and with evident sincerity maintain that there is nothing in Freemasonry, *so far as they know*, which interferes with a man's duty to his God, his king, his country, his family, himself. Nay, there have been cases in which, after conversion to the Church, such persons have conscientiously asserted that there was nothing in the principles of Freemasonry, as made known to them, which in their judgment militated against the system of faith and morals imposed upon them by virtue of their new allegiance. What is there to be said in answer to such facts ? Is it possible to assign any reason, appreciable by the common run of men and by those who are not versed in theology, why the Church has with unwavering severity condemned such associations ?

That men of lealty, honour, and virtue have enrolled, and do enrol themselves still, among the members of this Craft, cannot be denied ; that they would not do violence to their conscience by remaining in a body which they knew to proclaim a revolt against religion, constituted authority, and the moral law, we have no sufficient reason to doubt; that consequently they are excusable in the sight of God, if they are non-Catholics, may be confidently believed; that they may even use their fellowship with evil, hidden from their sight, for the more practical exercise of a noble philanthropy, few, if any, would be loth to acknowledge; yet it is undeniable, notwithstanding, that they are, however unconsciously, violating one of the most vital principles of the natural law by giving their name to a secret confederation. For nò man has a right to yield up his moral liberty into the hands of an unknown and self-constituted authority. It is not permitted to any one that he should take an oath in the dark, or unreservedly submit himself to an authority whose claims he is unable antecedently to gauge. Each one of us is individually responsible for his own actions; nor can such responsibility be transferred without sin, save to an authority constituted by God, and then only so far as is permitted by an express divine sanction. To promise silence with regard to teaching and a course of action about which we know absolutely nothing at the time we make the promise, is intrinsically evil. When, moreover, this secrecy is enforced by the sanction of an oath—the most solemn and indissoluble bond by which the freedom of the will can be fettered—the heinousness of the crime is proportionally increased. An example—hypothetical, if you please—will serve to illustrate what one would have supposed, save for the facts alluded to

above, sufficiently plain in itself. Suppose the case
of a man who, on entering a secret society, pledges
himself by a fearful oath not to reveal to any one the
teaching or commands which may afterwards be
communicated to him. After a time he gets to know
that he is associated in a widely-spread conspiracy
against kings, governments, property, and all forms
of religion as at present constituted. He receives,
later on, an order to dog the footsteps of a given
individual, till he can find a safe occasion to assas-
sinate his victim. What is he to do, if the principle
of right within him has not already been under-
mined? He can take no counsel outside the con-
clave of conspirators, because he has bound himself
to secrecy. His liberty of action is fettered, because
he has submitted to become the slave of an unknown
oligarchy. His conscience revolts against the crime,
but how can he escape from its commission? He
must either withdraw from the Society, with serious
inconvenience to himself; or violate his oath and
abide the certain consequences; or refuse obedience,
and incur thereby the terrible punishment which
irresponsible authority has decreed for such delin-
quency. He stands in peril of his life if he refuses;
poignant remorse and a gradual extinction of the
moral sense infallibly await him if he should consent.
No man has a right to reduce himself of his own
free will to the bare possibility of such a terrible
alternative. The act is intrinsically immoral, nor
can any possible combination of motives or circum-

stances lessen, much less destroy, its moral turpitude. It is true that implicit obedience, the surrender of free will, is, according to Catholic teaching, one of the evangelical counsels, but not to an unknown and self-constituted authority. The superiors whom the religious professes to obey are appointed according to fixed laws which have received the solemn approbation of the Church. Neither are there any secrets whose disclosure is reserved for after years. There are no *monita secreta* in any Orders or Congregations of regulars which have received the Church's sanction ; these are reserved for secret societies. On the contrary, the postulant for admission is submitted to a long probation, during which it is a duty enforced upon him to study all the rules and constitutions of the body, and to make himself practically acquainted with its life and aims. Nothing is kept back. Then, and not till then, is he permitted, should he still wish it, to take his vows. But even after his formal admission his obedience is not wholly unconditional. It is always understood·by all, and often expressly stated in the rules, that he is in no case bound to obey an order which he judges to involve the commission of sin. Thus ample reservation is made for the supremacy of conscience, seeing that the submission of the will extends only to actions in themselves either indifferent or good, and introduces those who yield it, so far as human weakness and infirmity in this its transitory state of trial may permit, to that highest degree of liberty, as St Austin defines it—immunity from sin. But to bind the will unconditionally to an unknown oligarchy, unsanctioned by civil or ecclesiastical authority,—to seal one's tongue for ever by a fearful oath with regard to an esoteric philosophy to be gradually revealed hereafter, is equally a violation of the natural law and of the divine commands; while it inevitably tends to weaken, and eventually destroy, the security of social, civil, and ecclesiastical institutions. It establishes a hidden empire within the empire, a hidden family within the family, a hidden sect within all religious communions. Such an association may strive to caricature the Church's catholicity, but it dares not be, like her, as a "city seated on a mountain which cannot be hid " (St Matt. v. 14).

There is another point about which Catholics must not allow themselves to be deceived. Freemasonry, wherever it may have taken up its habitation, and however it may be modified by the exigencies of the moment or the pressure of public opinion, is the avowed enemy of the Catholic Church. It is quite possible that here in England this secret confederation may have accommodated itself somewhat, for the present, to what it would call the prejudices of the people. But on this one question it is outspoken and unreserved, confident in the sympathies of a vast majority. At a meeting of the Provincial Grand Lodge of Warwickshire, held under the presidency of Lord Leigh, Brother J. C. Parkinson, Grand Deacon of the Lodge, and Grand Master of the Provincial

Grand Lodge of Middlesex, in responding to the
toast of the " Rulers of the Craft," said that while he
regretted the retirement of the Marquis of Ripon, he
could not share the naïve astonishment of some at
being told that a Roman Catholic might not continue
to fill a leading position in the Craft. *The fact was,
that the two systems of Romanism and Masonry were not
only incompatible, but were radically opposed.*"[1] Again,
at a meeting of the " Great City " Lodge, held at the
Cannon Street Terminus Hotel, the present Lord
Mayor of London, in response to the toast " Success
to the Great City Lodge," proposed by the same
ubiquitous Brother Parkinson, let drop, during the
course of his speech, the following remarks : "The present time was a most eventful one, and not the less for
the great contest raging between darkness and light.
Popery and the Pope himself were determined to
put down freedom and good-will ; but this country
and the Prince of Wales had determined that light
(Gnostic ?) should prevail, and that everything that
was good, and graceful, and beneficial should be put
forward, and stand before all mankind." Another
Freemason orator, Brother Hutton, on the same occasion, surpassing the Lord Mayor himself in the bold
fervour of his rhetoric, declared " it was well known
that the liberties of the world were threatened when
the Ultramontanes were taking counsel together, and
the broad issue was between the darkness of priestcraft and the intelligence and progress of our na-

[1] *Manchester Guardian,* October 8, 1874.

tion,"[1] as duly cared for and nourished, doubtless, by Masonic craft.

It is impossible that Catholics should, after these open declarations, complain of any reticence on the part of the officials connected with English Free-masonry. These latter tell the faithful, as plain as men can speak, that Freemasonry is incompatible with Catholic belief and practice,—that a contest had now begun in right earnest between the "darkness" of the Church and the "light" of their regenerating Craft, — and that the Prince of Wales, as Grand Master, is determined, in union with his brother Masons, to ensure the triumph of the light. Can it be credited, after this, that there are Catholics to be found simple enough to believe,—not that there are innocuous and estimable men among the Craft, which no one would be inclined to deny,—but that English Freemasonry is quite distinct from, and independent of, Continental Freemasonry in constitution and object? Can they for one moment believe that a society, whose only aim is the practical exercise of charity and mutual philanthropy, would require an oath of secrecy, adopt a peculiar ritual, establish methods of mutual recognition concealed from the profane, all for the mere purpose of organising a system of outdoor relief? Is there, or is there not, a solidarity between the home and foreign Lodges? Can it be denied that the most advanced and revo-lutionary Lodge in the whole Craft originally sprung

[1] *The Times,* March 22, 1875.

from British soil? English Freemasonry, indeed, has been contented in days gone by to pass for a mere benevolent society, for it could find no adversary worthy of its energies. But now that the Church is daily gaining strength and influence in our land, it has thrown the mask aside, and partially, at least, reveals its purposes. Catholics have themselves alone to blame if they continue to be duped by the declarations of mere novices, or by the show of moderation enforced till now upon the Craft by the tone of public thought.

But the present translation is not intended for Catholics only. All those who sincerely profess the Christian religion, and accept it as a divine revelation, are equally bound to inform themselves about the constitution and aims of an association which threatens the existence of positive religion under every form; while all those who love their country, reverence established authority, and realise the paramount influence of family ties in promoting the education, stability, and true happiness of a people, are in like manner bound to examine whether the accusations which have been made against Freemasonry are true, viz., that its endeavours are directed to the revolutionising of the first, the subversion of the second, and the entire extinction of the third.

It is quite plain, moreover, that every one who believes in the authority of conscience and in the existence of a natural law, however he may disregard the prohibitions of the Papal See, is never-

theless morally bound to determine within himself
whether it is right and lawful for him to become a
member of this Association before taking the irre-
vocable step. Is it ever permissible to join a body
which exacts on admission an oath of secrecy as
regards its proceedings, plans, aims, teaching? If
these are innocent, the oath is useless, and therefore
wrong; if they are not innocent, the oath is an immoral restraint of liberty, and therefore a 'graver
offence against the first principles of right. Furthermore, there is presumptive evidence in favour of the
second hypothesis; for it is a characteristic of evil
that it ever shuns the light: *cæcum omne scelus*.
Practices of mere philanthropy and Christian charity
can only be impeded by the introduction of a secret
oath, and can, therefore, never supply a plausible
reason for its imposition. Under such circumstances, no one can advisedly join a secret society
without violating the plain dictates of his conscience;
for to take an oath without a plain necessity is
intrinsically evil.

But the evidence contained in the little work which
is now set before the reader is of such a kind as to
exclude all reasonable doubt concerning the aims of
Freemasonry. It is plainly enough an organised
conspiracy against all authority, civil or ecclesiastical, and against the first principles of Christian
society as at present constituted, even though the
majority of its members may be kept in convenient
ignorance of the facts. The political and religious

millennium, which it is striving with fullest energy to introduce, has been partially realised already in the French Revolution of 1792, and in the temporary Communism which spread terror through the length and breadth of " Fair France " in more recent times. Its influence in this country is now being exercised in proportion to the strength and persistency of the Catholic revival, which is making itself more and more felt among us every day we live. Freemasonry in England is no longer quiescent, for the times and the condition of things are changed. It now stands forth partially unmasked, and proclaims an internecine war with the Church of God, whenever an opportunity presents itself. Yes ; for the moment, it is true, the Catholic Church is the one object of its machinations. But why ? Because, first of all, it knows too well that its avowed efforts chime in with the tone of public opinion in this country ; and then, in the second place, because it is fully persuaded that if it can but succeed against this its most formidable enemy, it will be able to make short work of all other communions professing themselves Christian. It is too astute not to perceive that the fate of Christianity is indissolubly bound up with the fortunes of the Papal See ; and with consummate craft it makes use of the divisions of Christendom to uproot, if that were possible, the faith and very name of Christ. The principles which it is disseminating everywhere under the rose with such signal success, are antagonistic to all supernatural religion under whatever form ; nay, even to the primary dictates of natural religion.

As many may feel inclined to be sceptical about the truth of these assertions, and of the dismal revelations made in the following pages, and as a yet greater number may still encourage in themselves the fond delusion that English Freemasonry is not chargeable with the revolutionary and atheistic intentions which, as they are willing to allow, animate the Continental Lodges, it will not be out of place to set the whole matter more clearly before the reader. Of course it cannot be expected that direct and formal proof of these assertions can be produced in the case of a confederation which conceals its inner teaching and designs from the public eye by a solemn oath of secrecy, imposed on all its members under the most fearful sanctions ; but it may be possible to arrive at a judgment, practically certain, in another way.

Suppose, for one moment, that the alleged charges against Freemasonry in general, and in consequence against English Freemasonry, as forming an integral part of, and remaining in communion with, the other sections of the Craft, are really true. For the sake of the argument let it be assumed that this secret brotherhood is bent upon subverting the altar, the throne, the family ; that it aims at destroying all authority, and at building up upon the ruins of Christian civilisation a universal communism from which all belief in God and in the fundamental principles of morality is to be rigorously excluded. The question, we will suppose, is mooted among the leading spirits of the sect as to how England can be best prepared for this atheistic millennium—as to the safest means to be adopted for inducing her eventually to aid in its establishment.   They know (as every one knows) that there is a deep religious sentiment embedded in the natural character of the people, that there is also a conspicuous respect for law and constituted authority; and, finally, that the spirit of the family, nowhere more cherished, has been of long time the salt which has preserved it from corruption and dissolution.   It is a nation more pertinacious in its prejudices than consistent in its logic—more influenced by its feelings than its intellect.   Proud of its traditions, suspicious of changes, distrustful of theories, eminently sensitive in its honour, wedded to home and ties of family, the secret directors of " the Craft " would see the un-wisdom of revealing to it for the present the veiled features of the false prophet.   But there is a weak point where the enemy perceives a possibility of en-trance—England is distracted by the conflicting claims of a thousand sects.   Its Establishment is los-ing day by day its claim to be the chosen religion of the great majority ; and because of that conservatism which is a necessity of its being, does not make full public proof of that power which it still retains.   The communions which have separated from it are jealous of its influence and clamorous against its privileges. Yet all are united in claiming the unrestricted right of private judgment, in denouncing what they term

Popery, and in opposing themselves to its reviving influence.

With such facts to deal with, how would Free-masonry prepare its plans of eventual triumph, if its aims be such as have been supposed ? It may, of course, attack the Catholic Church as openly and as vigorously as it pleases, for, in so doing, it is in perfect harmony with the spirit of the times. It may do its best also against Ritualism with equal safety, for the mind of the nation identifies this latter with the former. But further than this it dares not go at present. Open assaults on government, religion, social distinctions, rank, military establishments, may do very well in other countries, but they will not do here. The people are not as yet prepared for them, and, were their eyes to be prematurely opened, might become troublesome, if not dangerous. All hope, therefore, must be in the future ; and for the future generation provision must be made. Luckily the opportunity presents itself spontaneously. The whole country, within this present generation, has been agitated on the subject of primary education, and it was no sooner made apparent that the public mind was turned in that direction, than the matter, of course, assumed a prominent place in political programmes, and became at once what is called a party question. The main hindrance in the way of a final adjustment was what has been ˙called the religious difficulty. By an arrangement, however, which did credit to the eminent statesman who contrived it, the

difficulty was fairly met and overcome. It is true
that the legislative measure in which that arrangement was included confined religious and moral instruction within comparatively narrow limits, practically encouraged the neglect of it, and reduced it to
the level of a sort of after-dinner entertainment. Yet
it left the parents of the child free to send it to a
school whose training was in accord with the dictates
of their conscience ; while it provided secular schools
for the benefit of those who might consider that
religious belief had no legitimate place in the education of their children. Freemasonry, if its designs
are such as we have supposed, would have gained
much already from those concessions, for religion has
been thereby excluded from the schools supported
by the State, as a recognised and essential part of
their educational course. But this is as nothing
compared with what it would require for the eventual
accomplishment of its designs. It is perspicacious
enough to perceive that, while Catholic schools would
continue to receive State support, the provisions of
the Bill would offer little impediment to a Church
whose whole education is founded on a definite creed,
and on the basis of an objective and supernatural
morality. It is not blind to the fact, moreover, that
the English Establishment persistently endeavours,
in spite of its internal disunion, to nourish religious
ideas and obedience to the natural law among its
scholars. Under these adverse circumstances, what
is its best policy of action ? Agitate for a repeal of

the twenty-fifth clause—promote with unremitting energy the extension of purely secular schools in all our principal centres—prepare public opinion by degrees for a system of compulsory education—then, when all is ready, induce the State to recognise secular schools alone as answering to its imperial demands, and the triumph will be complete. The children of the entire population will be driven by force of law into schools where they will be, by stern necessity, brought up in utter ignorance of God, of Christian obedience, of Christian morality.

It is, indeed, a strange and most unpleasing fact that Freemasonry should have been aided in these its projects (if such they be, and there can scarcely be a doubt that such they are), by the even boisterous co-operation of political Dissenters. Strange, of a truth, that the spiritual heirs of ancestors who were worthily distinguished for their personal love of the Divine Redeemer should clamour for the exclusion of the very name of Christ and of God, of heaven and hell, from schoolrooms subsidised by the State, rather than consent that a single child, by means of aid from Government, should learn of Christ and duty from the lips of a Catholic or Anglican schoolmaster. It is idle to assert, considering what the tendencies of human nature are, that the influences of the Sunday-school, even were its sphere of action enlarged a thousand-fold, could supply the •need of moral and religious instruction. It is yet more idle to pretend that parents who are striving from early morn till

night to provide the bare necessaries of life for themselves and families, and return home only for food
and sleep, could take in hand this all-important duty,
or hope to succeed if they attempted it. If these
Nonconformist communions, owing to past remiss-
ness in providing for the education of the poor children belonging to their several persuasions, find to
their cost that the English Establishment and the
Catholic Church come in for the lion's share in the
distribution of State grants, would it not be nobler
and more honourable to acknowledge their former
deficiency, and enter upon a plan of generous rivalry
with the religious bodies above mentioned, by employing the vast funds at their disposal in the not
least solid, because least ostentatious, effort to spread
the knowledge of religious and moral truth among
their own people in accordance with their several
peculiar tenets, rather than to follow the example of
Samson, and submit to their own annihilation with
cheerfulness, provided that Catholic and Ritualist are
involved in the universal ruin? Let them be assured
that the powerful and widely-extended means which
Freemasonry has gained, and ceaselessly uses, for
influencing public opinion, have not been *as yet*
directed against themselves, because " the Craft "
knows full well that they will become its easy prey
when they stand alone in the arena; " it keeps them,
like an ape, in the corner of its jaw; first mouthed,
to be last swallowed ; when it needs what you have
gleaned, it is but squeezing you, and, sponge, you

shall be dry again." Are you, the Nonconformists of England, prepared to pave a way for its victory over religion, civil and social order, and the first princi-ples of morality? Are you really conscious of what you are preparing for your country and for your own co-religionists, while supporting with the weight you at present possess a system of what is called secular education, from which all mention of God and of future reward and punishment, and the sweet influences of your Redeemer's love, are rigorously banished? Do you wish to see England given over captive to an unfeeling infidelity, and all reverence for authority, all filial obedience, all distinctions of social grade, the pure influences of home, the recogni-tion of a moral law, universally cast into the limbo of obsolete prejudices and so-called mediæval supersti-tions? Yet, in the actual state of things, no more effectual aid could be given to such detestable designs than that which you offer by the policy you are pur-suing in the vital question of national education.

No Catholic would feel disposed to accuse even those Nonconformists who have adopted this un-happy policy of a complicity with such detestable designs ; and it would be yet more unjustifiable to lay it to the charge of the whole body of Dissenters, seeing that they are by no means unanimous upon the point in question. Moreover, their general pro-fessions of peculiar devotion to the world's Divine Redeemer, the life of unworldliness and piety which they advocate and strive to maintain according to the light that is in them, their system of home training, which, till recently at all events, rather discouraged secular learning than otherwise, on the ground that it was prejudicial to the principles of vital religion, would secure them from so hasty a judgment.   It was for this reason that, at the outset of the present digression, distinct mention was made of *political* Dissenters.   Nevertheless, repeated facts have unhappily conspired to prove that the policy referred to is more generally adopted by the members of these bodies than their religious professions would have led us to anticipate.   Can it be that here too in England, as in Germany and Switzerland, the Protestant sects are yielding up one by one the Christian tenets which they at first retained to the imperious demands of popular indifferentism and hatred of dogmatic truth ?

But, to return to the main subject in hand,—let us resume the hypothesis already made.   If it be true, Freemasonry in this country, as elsewhere, is bent upon the subversion, not of the altar only, but of the throne, of distinctions of rank, and generally of all civil authority.   It knows that it has undertaken a difficult task ; for the English are naturally a loyal people, cling to traditions of the past, and have an instinctive reverence for the authority of law.   How, under these circumstances, would it set about the work which it has proposed to itself, supposing it to be endowed with that astuteness for which its accusers give it credit ?   It would obviously take first

of all to mining and sapping, far too wise to venture
at once on an open assault. And what, it may be
asked, would be the safest method of conducting
this insidious strategy? The easiest step to begin
with would be to take advantage of the popular feeling in favour of what is called the liberty of the
press, and subject every action of government, every
judgment of the courts of law, every principle of
religion, ethics, philosophy, to an indiscriminate
criticism, scattered broadcast through the length and
breadth of the land. And we may imagine that the
secret orders of "the Craft" would be couched in such
terms as, these :—Habituate the unlearned to sit in
judgment on the learned, the ruled to question the
acts of their rulers, the hands to arraign the heads,—
train the people, uneducated and proportionally im-
pulsive, to claim to themselves the right of forming,
each one for himself, peremptory opinions upon every
subject, even upon questions whose perplexity appal
the wisest and most experienced,—accustom them
to put themselves on a fancied mental equality with
statesmen, diplomatists, legislators, judges, generals,
bishops, magistrates, doctors, lawyers,—help them
along this road of upstart folly by abundant use of
ridicule, of sneers, contemptuous depreciation, dressed
up in glittering and nervous style, directed against
those who stand at the helm of government, or are
found in authority of place and dignity. Much will
have been gained ; because modesty and self-knowledge will be thus expelled, in order to make way for

a spirit of self-sufficiency and ignorant imperiousness
of thought and will. After this, proceed to inoculate
the masses with the idea that they are the fountain
of all authority, and that the elected or hereditary
legislators of the country are the mere creatures of
their will and exponents of their wisdom. They will
soon learn to despise quality, and value quantity ; to
assume as a first principle that wisdom must yield to
numbers, right to might. By these means you will
have well prepared the soil. Now set on foot an agitation for universal suffrage and vote by ballot,—
claim a place for unlearned labour in the Senate of
the nation,—inculcate the fatal notion that the task
of legislation is not an onerous and responsible duty,
demanding from those who undertake it exceptional
qualifications, but an enviable privilege, easy and
open to all, even the least informed, the fitting toy of
popular caprice,—awaken a general prejudice against
old forms, pageants, guilds, civic institutions, which,
even when deprived of their original meaning, have
nevertheless so powerful an influence in associating
the feelings and imagination of a people with the
traditions of a glorious past,—modernise those
which, by reason of their acknowledged value, you
dare not overthrow,—throw contempt and ridicule
on all forms of religious belief that have strength in
them enough to vindicate God's presence in the
world,—put all the weights of wit, of sceptical criticism, of taking, epigrammatic style, of poetry, fiction,
periodical literature, in the scale of worldliness, ma-

terialism, and a loose morality, holding, moreover, an uneven balance,—make your way with ever increasing numbers into the staff of journalists, and cease not to inoculate the public with infidel conceits and emasculated ethics, borrowed from those superficial sophists whose reputation it has been your business to create,—the people will soon be made ready for the manifestation of the light. ' One great difficulty, it is true, awaits us yet, and it must be overcome by gradual and stealthy action. It arises from those influences of home, that spirit of the family, which have hitherto preserved England from the contagion of a revolutionary earthquake. One important advance has been made towards its destruction. The foundation of social life has been already shaken by the recent law which has legalised divorce, and given to the civil authority a power of putting asunder those whom God has indissolubly joined together. Follow up this advantage by an agitation for women's rights,—allure them to the platform and committee-room, while you seduce them from the nursery,—rob them of the needle, and substitute the lancet or the pestle,—strip them of that retiring modesty and refinement of feeling which make them a magnet of attraction round the family hearth, and transform them into boisterous men in all but the outward dress, and it will not be long before this last hindrance will be effectually removed.

Meanwhile excite, encourage every conflict of

labour with capital,—propagate trade unions, assume
the direction of them wherever you can,—unite them
in a general confederation, and practically affiliate
them to the Craft. Miss no opportunity that may
arise of bringing into contempt, and exciting popular
indignation against, the authority of judge and magi-
strate. Lastly, never lose sight of the principle that
the military forces are inimical to the success of the
Masonic millennium. Direct public opinion, therefore, in favour of retrenchment, push on every measure tending to extinguish that *esprit de corps* which
makes the English army and navy so formidable alike
to external and internal enemies, and use every effort
to bring the profession of arms into disrepute among
the humbler classes of society. Everything is con-
spiring to crown our efforts, brothers of the Craft,
with final success. Yet a little, and the time will
have arrived for the revelation and practical realisation of our great Gnostic secret; and we shall see
with our eyes the erection of our altar to the unknown on the ruins of an effete Christianity; while
from out the sepulchre of buried kings, of buried
governments, of a buried civilisation, shall arise the
Phœnix of one undivided Republic; one universal
Brotherhood, with the apron, mallet, triangle, and
two mystic pillars, established for ever as the world's
sole regalia.

It were here well, perhaps, to pause and examine
into the present success of the designs which we
have hypothetically attributed to the Masonic body.

There is a recent fact in our contemporaneous history which certainly merits the attention it has attracted. The son of a Wapping butcher undertook
to personate the heir, supposed to have been drowned
years ago, of an old English baronetcy. Two trials,
each of an unprecedented duration, resulted in the
conviction of the impostor, and his condemnation to
an imprisonment of fourteen years. It would be interesting, and probably instructive, to know (if the
facts could be thoroughly ascertained) by what
means, and through whose active intervention, the
funds were collected that were necessary to meet
such gigantic expenses ; but this is not the most
significative point in this disreputable romance of
real life. During the trial an extraordinary sym-
pathy was enlisted in favour of Orton among the
roughs of London. The fact might, perhaps, have
received a probable explanation, deducible from the
particular circumstances of the case, if it had not
been elucidated by subsequent events. No sooner
had sentence been pronounced, than the principal
advocate of the prisoner commenced an agitation in
favour of his release. Despite the exalted character
and legal ability of all the judges connected with
both trials, despite the unanimous verdict of an intelligent jury, chosen, as Mr Bright pointed out, from
the middle classes, despite even of the decided judgment of the English press, alike metropolitan and
provincial, which, with consentient voice, denounced
the agitation and its originator, the movement

gathered strength. It availed to carry the agitator, albeit just branded with the severest penalties which the legal profession could inflict on one of its members, and with an unusual token of royal displeasure, triumphantly into the Senate of the nation. The agitation spread in every quarter. Petitions were sent from different provincial towns, one signed by 11,000 persons, another by 14,000, requesting the disbarred member for Stoke to convene meetings in the several localities. A public demonstration had been previously arranged in London, and, according to the most moderate calculations, thirty or forty thousand persons responded to the summons. Now it is sufficiently notorious that the spontaneous ebullitions of a mob are not conspicuous for their organisation. One is curious, therefore, to know who prepared the petitions, marshalled the rank and file, gathered the workmen round the table, and put pen and ink in their hands after inducing them to give their names; and who they were, too, that conducted with such success the election at Stoke, and meanwhile created the extensive circulation of *The Englishman.*

However this may be, the facts of this humiliating drama are pregnant with warning. Dr Kenealy might have been somewhat hyperbolical in threatening us with an immediate revolution, and have justified those safe sneers at his expense which delighted a crowded House of Commons; but that he was not wide of the mark when he described us as walking gaily on the crust of an active volcano, is sufficiently plain from the commentaries which the leading journals in London have made on the proceedings. The *Times*, for instance, remarks, in a leading article to be found in its issue of April 26, 1875 :—

" If the member for Stoke has completely settled the question, as it affects his client and all the parties concerned in the trial, he has also thrown not a little light on another matter of some practical importance. We must give him credit for describing what is quite within his knowledge, and what he must have special facilities for observing and estimating, when he introduces us to the majesty of the people, terribly in earnest, and not to be put off by any delays or evasions of justice. No doubt his own constituency must be the impersonation of some such majesty as he describes. That there are a good many places like Stoke-upon-Trent, and that everywhere there has been found, *or could be raised,* an enthusiasm for the hero of a very remarkable drama, is boasted by Dr Kenealy, and admitted by those who reply to him It is, then, a melancholy fact, and one which Dr Kenealy has helped to bring out in striking relief and distinct form, that a very considerable, and in some places a preponderating part of the electoral body, is earnestly and passionately given to a belief and a line of action which the House of Commons, in the most solemn and decisive manner, unanimously pronounces foolish, worthless, and mischievous. The present utter failure of the last attempt to vindicate the Claimant reacts upon all who still believe in him, or who still profess to believe in him. *It warns us that there is in this sensible, sober, and calculating England, a stratum of society about as unaccountable and as little to be depended on as a quicksand or a quagmire. There is no saying what it may be terribly in earnest about to-morrow ; and when we do see it terribly in earnest, there is no knowing whether it is terribly in earnest with good reason or for none at all,—just some nonsense of its own imagination or some object of the grossest credulity. This is a sad conclusion to come to. We wish to believe in popular earnestness, and to*

recognise in solemnity of tone, gravity of demeanour, and com-
bined action, the natural vouchers for truth, reality, and sense.
But if we are to believe both Dr Kenealy and the House of Com-
mons, the majesty of the people is terribly in earnest for a
creature of its imagination, or, still worse, of its own corrupt
and dishonest will"

These statements are manly and outspoken: and
they convey a warning which is not given a moment
too soon. The *Spectator* for April 24, 1875, contains
an article entitled, "*The Orton-Kenealy Craze—Pes-*
simist View," in which are to be found the following
grave and pregnant observations :—

"The alarming side of this agitation, however, has yet to be
represented. *I cannot admit that, even as regards the moral side*
of it, it is without menace. No doubt the public mind of England has always been exceedingly susceptible to religious panic,
and worse things have been done under the spell of that panic
than under any other influence. But the danger of spasmodic
waves of popular passion, under the spell of religious feeling, is
one danger, and the danger of gross moral perversions of popular
judgment, under no such spell, quite another. We can appeal
from Philip drunk to Philip sober in the one case ; but if Philip
sober is as bad as Philip drunk, then there is no such appeal
possible. What has induced the people, without any spell of
self-interest or passion in them, suddenly to reject the judgment
of English judges as utterly untrustworthy, and to take up the
cause of a man who, whether on his own or Dr Kenealy's view
of him, is not a witness to be believed on his oath? . . . .
There has been not a little evidence of a great advance in the
popularity of Orton as his asserted or admitted rascalities came
out. So far from any disgust being felt at him for his assertion,
or rather fabrication, of the contents of the sealed packet, his
popularity definitely increased from the moment that that per-
jury was committed. . . . . Now, is there a more dangerous
form of popular sentiment than this delight in a ruffian's risks,
and hopes, and excitements, in which there is not any trace of

what is called 'poetical justice'? What would such a sentiment, if further developed, tend to produce? Would it not
tend to produce discontent with plodding industry, an impatience
for unwholesome audacities of one sort or another, a leniency
towards all grandiose forms of crime, and contempt only for the
squalid kind,—in short, an attitude of mind which excuses all
that is wicked, if it be also interesting to the morbid imagination of persons impatient of drudgery, and which judges crime
seriously only when it is on a petty scale, and therefore dull?
*And what temper would strike deeper at the root of English
character than that?* . . . . *The more definitely we refer the
delusion to a deliberate error of popular judgment, the more
likely it seems that that error will spread itself in ever-widening
circles, and result in breaking down all the buttresses against
popular caprice* ¹ . . . . And what can that end in, except a
growing estrangement between the people and honest political
intelligence, and the lapse of politics into hands which will make
political struggle a coarse and repulsive affair, from which all
pure, to say nothing of fastidious, minds will shrink? . . . .
*Everywhere there are signs that the respect for great national
institutions, for central as distinguished from local ideas, is
diminishing,* and that minute local notoriety has far more
influence in rendering, for instance, a candidate for Parliament
popular, than a great national fame. *Everywhere the self-sufficiency of popular opinion is increasing,* and the sources of political favour and disfavour are rapidly becoming pettier and
pettier. *Everywhere the difficulty of organising opinion is
growing,—the residuum, aided by the ballot, realising more and
more clearly that there is no true responsibility for political
opinion at all, and that an arbitrary* INCLINATION *to accord
support is at least no worse, if not a better, excuse for determin-
ing a secret vote, than a reason for thinking that that support
will result in public benefit. All the signs of the times go to show
that the people believe less and less that they have anything to
learn from their political leaders, and indeed hold that those leaders
are much rather their own instruments than their sagacious
and respected advisers.* . . . . *Look at it which way you will,
it seems to promise for England a period of mean and capricious*

politics. in which the least scrupulous men will come to the top, and the most scrupulous and most eminent will be cowed and silenced,—in which either the House of Commons will lose control of the wild whims of the people, or the wild whims of the people will gain control of the House of Commons ;—and which of these alternatives is the worst, it is hard to say."

The importance of the subject-matter offers an amply sufficient excuse for the length to which these quotations have been carried. These are startling facts, which are set before the reader by a paper, justly holding the foremost place among the weekly journals by reason of its talents, candour, and eminently polished as well as thoughtful articles. And here we have the volcano over whose thinly-crusted crater we can afford to dance and sing so merrily.

Well, then, if Freemasonry in England be the same in principle as it is confessed to be abroad, if its aims and designs be such as we have hypothetically assumed them to be, what could have been a greater godsend for the brothers of "*the Craft*" than this Orton-Kenealy drama? A Catholic baronet, of ancient lineage, is to be ousted of his property and title, and a Protestant butcher to be set up in his place. The legal institutions of the country, nay, the very House of Commons itself, are to be confronted with the angry denunciations and threats of the irritated masses. The Queen, too, and her Government can be reached by the movement; for a barrister, just deprived of his silk gown by royal authority, shall be returned to Parliament by a majority that will make the election the greatest practical insult offered at once to constituted authority, to the national senate, to the majesty of the law, and to the morally unanimous verdict of educated society. Surely, if Freemasonry had such designs as are attributed to it,. it could well afford to collect money, to send secret agents, to organise action for the purpose of strengthening an agitation so nearly affecting its own interests.

It would, of course, be folly to maintain that this or the other political movements which have been already referred to could have been produced solely by Masonic action. The same political sagacity which initiates a popular agitation can take adroit advantage of a temporary public sentiment, or a temporary dissatisfaction, to guide and shape both towards the promotion of, its own hidden purposes. What is certain is this : that if English Freemasonry should have designs upon this and upon all other nations such as our hypothesis assigns to it, it has done its work with remarkable success during the last thirty years.

But, after all, is the hypothesis reasonable ? Surely there must be some foundation for the belief, so widely spread and so persistent, that English Freemasonry is a society altogether distinct from, and independent of, the Continental Lodges. Besides, is it possible that eminent personages—including kings, princes of the blood royal, distinguished statesmen, diplomatists, men of high position and still higher character—should remain in a body whose professed object it is to overthrow the altar and to trample under foot all the crowns of Europe ?

It is necessary to confront these arguments openly and plainly.

Is, then, English Freemasonry entirely disconnected with the Continental Lodges ? Is it to be supposed that the *Daily Telegraph*, which is generally understood to represent more than any other paper the Masonic interests, would be well informed upon the point ? Now, a leading article of April 28, 1875—which, judging from internal evidence, has been penned by a brother of "*the Craft*"—supplies us with the required information :—

"While the Craft," observes the writer in question, "contend that its rites and ceremonies date from the time when Solomon's Temple was first designed, others, apparently without data of any sort, have declared that it is an English society of some two hundred years' standing, founded much in the same fashion as were other secret conclaves, outlasting them only because its tenets were purer, and its objects nobler. Against this latter supposition there are, however, the facts that Masonry is to be found wherever human beings dwell, and that the Persian suite of the Shah found in German Lodges a congenial home, albeit that their tribes had not had Masonic communication with the Western nations for well-nigh seven hundred years. That Masons towards the close of the last century were somewhat divided is generally admitted ; and that they were united under the leadership of the Duke of Sussex, who from that time forward till the day of his death ruled over the Craft, without fear of a rival, is also conceded. Be the history of this extraordinary Association, however, what it may, one thing is certain its influence spreads all over the globe. The Emperor of Germany boasts the title of Grand Protector in the Fatherland ; King Victor Emanuel, as Grand Master of Italy, bears sway in the Southern Peninsula ; Denmark, Sweden, and Norway have monarchs for their Craft chieftains ; Portugal and Spain, despite their allegiance to the Pontiff, boast fifty-six

Lodges ; in the Netherlands, the heir to the throne sways the baton of command ; four hundred Lodges own the sovereignty of the Grand Orient of France ; the Prime Minister of Brazil is Master of his Masonic countrymen in the Argentine Republic, Hayti, San Domingo, Mexico, Uruguay, Venezuela, and Peru. The most notable of politicians are the best known of Craftsmen. Canada and the United States are proud of powerful organisations and magnificent temples ; in Greece, the ' Children of Leonidas ' hold monthly congratulation at Syra ; Masons work amid the ruins of the Piræus, a Lodge assembles in Athens; and Patras, Corfu, and Chalcis help to swell the total of the Grand Orient of Hellas. Even Turkey contains thousands of brethren; India can tell of Lodges by the hundred; Australia and the South Pacific find symbols for the expression of fraternal feeling in the compass and square ; and African tribes, with wandering Arabs, claim the right to belong to *this singular brotherhood.*"

Singular brotherhood indeed, of good sooth ! " Why have the Gentiles raged, and the people devised vain things ? The kings of the earth stood up, and the princes met together, against the Lord, and against His Christ. Let us break their bonds asunder, and let us cast away their yoke from us " (Ps. ii. 2, 3).

Making all due allowance for the tall talk of an enthusiastic Craftsman, conspicuous throughout the whole of this remarkable paragraph, two incontestable facts remain ; to wit, the universal diffusion of this dangerous and baneful confederation in all quarters of the globe, and the unity and intercommunion of all its constituent sections, however locally or nationally distinct.

But there is little need of appealing to the authority of an anonymous writer, however friendly, for the

same fact is incontestably proved by the public proceedings that took place at the installation of his
Royal Highness the Prince of Wales as Grand
Master of English Freemasons. On that occasion
deputations were sent not only from the Scotch and
Irish Lodges, but also from that of Sweden ; while the
Grand Lodge of Italy sent its congratulatory address
through the well-known Brother J. C. Parkinson, and
"the Grand Orient Lodge of France sent a letter of
congratulation to his Royal Highness, as they had
done to his predecessors in office, the Earl of Zetland
and the Marquis of Ripon."—(*The Times*, April 29,
1875.) The Italian address is of such grave signifi-
cancy as to justify us in giving it in its integrity to
our readers. The document is headed by the following selections from the alphabet, A.G.D.G.A D.U.,
and opens with the following dedication, exactly copied
from the same number of the *Times*. It is worth
notice that those who authorised the publication of
the address in that journal thought fit to conceal this
introductory portion by leaving it in the original
Italian. The accompanying translation will suggest
a sufficient motive for a proceeding so unusual :—

" Massoneria Universale.—Communione Italiana."
(*Universal Freemasonry.—Italian Communion.*)
" Libertà, Fratellanza, Uguaglianza."
(*Liberty, Fraternity, Equality.*) The reader will probably
remember these watchwords in their connection with some
remarkable epochs in French history.
" Grande Oriente della Massoneria in Italia e nelle Colonie
Italiane."
(*Grand Orient of Masonry in Italy and in the Italian
Colonies*)

The rest of the letter from these brothers of Mazzini is given as follows :—

" To His Royal Highness the Prince of Wales, Grand Master of the Grand Lodge of England.

" May it please your Royal Highness to permit the Grand Master of the Grand Orient of Italy to unite the heartfelt applause of all our Italian brethren to that of our beloved brethren in England, who hail the elevation of their puissant Grand Master as one of the most auspicious and most memorable events of universal Masonry.

" By this event English Masonry, *which has already deserved so well of universal humanity,* will acquire ever fresh titles to the gratitude and admiration of the whole civilised world.

" Italian Masonry, therefore, rejoices at this new lustre shed upon *our world-wide institution,* and sincerely prays that between the two Masonic communities may be drawn *ever more closely* those fraternal ties which, through want of that *official* recognition which we venture to hope will soon be effected, have always bound us to our English brethren, whose profound intelligence and *unwearying activity* we constantly appreciate and seek to follow.

" Accept, then, Royal Highness, with all great wishes for your continued long life and prosperity, the expression of our profound homage and *fraternal affection."*

This letter, while it alludes to a present absence of official recognition by the English Freemasons of the Grand Orient of Italy, and prays that it may be granted, clearly establishes the fact that "the Brotherhood" is substantially one in all lands. It may be that the Italian Grand Lodge has not been officially recognised by the English Masons, because their Italian brothers have been imprudently premature in the revelation of the aims and action of the body, and because those ominous words, *Liberty, Fraternity,*

Equality, have still a somewhat ugly sound in this country.

Another significant fact, which adds to the weight of proof already given, is the appointment by " the Most Worshipful the Grand Master," after his installation, of Brother Wendt to be Grand Secretary for *German correspondence.*

The first objection proposed above has been, it may be presumed, sufficiently answered. There can be no reasonable doubt that there is a more or less complete solidarity between the English and Continental Lodges, and a community of aim which directs the action of the Craft in every quarter of the globe.

The next objection which has been made to the indentification of English Freemasonry with those fearful tenets, and yet more fearful conspiracy of action, that are detailed in the work now placed before the reader, is derived from the roll of names, partly illustrious by position, and partly distinguished by high public and private worth, which is to be found in the archives of this Society. How is it possible that emperors, kings, and princes would persevere in lending the sanction of their name to a body, one of whose acknowledged objects it is to overthrow every throne in Europe, and extirpate all social distinctions throughout the world ?

To begin with this last dilemma :—It can hardly be denied that there have been emperors and kings who have joined " the Craft," from the disheartening conviction that its power was too firmly established to be openly confronted by authority of established government; and they consequently assumed the apron with the delusive hope of being able *to direct* what they were unable to destroy. Others there may have been who, keenly alive to their own selfish interests, have tamely consented to cut off the entail, so to say, provided they could secure to themselves a life-interest in the regal power. But making every allowance for such cases as these, there still will remain a certain number of royal names, which cannot be included in either category. These, however, will take their place among the list of exalted and worthy personages who lend the authority of their name to this Association.

What is to be said in explanation of this fact? The reply is obvious: They have been deceived, and continue in the dark. It is thoroughly understood among the secret heads and chief agents of the body, that such brethren would not remain a single day in union with such a league if they were aware of its ultimate designs; so they have established for their convenience special degrees of honour and offices of seeming authority, where they may attract the uninitiated by the authority of their high character and exalted position, without enfeebling the secret action of " the Craft " by the demurrers of an over-scrupulous morality. The great universities of this realm are wont to confer on distinguished generals, authors, and other celebrities, the honorary degree of Doctor of Civil Law; but it is not commonly supposed that those who are selected for such a distinction have any deep knowledge of this particular branch of juris-prudence. If any one were anxious to obtain accurate information about English Freemasonry, and had received the requisite permission (as we will suppose) to get behind the veil, he would be more likely to gain his end by consulting, say, Brother Parkinson, than by submitting the Prince of Wales or the Earl of Carnarvon to his interrogatories. If any one should doubt the probability of this explanation, let him read the facts connected with Frederick, Prince of Orange, as given p. 60.

It still, however, remains to be explained how Englishmen in general should retain so strong a conviction that Freemasonry, in this country at least, is a harmless, nay, what is more, a useful and beneficent institution. That such an idea is generally entertained cannot be doubted. Thus, for instance, an article appeared in the *Times* (April 29, 1875), on the subject of the recent installation of the new Grand Master, in which the writer, in a tone of thinly-veiled contempt, gives expression to the judgment of popular opinion in the following terms :—

" The installation of the Prince of Wales as Grand Master of the Freemasons was an impressive, and, in some respects, an instructive ceremonial. Theoretically, no one knows what Freemasons are, or what are their ceremonies and principles ; but in practice we all know that they are very fair representatives of Englishmen in general, *and that their only peculiarity* is to discharge certain praiseworthy duties of humanity in a more picturesque and expensive manner than is thought necessary by other people. We would not for a moment disparage the value

of the 'Craft.' There is a singular passion in human nature
for anything in the form of order, association, and discipline.
Nothing of this sort can be too much for him, and in his enjoyment of the society of his fellows and of their common ceremonial, he is quite unconscious of the appearance he may present to the eyes of critical outsiders. *Grown-up men, however
grave, are still as happy as children in enacting some imaginary play, and, in one form or another, they insist on having
it.* . . . Ten thousand Englishmen wore their Masonic clothing
and performed their Masonic mysteries with unprecedented
effect. *It was a properly innocent enjoyment, and it is pleasant
to see that so many men can thus find genuine enjoyment in becoming very young again.*

"*But all this display seems to be the dress in which some of the
best impulses of good-fellowship and charity are clothed,* and as
the new Grand Master yesterday said, so long as the 'great and
ancient Order' confine themselves to those objects, they will
flourish. 'Loyalty and charity' are their watchwords, and so
long as these characteristics are maintained, they will be a useful, as well as an agreeable, Brotherhood."

This is somewhat tall writing, and, perhaps, sufficiently smart, but it can scarcely be pronounced
philosophical. It is quite true that the play-element
is an important constitution of our common nature ;
nor is it the wisest of things to aim at its suppression. It will be also easily granted that men ordin-
arily are attracted thereby to shows and pageants,
more especially those in which themselves are engaged
to take their part. But that kings, emperors, princes,
eminent statesmen, diplomatists, fierce earnest dema-
gogues, should seriously and unintermittingly lend
themselves to the world-wide propagation of a show,
—that Lodges should be established in every corner of
the habitable globe, and seventeen millions of reason-

able human beings should be united in one vast
confederation, with hidden signs and passwords,
sedulously concealed from the uninitiated, for the
purpose of occasionally wearing queer garments and
gay ribbons,—that distinguished members of the two
political parties in our English Houses of Legislature
should consider it consistent with their public position to be acknowledged partners in such a childish
farce,[1]—that all the bewildering diversity of offices
and grades, which have been recently exposed to the
public gaze, should be accepted by an Earl of Carnarvon, a Mazzini, a Louis Blanc, a Bismarck, as so
many marionettes devised for the entertainment of
playgoers,—that a secret oath of the most fearful
kind should be imposed upon the innocent per-
formers of these *tableaux vivants*, for the mere purpose of enabling them to practise in concert the
ordinary duties of " Charity and Loyalty," is an
assumption which one would hesitate to adopt, even
on the authority of the *Times*.

However,`though common sense would teach us
to reject an hypothesis so baseless and untenable,
it must be owned that the judgment of many wise
and impartial men, no less than the persistence of a
widely-spread opinion in the same direction, give
colour to the assertion that Freemasonry in England

[1] " In the appointment of grand officers, it is now no secret that the
City of London will have special honour, and it is believed that members of both political parties will be decorated with ' the purple ' of
Grand Lodges, not by reason of their position in the political world,
but as distinguished Freemasons."—(*The Times*, April 27, 1875)

has been greatly modified by the sobriety, loyal disposition, and practical solidity of our national character. We would fain hope that this may be the
case; and it is only an act of justice to call attention
to the fact, that the assertion receives some confir-
mation from the circumstance, alluded to in' the
Italian address of congratulation to the new Grand
Master, of there being no official relations at present
between the Grand Lodges of England and Italy.

Let us suppose, then, for the sake of argument,
that it is true. Believe, if it so pleases you, that
the Masonic " Craft " is, as actually constituted in
this country, an innocent, nay, praiseworthy society,
occupying itself only with the works of unostenta-
tious charity. Even so ; is the danger overpast ? Is
there any security that this formidable confederation
may not become, when popular agitation and internal
dissensions shall arise, what it has shown itself to be
in other countries while they were passing through
a like crisis ? Can you trust the fortunes of your
country and the safety of your families to men, however honourable and high-minded they may be, who
have committed themselves to the guidance of an
authority unknown to themselves, who are con-
federated under the most fearful sanctions of a secret
oath, and who are compelled to an inexorable silence,
even though tenets should be revealed and orders
transmitted from which their innermost soul recoils
with unutterable loathing ? Sick at heart, driven
half-mad at the revelation of the hideous secret, they

dare not go back ; and, oppressed with a deadening despair, they are forced to connive at deeds which they utterly abhor.

These are not mere dreams. They are based on the evidence of stubborn facts. Read the Masonic oath, as it is given in the *Irish Ecclesiastical Record* for April 1875. Here it is :—

> "*I swear, in the name of the Supreme Architect of all worlds, never to reveal the secrets, the signs, the grips, the passwords, the doctrines, or the customs of the Freemasons ; and to preserve with respect to them an eternal silence. I promise and swear to God never to betray any of them either by writing, by word, or gesture ; never to cause them to be written, lithographed, or printed ; never to make public anything of that which has now been confided to me, or of that which shall be confided to me in the future. I pledge myself to this, and submit myself to the following penalties if I fail in keeping my word. They may burn my lips with a red-hot iron, they may cut off my hand, they may pluck out my tongue, they may cut my throat, they may hang up my dead body in a Lodge till the admission of a new brother, as a scourge for my faithlessness, and as a terrible warning to others. Then they may burn it, and cast its ashes to the winds, to the end that there may not remain a single trace of the memory of my treason. So help me God, and His Holy Gospel. Amen.*"

If this be a true record,—and the respectability of the authority which gives it is a sufficient voucher for its truth,—how can any one delude himself with the idea that men bound to secrecy by such an oath can prove other than conspirators against public security ? It is no answer to produce the names of eminent and virtuous friends who are enrolled among them, and to rely on their testimony to the harm-

lessness of the " Craft." We firmly believe that by
far the greater number are in utter ignorance of the
secret designs to which they nevertheless stand
committed as apprentices in the body. But they have
bound themselves, blindfold, by that terrible oath ;
and, when the time for proof arrives, they *must* go
on, or abide the consequences.

Moreover, it is in violation of the natural order
and an ever-present menace to political stability,
that a body of men should exist within the state,
bound by obedience to an unknown and irresponsible
authority, and shielded from all possible supervision
either of constituted authority or of public opinion
by an oath of secrecy. " I consider," says Lord
Plunket, " an association bound by a secret oath to
be extremely dangerous on the principles of the
common law ; inasmuch as they subtract the subject
from the state, and interpose between him and his
allegiance to the king." And he speaks most truly ;
for it is an act of high treason against the most
fundamental principles of political and social life.

Finally, even should it appear that Freemasonry
has been misrepresented, and that the accusations
brought against it are full of exaggerations and perversions of truth (which, as we believe, the Brethren
will find it difficult to prove), the fact remains, notwithstanding, that the Masonic oath, as we have
already stated, is in itself a serious violation of
the natural law, which forbids us to abdicate the
freedom of our will in favour of an unknown

e

and self-constituted authority, and to bind ourselves irrevocably to the propagation of tenets, or to the blind execution of orders, about which we are in utter ignorance at the time, and are therefore unable to determine whether they are consistent or not with our moral obligations to ourselves, our neighbour, and our God.

Let those, then, who read this little work beware lest, out of an evil and unhealthy curiosity, they be induced to despise the voice of conscience, and to prepare for themselves, as so many unhappily have done before them, a life of misery, terror, and un-availing remorse. It is far wiser to remain in a safe and contented ignorance than to plunge into un-known dangers, and to refuse the temporal advan-tages which Freemasonry can undoubtedly secure, but only at the expense of that inestimable peace which fortifies us to endure with cheerfulness the troubles of this life, and assures us of that eternal bliss in the future of which It is itself a partial, though imperfect, instalment.

POSTSCRIPT.

AFTER the above introduction had been written, a
most valuable contribution to our contemporary
literature, touching the subject of this volume, from
the accomplished pen of Monsignor Dupanloup,
Bishop of Orleans, has come to hand. Any one who
is interested in this most momentous question—as
who is not?—should possess himself of the "Étude
sur la Franc-Maçonnerie." It will prove of special
interest to the English reader, since the proofs as to
the real designs of Freemasonry in Germany, and
generally on the Continent, collected in the present
work and in the Bishop's *brochure* from the most
authentic sources, are confirmed by the avowals of
English Freemasons which have been published in
the London journal devoted to their interests.

The evidence contained in the Bishop's pamphlet
gives such marked sanction to the course of thought
pursued in the above preface, and so completely
justifies the hypothesis therein developed, that the
latter might be supposed to have been suggested by
an attentive perusal of the former ; and, though the
suspicion is in fact groundless, this correspondence
between the two gives greater weight to both, for the
very reason that it is purely accidental.

One of the principal objects to which Freemasonry
throughout Europe is directing its most strenuous
efforts in preparation for the final construction of its

atheistic republic, is the establishment in every nation of compulsory State education, from which all religious instruction shall be rigorously excluded. In 1864, as the Bishop of Orleans narrates, a scheme of legislation issued from the Grand Orient of Belgium, drawn up in the form of twenty-three articles. The first two are couched in the following terms : 1. Suppression of all religious instruction ; 2. Obligation on the part of the father and widowed mother to force their children to the school " (1. Suppression de toute instruction religieuse ; 2. Obligation pour le père et pour la mère veuve, de conduire de force ses enfants a l'école). " The London Masonic journal, in reply to the Lodge at Antwerp, the Grand Orient of Belgium, and *The Rose of Perfect Silence* in Paris, declares that religious education is a poison, and consequently requires 'that parents should engage to withdraw their children from the virus of religious education.'"[1]

Who, then, can possibly doubt that such is the aim of Freemasonry here, as on the Continent? And, if we duly estimate the preponderance of Freemasonry in both Houses of our Legislature, and its profession by eminent and influential personages belonging to our two great political parties, the success of this educational scheme can be, humanly speaking, only a question of time. If some one of our representatives would move for a list of all persons connected in any way with Government, and of members of

[1] Étude, &c., pp. 34, 35.

either House, who are enrolled in this secret Society, the revelation might, perhaps, awaken public opinion to a sense of the perils by which we are surrounded. No one could, of course, suppose for one moment that any great number of our statesmen would be acquainted with the ultimate intentions of "the Craft;" if they were, they would not continue their connection with it for a day. The reader's attention has been already called to the fact that the full revelation is confided to comparatively few; while by far the greater majority remain either in total or in partial ignorance of designs to whose success they are unconsciously contributing. The Bishop of Orleans calls especial attention to the fact, and quotes the words of a distinguished Freemason, M. Louis Blanc, in proof. The testimony of this writer is so conclusive on the point, that its insertion here will require no apology. "It seemed good to sovereigns, to Frederick the Great, to handle the trowel and to put on the apron. Why not? Since the existence of the higher grades was carefully hidden from them, all they knew of Freemasonry was that which could be revealed to them without danger. They had no reason for concerning themselves about it, seeing that they were kept in the lower grades, in which they perceived nothing but an opportunity for amusement, joyful banquets, principles forsaken and resumed at the threshold of the Lodges, formulas that had no reference to ordinary life,—in a word, a comedy of equality. But, in these matters, comedy closely borders upon tragedy; and the princes and nobles were induced to offer the cover of their name and the blind aid of their influence to secret under-takings directed against themselves."[1]

Can any reasonable man doubt, after reading an explicit admission such as this from one who knew well what he was saying, that kings, princes, states-men, legislators, may be found in grades of high honour and dignity, provided by Freemasonry for their especial benefit,—may assume the first place in its public manifestations and the *external* direction of its government, and may yet remain in ignorance of its hidden designs as unconscious and complete as is that of the *profane* who are altogether excluded from its Lodges? Not without reason, therefore, has Leo XII. warned its unhappy dupes that, " Though it is not the custom to reveal what is most blamable in it to those who have not reached the high grades, it is notwithstanding plain that the power of these Societies, so dangerous to religion, is augmented in proportion to the number of their adherents."[2] The present Pope, in his allocution of September 25, 1865, incidentally bears witness to the same fact; for, speaking of previous monitions given by his prede-cessors, he remarks, " Unhappily these admonitions have not had the desired effect, and we have there-fore considered it our duty to condemn this Society once more, seeing that, *perhaps out of ignorance*, the false opinion might arise that it is inoffensive, that its

[1] Étude, &c., p. 65.   [2] Ibid. p. 83.

only aim is the practice of charity, and that consequently it could not be a source of danger to the
Church of God."[1]

One thing is certain. It is a 'mortal sin for a
Catholic to belong to it. It is almost as certain that
no one who professes to be a Christian can join its
ranks without peril to his salvation. Strange though
it may seem, Freemasons have themselves confessed
as much. For, when the Bishop of Autun affirmed
that, "If a man wished to remain a sincere Christian
he could not at the same time be a Freemason,"
the *Monde-Maçonnique*, the Paris organ of Freemasonry, openly admitted that " *The Bishop is justified in speaking thus. He is in his right. It is his
duty.*"[2]

TRINITY SUNDAY, 1875.

---

[1] Étude, &c , p 84   [2] Ibid. p 85.

ˏTHE SECRET WARFARE.

CHAPTER I.

INTRODUCTION.

THE war against throne and altar has bioken out
along the whole line. Liberalism in all its varied
hues, from peaceful Blue to fiery Red, is now master
of the field. Those monarchies which yield to its
sway allow themselves, half involuntarily, to drift
with the stream, and will find themselves, notwithstanding the protestations of devoted loyalty uttered
by the party in power, inevitably stranded on Republicanism. Not, however, the Republicanism of
Lamartine in 1848, but that of social democracy.
Such a result is doubly surprising, because the party
referred to is universally acknowledged to lack intellect and union. The only explanation of it is furnished by the organisation which conceals itself
behind Liberalism, namely, the Secret International
Society of Freemasons. This body, protected by
exceptional laws in its favour, has during the last

A

two centuries made such rapid strides, that it can boast a brotherhood numbering seventeen millions.[1] It is notorious that to it belong the principal members of the Liberal Ministries of Italy, Spain, Portugal, France, Belgium, and other countries ; to it are associated the most formidable democratic agitators, and the leaders of the Liberal parties in Parliaments : whilst the Liberal Press, consciously or unconsciously, is everywhere its instrument. This work has long been in preparation, and has been brought by tenacious perseverance to its present flourishing condition. One of the *initiated writes thus :—" The greatest and wisest men have bestowed on our Society a constitution which gives lasting proof of their sagacity. Shrouded in threefold night, we move among our adversaries, and, unseen by them, acquaint ourselves with their weak points, thus acquiring the mastery over their mind and heart. We use their passions

[1] If this number, which, in the summer of 1872, went the round of the papers, is not a rhetorical exaggeration, the affiliated societies, intended to prepare the mind of the masses for the reception of the doctrines of Freemasonry, must at any rate be included. With a view of rendering these doctrines popular, there have been established in North America alone, 100 such unions ; those most generally known are the Oddfellows, Goodfellows, Druids, Red men, Seven Wise men, Sons of Hermann, United Sons of Liberty, Harugaris, and Knights of Pythia. These form about 25,000 Lodges, with some 2,000,000 members. The last class has been within a few years introduced into Germany, and already has Lodges in Berlin, Stuttgart, Dresden, Zurich, &c. In France and America there are others of various grades, and Lodges of two different grades for ladies. (See the " Laacher Stimmen," 1873, No. 1, p. 100, *seq.*) Besides this, the International Unions, Leagues of Peace, Associations of Solidaires, Libres-penseurs, &c , are all more or less closely connected with Freemasonry.

as wires, whereby, without their being aware of the
fact, we set them in motion, compelling them to
work in union with us, whilst they ignorantly imagine
themselves to be merely gratifying their own wishes.
It would be unwise to engage in open warfare; the
spread of freedom of thought and independence of
action is the surest means of undermining the gigantic monument erected by ambition. Under the very
shadow of authority, the Mason works at the mighty
task committed to him. Freemasonry, great and
terrible, dogs your steps, spies out your proceedings, reads the thoughts of your inmost soul,
watches you when you imagine yourself enveloped
in impenetrable darkness. Its hidden and irresis-
tible influence shatters your plans, its powerful arm
wrests the dagger from your grasp. With your help,
brethren, it will strike off the chains which still bind
the peoples of the earth."[1]

We are very far from reckoning the entire Liberal
party, with all its members, as Masonic brethren, or
charging all Freemasons with consciously carrying
out the designs of their Secret Society; on the
contrary, we are convinced that the transactions
related in the following pages will probably give
umbrage to some of our readers, themselves members of this mysterious association, since they have
as yet heard of nothing of the kind in their Lodges.
This, however, in no way affects the question, for the

---

[1] " Wiener Journal fur Freimaurer," MSS. for the Brethren, 2d year,
No 1, p. 66.

duties of *all* the members are not confined to contributing money and attending at banquets. Further,
it is not a valid objection to say that since ruling
princes and members of their family have joined
the Masonic Lodges, the regard which is due to them
imparts a treasonable character to every word con-
demnatory of the Secret Society.[1] The very birds on
the housetops know that rulers and princes, even
if they are outwardly invested with the highest dignities in the various Lodges, are never Working Masons
or Architects, but Master Builders, and therefore stand
in exactly the same relation to their Lodge in which a
rich proprietor, who desires to have a splendid man-
sion erected for him, stands to the contractor of the
works, whose aim it is to become even a richer man
than the proprietor himself.   Noble natures—to their
credit be it spoken—are always the easiest to deceive ;
no one is more difficult to take in than a thorough-

---

[1] The oath administered to a Scottish Ancient or Chief Master and
Knight of St Andrew on his reception, is as follows —"I, N—— N——,
promise and swear to Almighty God, the Architect of the universe, to
my lawful Master of this high Scottish Lodge, before my Scotch
brethren here present, by a free oath of my body, that I will keep in
the most solemn manner possible all the secrets now confided to me,
and any conjectures I may form concerning them, and will not reveal
the least portion of them to any one whatsoever, *even were he the
Master of the whole Order*, unless I had recognised him in a rightful
high Scotch Lodge, or unless he had been made known to me as such
by my superiors of this Lodge " (Sarsena, p. 212. Eckert's "Die
Frage der Staatlichen Anerkennung des Freimaurer-Ordens in Oesterreich," 2d edit, Vienna, 1862, p. 5, &c) It is to be hoped that this
oath will suffice to render impossible any complaint of disrespect on
our part towards distinguished patrons.

paced rascal. Let us, therefore, not be accused of
disloyalty towards those royal personages who have
done Freemasonry the honour to enrol themselves
among its members ; our remarks will apply only to
the Architects who keep out of sight, not to any who
may be their Patrons.

And in fact it is high time to raise our voice, for a
great part of the Catholic body, in spite of signs
which thicken daily, refuse to see anything in Freemasonry but a harmless convivial meeting of Liberal
bon-vivants, or, at most, a secret association distracted
by internal dissensions.[1] This opinion, which may
perhaps formerly have had an appearance of justice,
is no longer tenable, the gravity of the situation
becoming every day more apparent. Dr Ketteler,
the Bishop of Mayence, in his pamphlet on " Liberty,
Authority, and the Church " (pp. 218, &c.), says very
aptly :—" The position claimed by Freemasonry
throughout the whole world is a peculiarly and radically exceptional one. It alone is never, except in rare
instances, discussed by the Press ; indeed, it refuses
to allow itself to be so discussed. Although priests
openly deliberate and pronounce upon all other points
affecting the general interests of mankind ; although
Christianity, with its system and doctrines, the State
with its laws and constitutions, are topics of free dis-

---

[1] We are aware that the author of the article entitled " Freemasonry " in the " Historico political Journal " (v. 8, 1841), wrote very
differently in the year 1873. From that and some similar articles
(1862) the Catholics of Germany have in a great measure learnt to
under-estimate the importance of the Lodges.

cussion ; although even the most intimate and personal concerns of individuals are made public—Freemasonry alone, by the universal consent of Europe,
is acknowledged to be a *Noli me tangere !* Every
one shrinks from speaking of it as of an uncanny
ghost. This phenomenon is an obvious proof of the
immense power Freemasonry exercises in the world."

In the following pages we propose to treat of the
covert warfare waged by this secret league—1st,
Against the Catholic Church ; 2dly, against Christianity ; 3dly, against Monarchy ; 4thly, against Social
Order ; and 5thly, against God Himself. We quote
for the most part from records and well-authenticated
utterances of the Lodges themselves, and shall studiously avoid all exaggeration, not allowing our deductions to go one whit further than the evidence adduced compels us to do.

CHAPTER II.

WE do not intend entering upon the history of Freemasonry, for to do so would lead us to overstep the limits of the task we have undertaken; we would only observe that writers on this subject frequently fall into one of two extremes. Some trace back the history of the League to the fratricide Cain, and thus give what is rather an account of the origin and development of evil amongst mankind in general,[1] while others assert the Secret Society to have been first set up in England by a natural philosopher named Desaguliers, a theologian called James Anderson, and one George Payne, although it is undeniable that documents exist of an earlier date.[2] Those writers are most to be trusted who trace its origin back to the Jewish Synagogue during the Christian era. This view is confirmed by the whole tenor of the accessory legends of Freemasonry, as well as by its general character and ultimate object. The name it bears,

---

[1] Thus, for instance, De Camille, " Storia della setta Antichristiana," Florence, 1872, 2 vols. Compare " Civiltà Cattolica," quad. 524, p 190

[2] *Vide* Schiodl, in the " Kirchen-Lexikon," edited by DD. Wetzer and Welte, under the heading " Freemason."

and the ceremonies in which Masonic tools are employed, are naturally an addition of later date.

As the aim of this society is to supplant Christianity, to usurp its place as far as external and internal
power is concerned, secretly to bring everything in
Church and State, in the community and the family,
as well as matters of opinion and custom, into subjection to itself, and to establish itself amongst mankind as the supreme and sovereign bond of union, as
the so-called "kingly craft," it becomes self-evident
that such an association must be the natural enemy
of that cosmopolitan society founded by the Son of
God, the Catholic Church.

I. Above all things, this hostility makes itself felt
in the domain of faith. The treasure of revealed
truth, the deposit of the faith (*vide* i Tim. vi. 20), has
ever been the Church's choicest jewel, and to preserve
this intact has been the chief object of her existence.
Throughout untold difficulties and struggles innumerable with the delusions of perverse minds, she has
proved equal to her task, permitting whole nations to
lapse from her maternal arms rather than yield up
one iota of her trust. She holds faith to be the root
and foundation of justification, the sure guide of daily
life, and she pledges her children to defend the least
of her dogmas at the cost, if need be, of their life. A
far-reaching chain of martyrs proves that she has been
understood and obeyed. And yet if we listen to the
apologists of Freemasonry, they would have us believe

no institution to be more tolerant of and considerate towards the Church than their own. In the German Quarterly Magazine (1841, No. 1) a "brother" goes as far as possible in this respect, saying—" It (the Society of Freemasonry) has always been able to steer clear of any active interference in political or ecclesiastical matters, and to recover its original glorious path, if influences external to itself have for a short time caused it to swerve aside." Plausible words like these were certainly not out of place as long as old-fashioned governments maintained to some extent their Christian character ; as long as they abstained from unceremoniously and publicly undermining the faith, although their administration often checked and hindered the free action of the Church. But times are now altogether changed, and the Secret Society is now no longer compelled to wear any such disguises ; it can fearlessly avow and carry into practice that hatred to the Catholic faith which was born with it, and which its written records long ago expressed. We will begin by referring to one of the oldest of these.

The celebrated document executed at Cologne in 1535, to which we find the signature of Philip Melancthon appended in his character of brother of the Order of Freemasons, asserts the existence of a secret society extending over every part of the world, and called previous to the year 1440 by the name of " Confraternity of St John," but after that date, and up to 1535, known under the appellation of " Free-

masons of St John," or "Fellowship of Freemasons."
A reform of this society took place in 1717, whereby,
while its original aims remained unchanged, it assumed
a more atheistic and democratic shape, modelling its
ritual after the modern English "Book of Constitutions." (*Vide* Eckert, "Mysteries of Heathendom,"
p. 329.) The following paragraph, taken from the Cologne document, stands under the heading *A* :—"The
confraternity of Freemasons united in the Holy Rule
of St John derives its origin neither from the Templars, nor from any other Order of Knights, whether
temporal or spiritual, but is older than all such Orders,
having existed in Palestine and Greece, as well as in
both divisions of the Roman Empire, before the time
of the Crusades. Our brotherhood was already in
existence at the time when, on account of the strife of
sects respecting Christian ethics (!), a small number of
initiated persons, who were acquainted with the true
doctrines of morality, and with the correct interpretation of esoteric teaching, severed themselves from the
mass. For at that time those learned and enlightened men, true Christians who had kept themselves
perfectly free from every infection of heathen error,
believed that a religion which was tainted with heresy
could only be a source of discord, and never of union.
On this account they took a solemn oath, binding
themselves to preserve henceforth more pure and
undefiled the fundamental truths of this religion,
which, conducive as they are to virtue, are indigenous
to the human mind, and to devote themselves entirely

to this object, in order that the true light might gradually emerge from the darkness, and dispel the mists
of superstition ; that thus the peace and prosperity of
mankind might be established on a firm basis, through
the regular practice of all *natural* virtues."

Under *B* we read :—" Although in the exercise of
our beneficent influence we admit no restriction of
creed or country, we have nevertheless hitherto considered it necessary, as a precautionary measure, to
receive no one into our brotherhood who, when mix-
ing in 'profane' and unenlightened circles of society,
is not prepared to profess himself a Christian." At
the close of the document stand the words, " 1535,
according to the era called by the name of the Christian Era."

By these unimpeachable documents [1] the whole
position of Freemasonry in its hostility to the Catholic faith is clearly shown.

1. It refuses to recognise in the earlier heresies anything more than disputes about Christian morality,
although, as a matter of fact, these heresies almost invariably had reference to some point of dogma ; consequently their importance, as bearing on matters of
faith, is studiously ignored, set aside as unimportant
and contemptible, or else their very existence is
denied.

---

[1] They are acknowledged by the Lodges. *Vide* "Jaarbœkje voor
Nederlandsche Vrijmetselaren," 5872 (1872), p 59, where, under the
year 5819, it is stated that a facsimile of the document was sent to the
Dutch Lodges.

2. The Church is placed on the same level with the sects.

3. Religious truth, it is alleged, can be found neither in the Catholic Church nor in the sects, but exclusively among a small number of the initiated, viz., the old Freemasons, who had separated themselves from the majority—that is to say, from the unity—of the Church.[1]

4. The true knowledge possessed by these men professes, however, to consist only in moral teaching ; consequently, religious dogma is openly represented as mere folly ; a toy to amuse the vulgar crowd.

5. Even their morality itself is not derived from revelation, but calls itself the "natural product of the human mind."

6. The Catholic Church is said to be infected with pagan error and disfigured by false doctrine ; hence she becomes the parent of strife amongst men, and can never give peace to the world.

7. Thus (and this is the necessary inference of what has gone before) every one initiated in the secret teaching pledges himself to combat the Catholic superstition with all his might, and to establish peace and prosperity amongst mankind by means of purely natural religion.

Such are the terrible designs of this dark sect. Have we then gone too far in imputing to Freemasons

[1] This idea has been poetically handled in the parable of the Three Rings in Lessing's drama of " Nathan," written in the interests of Freemasonry, to which body the author himself belonged.

a deadly enmity to the Catholic faith? Can it be said that the English edition of the Rules issued in 1717 is couched in more moderate terms? By no means. It is precisely in regard to this essential element of Masonry that its Conservatism is specially manifested; behind this smooth-sounding phraseology lurks the old hatred of the faith. The following are indicated as the chief duties and fundamental principles of the Freemason (Anderson's "Book of Constitutions," Frankfort, 1743, p. 298, &c.) :—"As a true Noachite, the Mason is obliged to conform to the Moral Law; and if he rightly understands his craft, he will neither be an atheist, nor openly irreligious and dissolute. It is now considered expedient, in contrast to the usages of former days" (charming fiction!), "to pledge the Masons to hold such religious beliefs only as all men share in common—that is, to return to the earliest form of Catholic (!) Christianity, calling on them to be good and true, honourable and upright men, and to observe all such reasonable commands of morality as meet with universal acceptation. Meanwhile 'each individual member is left free to adhere to his own particular form of religious opinion; all controversies and disputes about religion and politics are prohibited, and the Masons are desired to live as peaceable citizens, in obedience to the civil authorities. Nevertheless, a Brother who may have taken part in an insurrection against the State, without being guilty of any other offence, is not on this account cut off from connection with his Lodge. One essential law for all

the members is that of brotherly love, mutual help
and fidelity ; each is bound to look upon the others
in the light of equals and brothers, and upon the whole
society as a fellowship of humanity, philanthropy,
tolerance, and friendly intercourse."

It must immediately strike the thoughtful reader
that the Mason, considered in his character of
Noachite, not as the adherent of any positive religion,
is bound to observe such laws of reason and morality
only as are universally recognised as binding, and
to be honourable and upright in his dealings.   In
regard to everything else, he may, from prudential
motives, join in the outward observances of the
religious body of which he is a professed member, or
of whatever party expediency may point out to be the
best ; for instance, in England he will be an Anglican,
in Prussia a Protestant, at Rome a Catholic, in
Turkey a Mohammedan ; for, to speak more plainly,
all positive religion is an empty form.   If, however,
the Mason is a man of uprightness and honour, he
must, for consistency's sake, strive with all his might
to set his fellow-men free from religious errors,—that
is to say, from the mistake of having any religion at
all.   Hence, according to the very just remarks of
Jarcke (" Miscellaneous Writings," vol. 2, " Essay on
the Creed of the Illuminati ") :—"When Freemasonry
was founded for the second time, it at once assumed
a position of definite hostility to all that is positive in
the dogmas and forms of Christianity, for the task it
then proposed to itself was by no means limited to

uniting all its members, belonging to different Christian bodies, in the bond of civil and social unity, and bringing to bear on their external life the humanising influences of friendly intercourse. On the contrary, from the very first it set its face boldly in the direction of Indifferentism and Deism,[1] keeping in its own hands the power of regulating all that is positive in the belief of its Christian members, whilst allowing them outwardly to conform to any religious creed or opinion; since the only religion to which they were virtually pledged was a nominal one, reduced to a hollow form, drained of vital faith, and consisting merely of those universal laws of reason and morality on which all men are agreed." It is self-evident that the immediate result of views like these must be war to the knife against the Catholic Church and her sacred creed. Were she but once overthrown, the fragments severed from her in bygone times, the so-called sects, must inevitably share her fate, and then the dogmas of the "honourable man," the "universal religion of mankind," could drive its triumphal car over her ruins all round the world. Formerly it was sought to undermine faith by cold indifference, by assuming the disguise of an angel of light, and professing a certain general Christianity. All this, however, is no longer needed; in the present day hypocrisy is a superfluous trouble, for the Speculative or Blue Lodge equals the Red in its bold

---

[1] But even this was not its real object. We shall show later on that, in its ultimate aim, it goes very far beyond Deism.

avowal of enmity to the Catholic faith. As far back as 1841, the Freemason quoted above writes in the German Quarterly Magazine:—"The necessity of counteracting the influence exercised by Jesuits, and other opponents of the march of intellect, did perhaps render concealment needful at first, and the conscience of many an orthodox Catholic could only be set at rest by departing from our old simple ideal. For we must do the Roman Church the justice to say that she recognised the true aim and wide scope of the league, as well as its great importance, more clearly and at an earlier date than many of its members themselves, and held to her opinion with greater tenacity than they did." In order more fully to convince our readers, we will bring forward some additional testimony.

The "Journal of Freemasonry, printed for circulation among the Brothers" (Altenburg, 1823, i. 1, p. 95, *seq*), contains the following passages:—"The form of government or organisation of a Lodge realises the most perfect system possible; the constitution is democratic and the government representative. The members are divided into three classes—youths, men, and elders. The brotherhood is to be cemented by uniting the members of various religious bodies in natural religion, by equality of rights and claims, by common pleasures and common action in the interests of philanthropy."

In the Vienna "Freemason's Journal, for circulation among the Brothers," ii., 3, p 21, the Speaker of

the Lodge thus addresses the Brothers : " In early
times the inhabitants of Samothracia worshipped only
the heaven and the earth, because Nature was father
and mother to them, and there were then neither
priests nor despots to make them misjudge and hate
their divine parent, by craft and by force, by means
of superstition and oppression, by inward and outward coercion." On the reception of a Lutheran
preacher in Vienna, according to the same journal
(ii. 3, p. 184), the following was sung :—

> " What is there to choose between cross of gold
> Or breastplate as worn by high priest of old ?
> What if grass-green turban, adorned with lace,
> Or more elegant mitre the forehead grace ?
> Whether Pope of Rome his allegiance claim,
> Or pope of a place less well-known to fame,
> Of Hamburg or Stamboul, what matters the name ? "

The " Latomia " (vol. xii. p. 168) represents another speaker as addressing the Brothers in a somewhat similar strain :—" It is just as one-sided to be a
Catholic as a Lutheran, a Quaker, &c. The educated
man, especially the Mason, must be entirely free
from any such party-colouring."

II. A league which is diametrically opposed to the
Catholic faith, and has shown implacable hostility
towards it, cannot fail to prove an equally bitter
opponent where questions of morality are concerned.
By its own admission, it obliges its members to observe those rules only of reason and morality which
meet with universal recognition. But, in the name

B

of Heaven, how inconceivably wide that cloak of
morality must be, beneath whose folds the Chinese
adorer of Confucius and the Buddhist Malay, the
heathen Indian and the Turk, the fire-worshipping
Parsee and the Rationalist of the first water, the
Catholic and the Calvinist, can dwell together and
join hands in brotherly love! It is our firm persuasion that the League does not understand a single
one of the Ten Commandments in the same sense as
the Catholic Church, and that the fair dealing even
of " the honourable man" would suffer shipwreck, as
soon as Church property—and other property too—
had to be dealt with. Even the panegyrist of Freemasonry in the German Quarterly Magazine referred
to above, cannot entirely succeed in hiding its moral
nakedness when he writes in its exculpation :—
" Whilst it leaves dogmas untouched, and teaches
that every external respect and honour be paid to
the different forms of belief, the brotherhood derives
its spirit from the highest teaching of all, as proclaimed by its illustrious founder—a teaching which
is, alas ! too openly misunderstood—and which it endeavours to reduce to practice, and make fruitful in
daily life. Freemasonry may be termed the religion
of the full-grown man." But òf what nature can be
this morality of the full-grown—*i.e.*, the completely
independent—man, which, to use a common expression, puts both God and Beelzebub out of the question ? Much the same as that of the late Grand
Master Mazzini, who would giv the dagger into the
hand of the man he was about t send out on an

errand of death, and afterwards praise the assassin
for having one of those strong natures which allows
the influence of no third person to interfere between
himself and his conscience. The following important admission, found in an official apology for the
association, is remarkably similar:[1]—"Freemasonry
teaches how to be virtuous without the stimulus
of hope or fear, independently alike of heaven and
hell! The Mason looks for no future reward; he
has received his recompense in the present, and is
therewith content." In other words, as there is
neither heaven nor hell, consequently neither eternal
reward nor eternal punishment, the actions of men
are unshackled; we need only have due regard to
time and place, in order not to damage our reputation as respectable members of society. Thus Freemasonry carries us at one bound far back behind the
ancient Paganism of Greece and Rome in respect
to matters of morality. There is no Elysium to
attract, no Tantalus to terrify; man is absolute
master of his own belief and actions. Every one is
a usurper who issues laws restricting the unfettered
liberty which is every man's right, or prescribing the

[1] "The Attitude of Freemasonry in Relation to the Present Day:
An Open Exposure of the Object and History of Freemasonry,
together with an Answer to the most Recent Charges brought against
it, by E. E. Eckert, Barrister in Dresden, Leipzig, 1852." To repel
these charges a great Convention of the Order had been held, the
Grand Master of Germany himself being present, at which an apolo-
getic address for the benefit of the less-instructed brethren was delivered
It appeared under the above title. Cf. Eckert "On the Question of the
Recognition of Freemasonry by the State," 2d ed., Vienna, 1862, p. 45.

course he should take. With such premisses, it was easy for the writer in the German Quarterly Magazine already referred to, to say that Freemasonry was a League which had rendered itself illustrious by producing results such as cannot fail to be brought about by a League having for its object to unite together that which States, Churches, and social grades are the means of dividing, and to sing its praises as having triumphantly succeeded in levelling the boundary walls which so sharply define the different religious creeds. What attitude must this mode of viewing things cause it to assume in regard to Catholic morality? How will it look on the laws of self-denial, of mortification of the evil passions in the human heart, of Christian humility and purity, of obedience and forgiveness, and, above all, of that fairest blossom the Church can show—the evangelical counsels?[1] Must not the saints, those great heroes of the Church, appear fools in its eyes? Yes, we need not wonder if the apostles of this dark League speak of "pernicious Jesuit morality," and show for Gury's "Handbook of Morals" an abhorrence as strong as that shown by the Devil for holy water. They hug themselves in the fond belief that the

---

[1] On the occasion of the consecration of the Lodge Mataram in Djokdjokarta (Dutch possessions in India), the presiding Brother (Van Hengel) spoke thus on the second light being kindled—"Mataram, be strong and mighty! Be a bulwark against the inroads of prejudice, folly, and superstition. May this light guide you in the conflict on which you will soon have to enter."—*Jaarboekje voor Nederlandsche Vrijmetselaren*, 5872 (1872), p. 156.

Church, with all her dogmas and precepts, has been barren of results ;[1] and that their League has been the first to do something for the amelioration of mankind. But they deceive themselves, and, as we think, with their eyes open. The Catholic Church was, and still is, abundantly productive of the highest moral perfection ; not, however, in the case of those who allow their passions to legislate for them. We must not anticipate, otherwise we might here point out the moral abyss into which Freemasonry would precipitate the human race. This subject is reserved for our eighth chapter.

III. From what has been said, the tremendous hatred of Freemasonry to the Church follows as a natural consequence. Its owes its origin, to all appearances, to rabbinic animosity against the Son of God, put to death on the first Good Friday. The Cologne document of 1535 boasts the signatures of Philip Melancthon, of the unhappy Hermann von

---

[1] Menzel, in his " Neuere Geschichte der Deutschen," v. 10, p 312, Breslau, writes in a similar strain :—" It was the endeavour of Freemasons to recast in the mould of their Brotherhood those bonds of common interest in spiritual matters which had been slackened under ecclesiastical government, if not completely severed by schism, and converted into causes of discord. They hoped by means of mysterious rites to divert that love of dogmas and symbols which is easily excited in the human breast, away from the conflicting current of ecclesiastical opinions into the safe channel of a morality founded on reason. In fact, they aimed at supplanting the inefficient doctrines and rites of the Church by sound moral principles and social intercourse " This passage acknowledges the unconcealed warfare of the Lodge against Christian dogma, especially as presented in its most positive form by the Catholic Church.

Wied, then Elector of Cologne, and of Coligny, the
leader of the French Huguenots. Those by whom
Christians were most cruelly persecuted during the
first French Revolution were all Freemasons; and
every subsequent act of violence directed against the
Catholic Church has either been instigated by Freemasons, or has at least met with their approval and
moral support.   At all events, as long as their endeavour was, in strictly Catholic countries like Austria
and Bavaria, where Catholicism was upheld by law
and was the religion of the State, to destroy the power
of the hierarchy, slowly undermining it through the
tenacious perseverance of centuries, they spoke in a
high strain of the respect to be shown by every true
Freemason to dogma and forms of belief; tolerance
was lauded as the fairest jewel in the crown of princely
or civilian virtue ;[1] and under cover of such words
they sought gradually to blunt the edge of Catholic
fervour, and prepare the way for the introduction of
error. . And if from time to time an open attack was

---

[1] At first the Austrian Freemasons—to whose membership Francis
of Lorraine belonged, although he kept this secret from his noble con-
sort, Maria Teresa—represented themselves merely as zealous promoters
of enlightenment, and opponents of the abuses in the human element
in the Church, and as desirous of assisting the State to regain the rightful
position towards the Church which it formerly occupied.   They began
by interfering with old customs and by dictating in matters of ritual
observance, intending to proceed to raise a storm against the discipline
of the Church, to overthrow the former marriage laws, and abolish the
celibacy of the clergy ; the final aim being to destroy the foundations
of the Christian State.   Thus Brunner, " Mysterien der Aufklarung in
Oesterreich," Mayence, 1869, p. 151.

made on the Catholic phalanx, the plea urged was
the necessity of "counteracting Jesuits and other
opponents of progress." But now the day of concealment is past; the Church of Christ and the bastard
offspring of darkness stand face to face, with visors
raised. Edgar Quinet, a "Brother," openly and
boldly declares: "The Catholic religion must be
stifled in the mire."[1] Thus we find the Lodges of
both hemispheres uniting with the revolutionary
Cæsarism which assaults the Church, everywhere
directing their efforts to effect the separation of
Church and State, and the banishment of religion
from everyday life, to introduce undenominational
education, under the supervision of the State alone, as
well as civil marriage; in a word, to build up a State
without God. In order to be able to oppose confessors from the realm of darkness to the confessors
of Christianity, who should be the avowed offspring
of Freemasonry, the sect of the "Solidaires" was
formed; and since the funeral obsequies of Brother
Verhaegen at Brussels, it has celebrated its apotheosis
of hatred and contempt of the Church not only in
Belgium, but in the Free States of America, in
France, and in the Eternal City itself. When the
more aristocratic member of the Lodge fears to soil

---

[1] "Il faut étouffer la religion catholique dans la boue."—*V. La
Franc-maçonnerie dans l'état, par un ancien frère de l'ordre*, Brussels,
1859, 8, p. 40. In another speech, "Brother" Bello calls the Catholic
Church "a corrupt Church, and a faith which centres in a worship of
itself."—*Jaarboekje voor Nederlandsche Vrijmetselaren*, 5872, p. 174.

his hands, he calls in the assistance of his plebeian
step-brother from the affiliated Societies ; for occasions
constantly occur in public life when the bepraised
lower orders prove useful in doing dirty work, as, for
instance, forcing a majority in the Chambers in order
to turn out the Catholic Ministry in Belgium. If a
Government, such as the Austrian was up to 1866,
refuse to enact anything injurious to Christianity, it
is subjected to a series of annoying attacks from the
press, and other more influential agencies, until in
very desperation it consents to deliver over the Bride
of Jesus Christ to the unchivalrous Knights of the
Secret Society.

This hatred descends to the simple details of everyday life, not scorning even to pry into a railway *coupé*,
the unfortunate priesthood having to bear the brunt of
its most furious persecutions, as shown by the infamous lies of the " Chronique Scandaleuse," and by
the thousand difficulties daily experienced in the
performance of all religious functions. To preach
the truths of the faith is deemed folly, since religion
is defined to be the practice of morality ; to insist on
a Christian life is deemed intolerance ; and the refusal
to yield up rights common to all is branded as love
of power. Only the tepid, unorthodox, and worldly
priest is considered a true representative of his class,
and deserving of preferment. And with all their
hellish hatred of the Catholic Church, the " Brothers "
have yet the effrontery to complain that they are
" hunted down on all sides like wild beasts by royal

àvarice and Ultramontane fury."[1] If the crying intolerance of which they are guilty be pointed out to them, they become piously indignant over such a rash judgment, asserting that they highly esteem real religion, and only take up arms against "prejudice, folly, and superstition;" not being, of course, honest enough to confess that with these three opprobrious epithets they intend to designate our Holy Church. But cowardly hypocrisy and equivocation are ever the heritage of all Secret Societies.

Religious Orders are the fairest flowers in the Church's garden. Even an Order which has lost somewhat of its early fervour is always a great support to Catholic life, and a powerful agent for good. How much more does this apply to a zealous religious body! And as in the present day it is only zeal that enables the Orders to hold their ground, they are the object of the bitter hatred of Freemasonry. In speaking before one of the Lodges of Brussels, "Brother" Boulard declared that he would like to do away with convents and monks altogether, even though recourse to main force might be requisite. This intolerant utterance, at variance with the professed principles of the Society, was greeted with a deafening burst of applause.[2] A precisely similar onslaught on religious orders was begun in Austria

---

[1] These are woids uttered by Brother Juge, editor of the Masonic paper *Le Globe* " Traqués de toutes parts comme des bêtes fauves par l'avidité royale et la rage ultramontane."—*Cf. Le danger de croire facilement aux prophéties*, Brussels, 1872, p 66.

[2] "La Franc maçonnerie dans l'Etat," p 40.

by the Freemasons of that country in the time of the
unhappy and misguided Joseph II., and was unfortunately only too successfully carried out.   In order
more thoroughly to uproot the Catholic Church, it was
necessary to put a stop to the influence exercised by
convents over the education of the rising generation
upon Christian life in the world.   For this end a
host of infamous writers employed lies, calumnies,
and contempt, representing places consecrated to the
life of perfection to be abodes of darkness and superstition, thus to make their spoliation and destruction
more sure.   Amongst these writers, the founder of
the Vienna Lodge of "True Unity," named Born, a
member of the Imperial Council, and personal friend
of the Emperor, distinguished himself by his cynical
hatred and unscrupulous mendacity.[1]   With him, and

---

[1] In his infamous "Monachologia," for instance, he thus expresses
himself : "The race of monks may be divided into three families, viz ,
those who eat flesh, those who eat fish and flesh, and those who eat
fish alone.   A monk may be described as a creature resembling man,
who wears a cowl, howls at night, and is always thirsty.   Man is
possessed of speech, reason, and will ; the monk is dumb at times, and
is devoid of judgment or will.   Man gains his bread in the sweat of his
brow ; the monk fattens in idleness.   Man dwells among his fellow-
men ; the monk loves solitude and shuns the light.   Hence we see
that the monk is a species of mammal differing from man, a kind of
cross-breed between men and monkeys,•most like the latter, since
speech and food scarcely suffice to distinguish him from them.   How
much he resembles the ape, that most hideous creation in the animal
kingdom !   The use of the monk is this,—to fill space and to eat."
This lampoon, written in Latin, and afterwards translated into German,
was distributed in thousands by the "Brethren," and, as a matter of
course, reckoned among "the most famous products of the human
mind."   Cardinal Migazzi, Archbishop of Vienna, presented to the

under him, throughout the wide provinces of the Danube, Apprentices, Fellow-crafts, and Master-masons worked on the same plan, bringing upon Austria the evils under which it still smarts. Similar effects springing from the same causes are to be seen in our own day. The outburst against Jesuits in Germany is the work of the Lodges, whose fury will soon extend to all other religious communities in the Church ; the final results—so these hellish adversaries are fain to hope—will follow as a matter of course.

For ecclesiastical dignitaries, especially the bishops and the Pope, no better fate has been reserved by the

King a memorial couched in most moderate terms, but to no avail. On this account Joseph II. met with most enthusiastic applause from the Freemasons, *e g*, '' Were Christ to come to earth again, the first thing He would do would be to betake Himself to Vienna to seek out the great Joseph ; He would fall on his neck, embrace him tenderly, and say, ' Dear Joseph, My beloved son, thou art he whom My Heavenly Father has placed as a sovereign upon the earth in order to restore to its primeval splendour My holy religion, which the godless monks and priests who, perhaps, wish to crucify Me anew, have defaced with a thousand superstitions. Thou, Joseph, art the man chosen by My Father for this important work, and since neither the Pope, My representative, nor the bishops, will support thee, as their duty binds them to do, in thy ordinances and wise appointments, I have been sent once more to earth to give a helping hand to the undertaking.'' By the way we may remark, that nothing tends more to trample majesty into the dust, and render it contemptible, than clumsy flattery of this sort, the folly of which must be apparent to the simplest man among the people. " Brother " Ratschky congratulates the Emperor on his conquest over "that hydra of monasticism, and because the greatest prince now occupying a German throne protects Freemasonry with his shield "—*Cf. Seb. Brunner, Die Mysterien der Aufklarung in Oesterreich,* 1770, 1800, from archives and other sources hitherto untouched. Mayence, 1809. Also, " Theologische Dienerschaft am Hofe Joseph II." Both works are worth reading at the present time.

Secret Societies, since the shepherds must first be slain before the sheep of the flock can be scattered far and wide. Let us confine our attention to the past, as to-day is but a development of yesterday. In 1781, when Joseph II. sat upon the throne, the Austrian " Brothers" first began to pour their flood of unmitigated contempt upon the best bishops of the realm. While they mutually extolled one another as " men of honour," they made furious sallies against all " opponents of the light, against priestly rogues and deceivers," demanding that the Emperor should put down these "good-for-nothing clerical Mandarins, and unearth the political moles who were burrowing under the State with their crooked ways and cross-grained faces." [1] Hence we see that the hostile sentiments with which the clergy were credited were punishable even then, and that priests were considered to be dangerous to the State (*staatsgefährlich*) a hundred years ago. There is nothing new under the sun ; nothing is learnt or forgotten by Masons. Had not the " German Library " established by Nicolai in Berlin the

[1] The pages of the " Katholische Phantasien-und Predigeralmanach," published by the members of the Union, were filled year by year from beginning to end with the most scurrilous attacks upon religion and the bishops. A Life of the Blessed Virgin is reviled in this almanac in passages such as the following " In chap 14, Christian blockheads are made acquainted with the perfections or virtues which adorned Mary during her life in the temple." Of Bishop Felix of Ypres is said, " He has a special attraction to the devotion of the maternal heart of Jesus, a devotion which even fools see to be folly. . . . . In its honour he established a particular Confraternity, confirmed by that hawker of indulgences, Pius VI , among the Benedictines of Ypres " And the bishops who paid then homage to the venerable Pope Pius VI., on his arrival in

self-same object in view? A similar hatred was displayed, and the same weapons were employed, in the
persecutions carried on against the Catholic faith by
the accursed sect of the Illuminati, established by
the Freemason F. A. Weishaupt, the parent of that
wretched class of individuals who, at the present
day, are thrusting themselves into notice in Bavaria.
It is true that, later on, many Freemasons were
ashamed to acknowledge such sorry comrades, but it
cannot be denied that Weishaupt was a Freemason,[1]
that his doings, far from being disowned, were approved of by the Lodge, and at the Convention of
Wilhelmsbad the Illuminati were able to boast that
there was not one of all the Lodges legitimately
established in Germany which was not in correspondence with their Order.

It is natural that the most intense hatred should
concentrate itself on the central point of Catholic
unity, the Papacy. For ninety years past the Secret
Society has plainly been striving to wrest the States of
the Church from the dominion of the Pope. We find

Vienna, were scoffed at in the most disgraceful manner by the organs of
Freemasonry—*e g*, the "Realzeitung," and Vienna "Freimaurerjour-
nal." The Pope himself fared no better during his residence in the
Austrian capital. V. Brunner, "Mysterien," p. 199, also his "Theolog.
Dienerschaft," p 423, and other lampoons of the time. Besides the
above named Born and Ratschky, Reinhold, Haschka, and the notorious
Blumauer were amongst the active Masons. Brunner tells us that in
1783 there were already forty volumes of Masonic songs, many of them
printed with music, which were sung at the Masonic religious services

[1] "V. Jaarboekje voor Nederlandsche Vrijmetselaren," 1872, p. 54,
under the year 5785 = 1785.

" Brot   Haschka[1] inciting the Emperor Joseph II.
to aid ₋his project; and other pamphleteers during the

[1] Brunner, "Mystenen," p. 107. We will quote one verse only of
Haschka's rhymes :—

> "Accomplish the work ! nor let Papal guile,
> Nor its fawning slaves with their Jesuit smile,
> Wearing piety's cloak, but assassins at heart,
> Deter you from acting so noble a part "

Another wearer of the leather apron writes thus :—" What should
we do if our Emperor were to be excommunicated ? Why laugh, laugh
with all our might ! O Joseph, great immortal Joseph ! The nations
of the future, whose emancipation thou alone wast capable of effecting,
will thank thee in years to come, will pay to thy ashes the tribute of
copious tears, like clouds of incense ; and no true-hearted German will
pass thy tomb without arresting his steps, and thinking with a sigh
Here lies Joseph, the greatest Emperor ever known."—*Brunner*, p 220.
In proof that the hatred of the Lodges to the Papacy has, if possible,
increased in our own day, we transcribe in the original the following
verses, sung at a Masonic banquet in Belgium.

L'EXCOMMUNICATION.

A ce Banquet où l'amitié préside,
J'avais dessein d'apporter ma gaîté ,
Helas ! la peur me rend la voix timide
Du Vatican les foudres m'ont heurté
Un jour l'Enfer décuplera sa dîme
Sur les maçons que je vois assemblés
Freres pour vous, ah ! ma pitié s'anime,
Vous êtes tous des excommuniés.

Vous méprisez *une idole pourrie,*
Devant laquelle un peuple est à genoux ;
Il existait dans son temple blottie,
Une Hydre obscène ayant les yeux sur vous
Le vieux serpent aujourd'hui se ranime,
Son noir venin vous a tous effleurés
Freres pour vous, ah ! ma pitié s'anime,
Vous êtes tous des excommuniés.

Quoi vous riez du courroux du St-Père
Et vous raillez du nouveau mandement,
Tout comme si, *pour son épouse altière,*
Dieu dût faillir au dernier jugement

Si la creance était illegitime,
Que de dévots auraient un pied de nez
Frères pour vous, ah ! ma pitié s'anime,
Vous êtes tous des excommuniés

Vous reveillant d une terre maudite,
Que direz-vous au portier des Elus ?
Quand près de Dieu la vertu seule acquitte,
Au goupillon St-Pierre tient bien plus
En vain il voit les pauvres soulagés
Frères pour vous, ah ! ma pitié s'anime,
Vous êtes tous des excommunies

Mai je me tais, j'entends votre murmure
Qui vient me dire Irions nous au taudis
Ou *Borgia* promène sa souillure ?
Pape infaillible il est en Paradis
A libre choix, nous preferons l'abyme
Ou De Voltaire est au rang des damnés
Point n'est besoin que ta pitié s anime,
Nous voulons tous être excommuniés

Par un jeune F .   de la Persévérance.

reign of the same monarch making merry beforehand
over the excommunication which their "immortal
Joseph" would incur in the event of his following
their advice. When the Grand Master of the Grand
Orientals of France, Prince Murat, voted in the
Senate for the temporal power of the Holy Father,
such a storm was aroused by the heretical boldness
displayed in this anti-Masonic action, that he was
forced to resign his post in favour of Marshal Magnan. ("Laacher Stimmen," February 1872, p. 118,
&c.) The sacrilegious act perpetrated on September
20, 1870, as well as the whole success of revolutionary principles in the South, is to be attributed
to Freemasonry, this triumph having been promised
to it five and a half years before, as a reward for
services rendered elsewhere. The remarkable
lethargy displayed by European diplomatic circles
on the occasion referred to may be traced to the
same source.

IV. Heresies and schisms are no unimportant auxiliaries in carrying on war with the Church of Christ;
therefore Freemasonry fosters and promotes every
heretical rising within the realm of Catholic Christendom. By it the Jansenists and Febronians of former
days were petted and caressed ; the Josephinian
excitement was for the most part the work, long
prepared, of the Austrian Brothers of Beelzebub ; and
the same may be said in the case of the heresies
disseminated on German soil by fallen spirits during

the last few years. The tremendous outcry invariably accompanying their miserable attempts, calculated, if possible, to deceive the very elect, must be traced to the same dark agencies. Let us hear the testimony of two witnesses.

Jochmus-Muller, President of the German Catholic Community in Berlin, writes thus in his " Kirchenreform " (vol. iii. p. 230) : "Every one is aware that Freemasonry has exerted a favourable influence on the development of German Catholicism, which has contributed so many valiant recruits to its ranks, and that no attempt is made by either side at concealing the perfect concord existing between them on religious matters. Together with this admission, we must express our firm conviction that these common principles form the religion of the future, which, in spite of excommunication and compulsion, of skill and cunning, will soon be believed explicitly, as they already are implicitly, by the majority of educated people."

Giese, a member of the Lodge of Halle, and pastor of the German-Catholic, called later the Free, Church of that place, declares in the Berlin "Allgemeine Kirchenzeitung" (1847)—" The doctrines of the Free Church are a sort of popularised Freemasonry. Moreover, all Civic Unions, Trade Unions, Polytechnic Societies, Sunday Schools, Musical Clubs, &c., pursue the same end, and only apply the great principle of Freemasonry, of which they are Associates and Sister-societies, in a somewhat different manner and form." If we cannot interpret these words in their fullest meaning, they are, at any rate, more than sufficient to prove our assertion.

And now look at the apostates of later days. How tender is the friendship that binds them to the heroes of the trowel and plumb-line! They have even taken the pains to learn Masonic slang, and are as proud of this accomplishment as a negro can be of the glass-beads for which he has just bartered true gold. They are rewarded by being received as Brothers, and having fresh life communicated to them. We will give one example of the mutual similarity in thought and speech of the different Lodges. On the occasion of the dedication of Lodge "Mataram" in Djokdjokarta, the speaker thus expressed himself :— " Freemasonry aims at the amelioration of the human race, the development of man as a rational being, capable of thought, will, and action, and the advancement of society on the path of culture, science, learning, morality, sociability, and philanthropy " ("Jaarboekje," &c., p. 159). Are not the sounds re-echoed from Dutch Java identical with those heard in the petty congresses of modern Protestants, and the sapient utterances of their Patriarch ? *Quomodo cecidisti!*

In times when storms rage high against the Catholic Church, the Secret Union gains immensely in the number of its members, in its power over fashionable society, and in its influence in ruling circles.[1]

[1] We have inserted in the third division of this little work a list of the

C

The ill-will which would lead it to wage war to the knife with the Church is never wanting. It has ever at hand an innumerable array of confederates, composed of craven souls who lack the courage to stand up for Christ; of worldly-minded persons, who esteem gold of greater value than virtue; of liberal Catholics, who, in the heat of the strife, would make peace on dishonourable terms; of all those professing Christians outside the Church's pale, who, in the dim twilight of their false creed, bore holes in the bottom of the great ship on which their own little bark is carried. It were culpable negligence in us Catholics to under-estimate our enemy because he works in silence, and to speak slightingly of him even in the present day, when the successes he achieves are trumpeted abroad. The Popes have judged very differently of the Secret Society. Clement XII., as early as 18th April 1738, issued a bull threatening all secret sects with the severest penalties of the Church, especially that of the Freemasons. The menace was confirmed and renewed by Benedict XIV. in a fresh bull, March 18, 1751. Pius VII. raised his voice against the Carbonari, one of the Masonic Parties of Action, in his bull of September 13, 1821. Leo XII. also denounced Freemasons in a bull of March 13, 1826. Gregory XVI., too, in his Encyclical (August 15, 1832), enlightened the Christian world in regard to the danger that

principal European and American Lodges, taken from an official Masonic source

awaited it; and Pius IX. has repeatedly done the same.[1] Obedient to the warning cry uttered by their Chief Shepherd in 1837, the Belgian bishops collectively declared all Freemasons to be excommunicated. The more the secular power acts as if it were deaf to the sounds of these sappers and miners, the louder must all Catholics raise their voice; and they must no longer refuse to see more than a convivial and bacchanalian club in a society spoken of by the Popes as seriously endangering the salvation of souls and the work of the Church. Did not the Freemason whom we have already so often quoted, himself acknowledge in the German Quarterly Magazine— "In justice to the Roman hierarchy, it must be said that they recognised the true aim and wide scope of the Society, as well as its great importance, not only more clearly, but at an earlier date, than did many of its members themselves, and they held to their opinions with greater tenacity."

Thus the days have now come of which the first Pope wrote these words:—"There were also false prophets among the (Jewish) people, even as there shall be among you lying teachers, who shall bring in sects of perdition, and deny the Lord who bought them, bringing on themselves swift destruction; and many shall follow their luxuries, through whom the

[1] In the Encyclical *Qui pluribus*, November 9, 1846; the Allocution *Quibus quantisque* of April 20, 1849; the Encyclical *Noscitis et nobiscum*, December 8, 1849, the Allocution *Singulari quadam*, December 9, 1854; the Encyclical *Quanto conficiamur moerore*, August 10, 1863. Cf. *Syllabus*, sec. iv.

way of truth shall be evil-spoken of; and through covetousness shall they with feigned words make merchandise of you " (2 Peter ii. 1–3).

The public action of the Church is already much hampered, if not altogether checked, all over Europe, but the work is as yet incomplete ; erelong she will be completely thrust back into the Catacombs, there, like a criminal, to call her children together in secret, while the birds of night greet the grey, dim light—so uncongenial to man—and rejoice in it as in the glorious brightness of noonday splendour.   Maxentius and Constantine the Great once more stand opposed to one another, and victory is once more reserved for him who obeys the heavenly voice : *In hoc signo vinces.*

CHAPTER III.

STATISTICS OF FREEMASONRY IN THE YEAR 1871.

N.B.—The following list does not pretend to be a complete one. We have endeavoured to give such information only as we could gather with absolute certainty from the books of the Freemasons themselves.

Prussia.	(a) Grand National Parent Lodge of "The Three Globes," in Berlin.	(a, b, c) William I, Emperor of Germany and King of Prussia. *Representative* — Frederick William, Crown Prince of the German Empire and of Prussia	C. F. Von Messerschmidt.	..	108
Do.	(b) "Royal York Friendship" Lodge, in Berlin.	*Hon. Gr. Master*—Lewis William Augustus, Prince of Baden.	J. F. Schnackenburg.		46
Do.	(c) Grand Patriotic Lodge of Germany, in Berlin.	*Master of the Order*—Frederick William, Crown Prince.	C. Von Dachroden.	For Prussia at Konigsburg, Mecklenburg at Rostock, Silesia at Breslau, Lower Saxony at Hamburg, Pomerania at Stettin, Rhenish Westphalia at Crefeld	77
Saxony.	Grand Patriotic Lodge at Dresden.		G H Warnatz.		18
Hamburg.	Grand Lodge of Hamburg.		H. W. Buek.	To this belongs the Provincial Lodge of Mecklenburg-Schwerin and Strelitz at Rostock	29
Frankfort-on Main.	"The Eclectic Union."		H. Weismann.		10
Hesse-Darmstadt.	"Of Unity."		A. Pfaltz.		9
Bavaria.	"Of the Sun," at Bayreuth.	Lewis, 3d Grand Duke.	F. Feustel.		15 [1
Switzerland.	"The Alpina"		A. Humbert, in Neuchâtel.		28

	Grand Lodge	Patron	Grand Master	Remarks	
Austria, Cis-Leithan	Not known.				
Do. Trans-Leithan	Grand Lodge of Hungary, at Pesth.		F. Pulszky.		14
Luxemburg.	"Suprême Conseil"				2
Netherlands.	Dutch National Grand Lodge.	William Fred. Charles, Prince of the Netherlands.[2]	M. L. Schroblgen, Europe: J. J. F. Noordzaek, at the Hague; India: T. H. Der Kinderen in Batavia	Empire, Colonies (Surinam, Curaçoa, and Capland).	67 work 15 pass.
Belgium.	(a) Suprême Consel.		Wasselaer.		17
Do.	(b) Grand Orient.		Van Humbeek.		60
France.	(a) Grand Orient.		{ The Grand Mastership abolished in 1871		292
Do.	(b) Suprême Consel.		Crémieux.		50
Great Britain.	(a) Grand Lodge of England, in London.		Lord de Grey and Ripon.	42 Provincial Grand Lodges, of which 25 are in the Colonies	1334
Do.	(b) Grand Lodge of Scotland, in Edinburgh.		Lord Dalhousie.	44 Provincial Lodges, of which 14 abroad.	385
Do.	(c) Grand Lodge of Ireland, in Dublin.		Duke of Leinster.	19 Provincial Grand Lodges, of which 6 abroad.	337
Sweden.	National Grand Lodge at Stockholm.	King Charles XV.	Oscar Fred., Grand Prince (now King)	3 Provincial Lodges.	16
Denmark.	Grand Lodge at C'hagen		Trap		4
Portugal.	Grande Orente Lusitano Undo.		Gr. de Paraty.		33
Spain.	(a) Grand Orient at Mad		R. M. Calatrava.	Unknown.	Unknown
Do.	(b) Grand Lodge de España		M. R. Zorilla.	Do.	Do.
Italy.	Grand Orente at Rome	King Victor Emmanuel.	Jos. Mazzoni.	Do.	150
Greece	Grand Lodge of Greece				12

[1] There is besides the Association of German Freemasons—President, R. Seydel. Secretary, J. G. Findel

[2] The Prince resigned in the autumn of 1872; the members of the Lodge wished to elect in his place the brother of the King, Prince William Frederick Henry, born 1820, to the great annoyance of the Catholic population

B —SUMMARY OF THE PRINCIPAL AMERICAN
IN THE YEAR 1871.

I.—UNITED STATES.

State	Grand Lodge at	Grand Master
Alabama	Montgomery	G. D. Norris
Arkansas	Little Rock	A. A. English
California	San Francisco	Prutt
Colorado	Central City	H M. Feller
Columbia	Washington	R. B. Donaldson
Connecticut	New Haven	E. S Quintard
Delaware	Wilmington	E. F. Hoiner
Florida	Tallahassee	S. Benezet
Georgia	Macon	S Lawrence
Idaho	Idaho City	G Coe
Illinois	Springfield	D. C. Gregier
Indiana	Indianopolis	M. H. Rice
Iowa	Des Moines	J Scott
Kansas	Leavenworth	J H Brown
Kentucky	Louisville	W. C. Egington
Louisiana	New Orleans	S. M Todd
Maine	Portland	J H Lynde
Maryland	Baltimoie	J. Coates
Massachusetts	Boston	W. S. Gardner
Michigan	Adrian	J W Champlin
Minnesota	St Paul	C W. Nash
Mississippi	Jackson	Th. S. Cathright
Missouri	St Lewis	W D. Muir
Montana	Mountain	L W. Frary
Nebraska	Plottsmouth	H. P. Deuel
Nevada	Virginia City	G. W. Hopkins
New Hampshire	Concord	A. M Winn
New Jersey	Trenton	W E. Pinne
New York	New York	J H. Anthon
North Carolina	Raleigh	R. B Vance
Ohio	Cincinnati	A. H Newcomb
Oregon	Portland	D. G. Clark
Pennsylvania	Philadelphia	A. R. Lamberton
Rhode Island	Providence	T. A. Doyle
South Carolina	Charleston	J Comer
Tennessee	Nashville	J. W. Paxton
Texas	Houston	P. C. Tucker
Vermont	Burlington	L B Englesby
Virginia	Richmond	F. Th. Owens
Washington	Olympia	W. H, Troup
West Virginia	Wheeling	W. J. Bates
Wisconsin	Milwaukee	G. Bouck

American Lodges.

State	Grand Lodge at	Grand Master
New Brunswick	St John	L. Peters
Canada	Toronto	Stevenson
Quebec	Montreal	J. H Graham
Nova Scotia	Halifax	A. Keith
British Columbia	Victoria	Heistermann
Peru	Lima	P. Galvez
Chili	Valparaiso	J. de Dios Artegui
Brazil	Rio Janeiro	J M. da Silva Paranhos
Venezuela	Caraccas	T. J Sanavria
Columbia	Bogota	J. de Dios Riomalo
New Granada	Carthagena	F. de Zubirias
Uruguay	Monte Video	E. Perez
Argentine (La Plata)	Buenos Ayres	D M. Cazon
Hayti	Port-au-Prince	A. T. Boucherou
San Domingo	San Domingo	J. de Castro
Cuba	Santiago	De Castio
Mexico	Mexico	J C. Lohse
Liberia, a N American free Colony of Negioes in Africa	Monrovia	J J. Roberts

CHAPTER IV.

THE COVERT WARFARE WAGED BY THE SECRET
SOCIETY AGAINST CHRISTIANITY.

FREEMASONRY can always reckon on the co-operation of Protestantism when attacking institutions exclusively Catholic. As a rule, in carrying out its plans for the remodelling of the world, it can find employment for workmen of every kind, from the liberal Catholic to the avowed atheist. There are, however, different grades in the service. In order to remove the possibility of any divisions arising in the ranks of its employés, and, at the same time, to ensure the Secret Society appearing to outsiders to be a harmless association of philanthropists, those rules which are made public contain a special proviso that the discussion of religious questions shall be banished from the meetings of the Brethren. Outpourings of hatred to the Catholic hierarchy, to the doctrinal authority of the Pope and the Religious Orders—above all, the Society of Jesus—naturally come under the head of' purely secular and everyday topics.

But the prohibition of all religious discussions in a circle of *friends* strikes one as peculiar, to say the least of it. We can understand the necessity of prudential measures of a similar nature in meetings of persons holding widely different religious views, or in associations having for their object the promotion of the temporal welfare alone of the community ; but it is incomprehensible in the case of Freemasons, who openly boast that they aim at nothing short of perfect unanimity amongst themselves on all most important questions. Take one example in proof of this. The ritual for the admission of a Scotch Ancient or Grand Master in the Chief Patriotic Lodge of Germany runs as follows :—" Friendship is the sacred bond which unites together all the Brethren of our Craft ; for, however much scattered over the face of the earth, they all compose one only body; because one is their origin and one their aim, one the mystery into which they are initiated, one the path by which they are led, one the gauge and measure applied to each and all of them, and one the spirit by which they are animated " (Eckert, " Die Frage der Staatl. Anerk ," p. 12).

According to this, we can come to no other conclusion than that there exists a secret union, which, while taking the field in the most decided manner against every positive religion, and singling out the Christian religion as its chief foe, refuses, in the ordinary intercourse of its members, to allow a word to be heard about religion. But lest it be thought that we are indulging in a merely malicious suspicion when using such language, we will cite the official utterances of the Society. The Freemasons' Journal of

Vienna (2d series, No. 2, p. 143) thus reports the speech of a Master, addressing his Brethren from the chair of office :—" What is the false religion so eagerly forced upon mankind in mosques, synagogues, temples, and churches, except a jugglery carried on by imaums, popes, and priests ?   And are we to hold our tongues about it all, until defective education, long habits of slavery, superstitious prejudices, un-reasoning endurance, shall at length have deprived men even of the power to see the real state of affairs ? "

    We are now in a position to assert that Freemasonry is the sworn enemy of Christianity in general.   We know well how heavy is this charge which we bring against it, and we are bound in common justice to prove all we say from the documents of the Lodges.   If we are able to make good our cause (and we have little doubt of accomplishing this), every Christian, without distinction of creeds, will feel it incumbent on him to take up arms against the common foe, and Free-masonry will no longer be able either secretly or openly to administer its soothing narcotic, and per-suade men that it strives only to overthrow Ultra-montanism, Jesuitism, and the Papacy.   In such a case, all Christians must make common cause.   Were the Lodge ever to propose, even to the most zealous Jesuit, to completely exterminate Protestantism, the answer returned would surely be this—" The boon you offer is an insidious and treacherous one.   I will not accept it at your hand.   As far as lies in me, never shall you lay a finger upon Protestantism ; for you hate it, not because it has fallen away from the one true Church, but because you cannot tolerate those portions of Christian truth which still cling to it."

We can here, of course, only touch upon such points as have been common to Christendom in all times and in all places, concerning which, consequently, all denominations are at one, and we must prove Freemasonry to be antagonistic to them all. Now all bodies of professing Christians must assent to the four following propositions :—

1. The Christian religion is holy ; therefore its external forms are to be respected, and the social life of all nations professing Christianity must be regulated according to its maxims.

2. The Bible is sacred, and a fountain-head of truth.

3. Christ is truly God, and the Son of God.

4. The maintenance and spread of Christ's kingdom is to be desired.

The work before us divides itself naturally into these four heads :—

I. The attitude of Freemasonry in regard to the externals of Christianity.

Now, in places where it is expedient to keep up an outward appearance of Christianity, Freemasonry not only allows, but desires, its members to conform to the religious usages of the country in which they may chance to be residing. It was for the interests of the

Society in general, not merely for his own private interests, that Brother Verhaegen, whose sad end created
such a stir in Brussels, should have the reputation
amongst the people of being the ablest man in the
country, and the king's most trusty counsellor ; on this
account he might be seen every Sunday and holiday
ostentatiously wending his way to High Mass, with a
prayer-book conspicuous under his arm. Similar sights
may now be seen in Belgium in the very towns where
Freemasonry is known to have a large number of adherents.   Prudential motives have likewise actuated
the National Parent Lodge of the Three Globes in
Berlin to deny admission for many years past to any
but Christians ; though since 1868 it has seen fit to
receive unbelievers as associate brothers.[1]   As yet,
Jews must, for form's sake, make good their reception
in Leipzig or Hamburg, if they would be fellow-
workers with the Lodge in Berlin.[2]   On the other hand,
no opposition is offered if a newly-admitted brother
feels called upon to fulfil his religious duties, for although he has not yet been initiated into the higher
degrees, he can still be of service in his own place,
if only by his opposition to that religious fervour
which Freemasonry so cordially detests.   We can
safely take for granted that during all those centuries
when Governments were Christian, the work went on

[1] Zaarboekje voor Nederlandsche Vrijm , 1877, p. 85, year 5868
(1868).

[2] The last barrier in the way of Jews is now broken down.   On
November 28, 1872, for the first time, four Jews were admitted
directly into the Grand Lodge at Berlin.

secretly, but all the more surely, although the externals of Christianity were not openly attacked. The mole burrows best far away from the regimental band.

The modern English "Book of Constitutions" speaks still more plainly (Eckert, p. 25) :—"In olden times, Masons calling themselves Christians were, into whatever land they might be led by business or pleasure, bound to conform to the Christian usages of the country; but now a Mason, in his character of a true Noachite, is bound to observe only the moral law." [1]

Now, what is to be understood by these laws of Noah ? The modern English "Book of Constitutions" says—"As a true Noachite, the Mason is solemnly pledged to keep the moral law, and to fulfil the precepts of that religion in which all men agree ; for to the three great maxims of Noah no one can refuse assent." The York "Record" and the above-named "Book of Constitutions" give us three antediluvian and three postdiluvian commands of God to Noah. Those given subsequent to the Flood, founded on Genesis ix. 1, &c., are thus embodied :—

1. "The world is given to man that he may enjoy it." A maxim which the epicurean well knows how to appreciate.

---

[1] From the writings of the Craft we gather that the Noah of whom they speak is a very different being to the Patriarch of Scripture. As looked upon from a naturalistic point of view, he has more analogy to the Bacchus of the Greeks or the Osiris of the Egyptians. (*Cf.* Eckert, "Die Frage der Staatl. Anerk.," p. 34, &c.)

2. " Man is bound to abstain from shedding blood ; " and, also—

3. " From eating flesh with blood."

But the special, the "great" Noachian laws are those given before the Flood, viz.—

1. "To build the Ark" (that is, to help in con-structing *our* Ark, the Craft, a structure destined for the whole world).

2. " In it to abide the chastisement about to come on the world" (that is, remain true to our Craft while the state of things around us is involved in destruction).

3. "To re-populate the earth after the Flood " (that is, find the highest bliss in sensual enjoyment).

The Modern English " Book of Constitutions " fur-ther explains—" As the destruction of the world drew near, God commanded Noah to build the Ark, or floating fortress, in which work his three sons assisted him, one as Deputy-Master, the other two as Master Masons.   Although the material employed in its construction was but wood, the Ark was as geometri-cally correct as if made of stone, and when complete, formed a splendid masterpiece of architecture.   This wonderful edifice was 300 cubits long, 50 wide, and 30 high ; it was of cedar-wood, and was divided into four stories, in each of which there were chambers, separated by partitions.   Thus the whole present race of mankind derived its origin from these four Free-masons, or Grand Functionaries. . . . . After the Flood Noah and his three sons preserved the know-ledge of the arts and sciences, transmitting them to their descendants. They dwelt together in the Land of Sennaar, as Noachites; such being, according to some old chronicles, the name originally borne by Freemasons."

What most forcibly strikes us here is the supercilious manner in which the whole system of Christianity and the Mosaic revelation are ignored, the latter being put out of the question from motives of prudence. The statement of the greatest importance, and which gives a key to the whole mystery, is this, that the Mason, as a true Noachite, is solemnly pledged to keep the moral law, and to fulfil the precepts of that religion in which all men agree, and which consists precisely of the three laws of Noah. No mention is made of dogmatic faith, just as if it did not exist; the whole religion of the Freemason consisting in the moral law; and even this is condensed into the three notorious articles, which neither Rationalist nor Buddhist would feel the least hesitation in signing But as since the time of Noah the dogmas of faith and the laws of morality have been revealed by God for our guidance, first by the mouth of Moses, and afterwards by that of His only-begotten Son, it is an act of rebellion against the Supreme Lawgiver to hold exclusively to the earlier injunctions, and pertinaciously ignore the later. A soldier would be as much justified in addressing his Commander-in-Chief by the title of Captain, because he formerly held that rank in the army, as one is in speaking of the Noachian precepts as the true religion, now that the light of

Christianity shines upon the world. Those, nevertheless, who act thus, afford incontrovertible proof
that they repudiate the whole system of Christianity,
regarding it as a nursery tale for the amusement of
the populace. Such a degradation of all that is most
sacred can be looked upon with indifference by no
body of Christians; this is a gauntlet which no one
on whose head the waters of baptism have been
poured can refuse to take up.

We see, moreover, that in the Masonic view man is
regarded exclusively in the condition in which he was
at the time Noah left the Ark, namely, in his purely
natural condition of a rational biped. He who requires man to be more than this, sins against the one
true faith, the three laws of Noah; consequently the
social life of mankind cannot be expected to be more
than merely natural. All that is supernatural must
therefore be carefully eradicated from the soil of the
State and of society, or at most tolerated there for
the present, just for the sake of those troglodytes who
call themselves Christians. Thus, the Christian State,
denominational education, Christian marriage, in a
word, the whole influence exercised by Christianity
upon daily life, becomes an insupportable tyranny,
practised by benighted birds of prey on the majestic
and keen-sighted eagle; and man must put forth all
the powers of his mind to free social life from such
debasing fetters, giving himself no rest until he sees
a godless State, secular compulsory education, civil

marriage, and other things of a like kind, become inviolable articles of the constitution.

It is from such a standpoint as this that the political phenomena of our own day must be viewed. In point of fact, it is not the Liberals who agitate vehemently for a radical reversion to a state of things existing five thousand years ago; the majority of them entertain ideas differing *toto cœlo* from these. It is from the Masonic Lodges that the whole impetus comes of a movement which almost succeeds in carrying us along with it, for we know that, come what may, this consoling fact ever remains, Christianity is certain to outlive the storm. The dilatoriness displayed by the good, and the cowardice of the half-hearted, have brought Christendom under the yoke of Freemasonry, and Christianity will soon be afraid to show itself openly. Let us proceed to bring forward proofs of this.

Brother Gotthold Salomon, D.Ph., preacher at the new Synagogue at Hamburg, member of the Lodge entitled " The Dawn in the East," in Frankfort-on-Main, thus writes in his " Stimmen aus Osten " MSS. for the Brethren :—" Why is there not a trace of anything appertaining to the Christian Church to be found in the whole ritual of Freemasonry ? Why is not the name of Jesus once mentioned, either in the oath administered, or in the prayers on the opening of the Lodges, or at the Masonic banquets ? Why do Masons reckon time, not from the birth of Christ, but

from the creation of the world, as do the Jews? [1]
Why does not Freemasonry make use of a single
Christian symbol? Why have we the compasses, the
triangle, the hydrometer, instead of the cross and
other emblems of the Passion? Why have Wisdom,
Beauty, and Strength superseded the Christian triad
of Faith, Hope, and Charity?"

In what light, then, does a member of the Craft look
upon Christianity? He looks upon it as he looks upon
the ·Christian State—namely, as a chain forged by
deceit and imposed by force, which it is the business of
his life to break and demolish. In the "Latomia," vol. ii.
p. 176, we are told that the memorial entitled " Banquet on Occasion of the 25th Jubilee of the ' Aurora '
Lodge in Frankfort-on-Main," was printed for circulation amongst a portion of the Fraternity. This contained, besides other essays, one called "The Spirit
of Freemasonry," by a Jewish member of the literary
world, Dr Herz, from which we give the following
extracts:—"To call Masonic Lodges Christian institutions is to overlook the essential mission of the Craft,
which is to fill up the chasms cleft by differences of
religious opinion and of social grades in the fabric of
humanity. If Freemasonry ceases to keep this its

[1] The Cologne document likewise, handed down from the sixteenth
century, is dated in the following expressive terms —"According to
the system of chronology called the Christian system, in the year 1535."
In general, Freemasons simplify chronology, as they reckon 4000 years
B C., so that 5872=1872 A.D. We shall frequently have occasion later
on to refer to this negation of the Christian era, which speaks volumes,
and of which the records of the Craft boast more than is at all necessary.

vocation steadily in view, it will only serve to strengthen prejudice and error. It is true that now one stone after another is being thrown down from the thick wall, cemented by darkness, constructed of hallowed impostures and false maxims, of myths and legends, of sham traditions and sacred symbols, that was raised in order to exclude the light of reason, and to screen with zealous care blind credulity and its natural offspring, blind obedience. And that no man might dare to lay hands on the fabric of their deceit and tyrannical power, and undermine its buttresses, they entered into a covenant with the secular power, and wove the scheme of a State religion, thus attaching temporal advantages to an external profession of religion, introducing into society a legalised deception, and encouraging such deception by promising to reward it. . . . . But men had access to the treatises of antiquity ; they could peruse the revelations made to the master-spirits of Greece and Rome, and of the little country of Judæa,—and very different were the doctrines found inscribed in those pages from those which priests, monks, and rabbis have taught. Hence one Samson after another has arisen to shake with no feeble hand the pillars which support the ancient structure ; already they have begun to fall, and through the crevices thus formed the noonday brightness was poured in—' and there was light !' . . . And it was in the halls of the Craft that, under cover of the mystery which enveloped them, noble minds of every class and every rank first called into activity, and communicated to others, those principles which in the profane circles of society were still denounced as heretical and unwarrantable innovations. To English Freemasons belongs the honour of having been the first to re-instate mankind in the rights of which they had been deprived through the encroachments, sanctioned by long custom, of privileged castes, and the tyranny exercised by priestcraft over the consciences of men. Long before the ruling spirits and the great events of the last century had made the rights of man the solid basis of government, they had been recognised and proclaimed by a genuine Freemasonry in her statutes."

In this way the entire Christian organisation of the State and of society is repeatedly rejected as in-jurious to mankind, and the principles of the great Revolution are extolled as the highest of all, as a trophy won by Freemasonry ; the expulsion of the last vestige of Christianity from social and public life being not merely approved of, but openly proposed as the goal to which the efforts of the Masonic body ought to tend. People often wonder, nowadays, why the leading party, in spite of the songs which it is for ever singing in praise of liberty, constantly calls for despotic measures with regard to Christian institu-tions, laying itself open to the reproach of the most crying inconsistency, and even thereby imperilling its own future. But the passages we have quoted ex-plain the apparent contradiction. The point at issue is not freedom *with* Christianity, but freedom *from* Christianity. Let the scales once fall from the eyes of the multitude, and society will be divided into two camps only—that of Christianity, and that of modern Paganism. Every day the hour draws nearer when the present generation will be compelled to face this alternative, and compromises are things of ephemeral existence.

II. The attitude of Freemasonry in regard to the Bible.

The Scriptures of the Old and New Testament are — for all Christians of every denomination — a sacred volume written under divine inspiration, and for this very reason distinct from all other books of mere human authority. The Bible is, indeed, laid on the so-called "altar" in the Lodge,[1] and plays a part in the initiation of each new member of the Order of Light. But from what has been already said, it is plain that its use is a mere external ceremony borrowed from Christianity, and intended to hoodwink the new adept, whose eyes are as yet incapable of bearing too strong a light. In accordance with Christian custom, the oath is sworn upon the Scriptures, opened at the first page of St John's Gospel. If the Bible were the same in the hands of the Freemason as it is in the hands of the Christian, it could never serve the purposes of an Order which recruits its ranks from amongst the adherents of every creed. What would the Jew think, to whom the New Testament is an abomination? The Mussulman, who recognises the Koran alone? The Indian, who swears by his sacred Vedas?

[1] This custom is not universal. *Cf.* "Jaarboekje," p 192.

No; Freemasonry does not regard the Bible as a sacred volume, but as a mere ritualistic accessory, entirely without any internal value of its own. "Brother" K. Chr. Fr. Krause—who, for having divulged the secrets of the Craft, was expelled from the Fraternity in 1810, and persecuted by his former Brethren until his death—speaks thus, "However Masons may formerly have regarded the Bible, they now, at all events, know how to put it in its proper place. The Mason should be entirely free from all blind adhesion to any dogmatic belief whatsoever, just as Jesus appears to have been." In other words, Masons consider the Bible as an interesting book, but see nothing sacred about it to make them believe in it. From an address delivered by Marbach, the chairman of the Leipzig Lodge (2d ed. "Leipzig," 1862), we gather that he had been blamed for having quoted the Bible too frequently, this being at variance with the first principles of Freemasonry, which does not view the Bible, as the Church does, as a text-book of religion, but as a symbol of faith and religious persuasion. Thus the religion of the true Mason differs entirely from the religion of the Bible, and the Bible itself is not looked upon as a sacred and divinely-inspired volume. Marbach completely admits these principles, and thus answers the objection raised, " But, my Brethren, the question may arise in the minds of some amongst you; if we are always being referred to the Bible as the rule and guide of our faith, what becomes of the proud boast of Freemasonry, that it

heeds no differences of creed, and gives the title of
Brother alike to Christian and Jew, to heathen and
Mohammedan, in a word, to every one who bears the
name of man? O my Brethren! will you be put to
shame by your Mohammedan Brethren, who are
willing to see your Bible upon the altar instead of
their Koran? I tell you, Were a heathen or a Mussulman to come forward, and take exception at hearing
these walls resound with the words of Scripture, employed in order that we may adore God in spirit and
in truth, I should pronounce him to be no true Freemason, even could he boast a tenfold acquaintance
with sign, password, and grip. And I tell you once
again, Were a Christian to stand forth in this assembly, and take you to task for quoting words from the
Koran, from Sophocles, or from Goethe, used to
enable us to adore God in a universal spirit and
in truth, he would no better deserve the name of
Freemason, since all writings inspired by God are
profitable to teach, to reprove, to correct, to in-
struct in justice. Where the Spirit of God is, there
is the Bible."[1] Strip these words of their rhetorical
bombast, and they will be found to mean that the
Bible is worth as much to the German Mason as to
the heathen Mussulman, *i.e.*, absolutely nothing, and
is to be ranked with the Koran, with Sophocles, and
with Goethe, as an intellectual storehouse of quotations, a purely human production.

[1] This, as well as the preceding quotation, is taken from Eckert, as
quoted above, p. 38.

We find that from the so-called altars of many of
their "temples" the members of the Craft have been
honest enough to remove the Bible ; they are also
beginning to employ their pen to procure its final
banishment from them.

Respecting " The Bible in the Lodge," an article
appears in the " Jaarboekje," *i.e.,* in the official Dutch
Freemasons' Almanack for 1872, by Brother C. Van
Schaick, from which we take the following extracts :
—" As matters now stand, the presence of the Bible
on our altar is an empty form. . . . . From whatever point of view we regard the Bible, we do not
hesitate to declare openly, that in our reunions it is
out of place, once and for ever, since the doctrines of
humanity now occupy the most prominent position,
and are taught as the best method of ameliorating
the condition of mankind." We must do the man.
the justice to add, that he stands up boldly to protest
against hypocritical disguises, that he will " have
nothing to do with misleading any one, oppressing
any one, or depriving any one of liberty of conscience." But the question must present itself to
every man who attaches any value to the name of
Christian, whether he can now take one single step
in union with an association which altogether re-
pudiates the divine origin of Holy Writ, and sees in
it nothing but an accessary to its ceremonial? Human
intelligence, not divine revelation, is their rallying-
cry, and the attack is now directed against the last
outpost of Christianity.

III. The attitude of Freemasonry in regard to the divinity of Christ.

As the Secret Society ignores the whole body of Christian dogma, and only understands by religion some general principles of morality prescribed by reason, in which all mankind will agree, it is easy to understand that from the very outset it has been antagonistic to the divinity of Christ. In fact, how can he who denies the sacred character of the Bible retain for a single moment this, the fundamental dogma of all Christian societies which agree in accepting the two oldest creeds ? And if it can be proved that Freemasonry is an institution of the Synagogue (a point upon which we will not now enter), and dates from the time when, after her heroic sacrifices were accomplished, Christianity became triumphant, it would follow as a matter of course that the point against which the Society directs its fiercest attack should be the doctrine of the Divinity of our Lord. And if, indeed, all Christian belief is to be banished from the world, and "the interest which men can so easily be made to feel in dogma and symbolism" is to be diverted by means of a mysterious cultus from the channel of dogmatism into that of morality,[1] and Christian charity is to be replaced by certain social forms,—then we consider ourselves entirely justified in asserting that Free-masonry denies the divinity of Christ. This denial

[1] K. A Menzel, "Neueie Geschichte der Deutschen," Breslau, 1843, B. 10, p 312.

can easily be discerned through the mist of its fanciful legends.

Frederick, Prince of Orange, the second son of
William I., King of the Netherlands, was chosen on
the 4th June 1816 (when he had scarcely attained his
nineteenth year) as National Grand Master for life of
the Grand Lodge of the Hague.   The next year he
was also elected in the Grand Orient, in Brussels, to
the Grand Mastership of the Southern, now called the
Belgic, Lodges.   Although he had only been made
acquainted with the fantastic Jewish legends of the
Craft, his upright mind, thoroughly imbued as it was
with Christian sentiments, suspected the rabbinical
hatred lurking behind them, and led him to resign
the post of honour he occupied.   We will give some
passages from the reasons for this step, which were
sent by him to the head of the Lodge.   In them he
thus speaks of the fourth higher grade, that of Rosicrucian (Souverain Prince Rose-Croix):—"I am a
Christian, and will ever remain one.   Everybody will
understand how extremely painful it is for me to be
compelled to speak of the abuse made in the Masonic
legend of the teaching of my Divine Master, the Son
of the Heavenly Father, who, having assumed a
human form, became at the same time the Head of
the human race, and in this character gives to mankind those holy laws which first teach us men our
true dignity ; who willingly endured the dreadful
death of the Cross, and could say with justice of His
work, 'It is consummated!'   How could I write the

story of Thy life, O divine Jesus, and then call this
story the Legend of the Degree of Rosicrucian? Those
who know no better perhaps might exclaim, What
more could be claimed for any legend? But right
reason and profound reverence bid my pen stop here.
Is it possible to degrade this hallowed story so low
as to turn it into a mere legend? And can any one
fail to perceive that in such a case it would become a
simple parable, like the fable of Zorobabel, fit to be
ranked in the same class with it, and that the death
of Jesus Christ would in like manner be reduced to
the same level as that of Adoniram? But where is
the real Christian who could find it possible to doubt
the history of our Lord as contained in the New
Testament? Where is the Jew who will venture to
deny the Crucifixion? It is a fact which even a
Mohammedan does not call in question. And can it
be that the Brethren of the Craft meanwhile regard
this death as a parable, and range it with the mass of
fictions which are successively set before them? Let
us not deceive ourselves, my Brethren, and dissemble
the fact, that the Legend of the Grade of a 'Sovereign
Prince Rosicrucian' is no other than the history of
Jesus Christ! Enough has been said on this point,
perhaps too much; for who will pretend that it is not
utterly unjustifiable to place the life and death of
Jesus Christ side by side with fables? And we further find, to our indignation, ceremonies in connection
with the reading of the legend of this grade which are
in direct opposition to the teaching and character of

the Son of God, and to His holy law.   For instance,
an axe is swung above the head of the candidate at
the moment he pronounces his oath.   Now, the words
of Jesus breathe gentle persuasion; while the Rosicrucian, on the contrary, employs emblems denoting
power, force, and violence." Lest we should weary the
reader, we are compelled reluctantly to break off the
words of the young Prince, the purity and simplicity of
whose mind enabled him to see through the disguises
in which hatred of Christ had clothed itself.   In opposition to the false pretences of Freemasonry, the
Prince proceeds to prove that the grade of Rosicrucian cannot be accepted by persons belonging to any
religious persuasion, since it is accompanied by a
ceremonial equally repugnant to the Jew, the Turk,
and the Christian.   We quote his own words :—" Ask
the Jew if he can become a Rosicrucian, and he will
reply, 'How can you require me conscientiously to
pay homage to Jesus?   Our histories and traditions
teach us that he was a deceiver, who pursued his own
selfish ends, and sought to raise himself to the highest
rank amongst men. You yourselves intimate as much,
by giving him the name of J. N. R. J., and designating
him in your ritual by this appellation.'   What would
the answer of the Mohammedan be?   Almost identical with that of the Jew."   "Why," continues the
Prince, "should I allow others to force from me a
promise to veil the teaching of my Divine Master
from the eyes of my fellow-men ?   Did He not bid us
'Go and teach all nations'?   Of what use, then, is

this symbolic dressing-up of the Sovereign Prince
Rosicrucian? We have in the New Testament the
life and death of Jesus Christ, and, above all, His
teaching, set before us in such plain terms that they
need no further explanation. What do I want with
all your symbols, some of which are, to say the least,
objectionable?" Somewhat further on the Prince
excuses himself for his non-obseivance of the secresy
prescribed by the Craft in regard to this portion of
its teaching; for if the doctrines heard in the Lodge
are the doctrines of Jesus Christ, he may and must
proclaim them openly; if not, he has no right to
accept them. "You say, for instance," he writes,
"that the name of your Chief Master, *i.e.*, Jesus
Christ, is Jesus Nazarenus Rex Judæorum. No, my
Brethren, you deceive yourselves; it is not so. Jesus
Himself testifies, 'My kingdom is not of this world;'
and if these words are not enough for you, you know
full well that the actions of the lowly Jesus prove
Him to have sought not His own interests, but those
of humanity."[1] The ex-Grand Master was not far
wrong. In so far as the Divine Redeemer appears
in the said Masonic ritual, He is nothing more than

[1] "Annales Maçonniques," ii. 89, iii. 610; "The Legend of Rosicrucians," ib iv. 60–144. A considerable part of the Prince's Memorial is inserted in "La Franc maçonneiie dans l'Etat," Bruxelles,
1859, p 58, *suiv.* ; Barruel, "Mémoires pour servir à l'Histoire du
Jacobinisme," in the Hamburg edition of 1803, vol. ii. p. 203. But
why did not the Prince see thiough eveiything? *Cf.* Barruel, as above,
p 214

a selfish seditionary, who was overtaken by justice at the very moment He was about to seize the crown. The battle-cry of this anti-Christian militia, in the sacrilegious warfare which it wages with God and His Anointed, is in complete harmony with the delusion which has possessed the blind Jewish nation ever since the first Good Friday.

But more unequivocal expressions on the part of Freemasonry are not wanting. Later on we shall bring forward a French document, which breathes the Pantheistic spirit of Spinoza in its teaching about God, of whom it asserts that His existence is coeval with that of matter, and that He cannot be divided into a plurality of persons, nor be made subject to human infirmities; consequently neither has died, nor can die. Furthermore, it is boldly alleged, in the name of the Craft, that it was impossible for Christ to have been God, or, indeed, anything more than a being of superior intelligence—a philosopher or a sage. If Freemasonry were really in earnest, as it professes to be, in its determination to exclude all religious discussions from its gatherings, and if it did not fully agree, even in its higher grades, with the opinion here expressed of Christ, it must necessarily have risen as one man to repudiate such an assertion. But this it did not do, and, what is more, this it could not do. It was not until 1865 that the "Grand Orient" of Paris, considering the excited state of public opinion, thought fit to declare, after passing its statutes in review, that it recognised the existence of a God and the immortality of the soul.[1]

The same phenomena are to be met with in Germany. Brother Jochmus-Muller, President of the late German-Catholic Church at Berlin, says in his "Kirchenreform" (vol. iii. p. 228)—"We have more in common with a free-thinking, honest Paganism, than with a narrow-minded Christianity." By this he means a Christianity which still believes in the divinity of its Founder.

A kindred soul (Bastide) says much the same thing in the *Universal Church Times* of Berlin (Eckert, p. 51), addressing the editor :—" It cannot be new to you that the Mother of the Saviour has taken the place of Isis and Alcmene ; that the festival of the Saviour's birth has superseded the joyous saturnalia attending the middle of the winter solstice ; that the mysteries of Holy Week and Easter have replaced those of the death and resurrection of Adonis, when the awakening of Nature at the time of the vernal equinox was also celebrated." Thus Christ becomes a mere mythical personage, like Hercules, Adonis, or Osiris, or whoever may be chosen to personify the sun in his annual course.

It is plainly apparent that doctrines such as these are fraught with much danger to the beliefs of Pro-

---

[1] Jaarboekje, p 73, year 5865. It may be added that this manifesto was intended to deceive, and that it was expressed in terms admitting of Pantheistic interpretations

E

testantism.   On account of this, the Protestant Con-
sistory in Hanover was only acting in self-defence
when, in the year 1745, it decreed that any preacher
who was already a Freemason should receive a strict
injunction, with which he should be compelled to
comply, immediately to resign his membership, and
abandon all practices connected with it ; and that
in future the clergy should be forbidden, under
strict penalties, to join the Craft, since for them, above
all other men, it was most unjustifiable to become
members of a society which denied them the right of
making themselves acquainted with its laws and regulations previous to binding themselves to it in the most
solemn manner.   And this prohibition was to hold good
even if it were alleged that the chief object of the
society was to unite Christians in a bond of charity ;
for in Holy Scripture they have so strong a bond that
they can need no other.   " Nevertheless Freemasonry,
as the Protestant ecclesiastical historian Guerike de-
plores, has exercised unbounded influence on the destinies of positive Christianity ; has sought, as far as
possible, to strike it with its hammer, and shatter it into
a thousand fragments ; has endeavoured, finally, to
construct a new system of worship in the place of that
established by Christ. . . . . In order to attain this
end, it has employed those principles of brotherly
love, mutual help, and fidelity on which the Society
rests, to effect a widespread system of corruption,
and obtain a monopoly of all posts and offices

capable of influencing Christianity, science, or the Church. "[1]

In order, under cover of the spread of so-called science, to render the denial of Christ's divinity more and more universal, the German Protestant Association was founded by men known to be leaders of Freemasonry, on principles in striking harmony with the religious views of the Craft ; in fact, its very language recalls strongly the jargon of the Lodges. Christian feeling does occasionally rise up against the preachers of this party when they give too great publicity to their heterodox opinions ; but the day is now past when faith was upheld by authority, and when Freemasonry was a thing tolerated, indeed, but forced to keep out of sight. Now, on the contrary, it boasts openly of an influence never greater than at present. The old Lutheran Congress at Kammin showed a just appreciation of the position of affairs when it enacted that its clergy should be forbidden to join either the body of Freemasons or the Protestant Association.

The proceedings of the Secret International Congress of Freemasons, held during the first three days of November 1872, evinced a similar desire to exterminate the belief in the divinity of Christ by means of democratic revolution, and to give the force of constitutional law to the opinions of Freemasonry as

[1] Guerike, " Handbuch der Kirchengesch ," 4th ed , Halle, 1840, vol ii p. 553. *Cf* Schrodl on "Freemasons" in the Kirchen-Lexikon of DD Wetzer and Welte.

to what ought to be called religion. The Congress
met at a villa near Lucarno, and sat each day from
4 P.M. until midnight. One of the subjects deliberated
upon was the nature of the worship to be introduced.
It was unanimously agreed to throw into a cate-
chetical shape the democratic Bíble of the Socinian
Renan, and to make this the handbook of the religion
to be publicly recognised in the social and democratic
republic of the future.[1]

We leave all those Christians who are separated
from the Church to decide for themselves whether
the designs of Freemasonry are directed against the
Church of Rome alone.

IV. The attitude of Freemasonry in respect to the
maintenance of Christianity.

Even at the time when the Archangel Gabriel
announced to the most Blessed Virgin the incarnation of the Son of God, he wound up with these
words—" And of His kingdom there shall be no
end " (Luke i. 33). The fathers assembled at
Nicæa took up the strain with the joyous confidence of undoubting faith, and closed the Christo-
logical portion of their creed with the same words—

---

[1] This Congress, in which the preliminaries were arranged of the
transactions enacted in Rome on November 24, 1872, was attended by
the chiefs of the Freemasonic party of action, the secret of its proceedings being divulged in several letters published in the *Univers*, particularly in the numbers of the 12th and 19th November 1872   The
Congress was attended by delegates from the Grand Lodges of Palermo,
Naples, Rome, Florence, Turin, and Genoa ; also from those of France,
Hungary, Germany, and Switzerland.

Cujus regni non erit finis. All bodies of Christians
earnestly desire the maintenance of the religion of
Jesus Christ, and do their utmost to spread it, while
their united supplication ascends to heaven—" Thy
kingdom come." On this point we once more discover
Freemasonry to be the very antipodes of Christianity.

Freemasonry is, by its own confession, the representative of Paganism, and is about to renew once
more the struggle with Christianity, which must be for
life and death.

Le Globe,[1] a Masonic journal, issued from 1839–
1843 by L. Th. Juge, one who had himself been initiated into the highest grades of Freemasonry, has
been pronounced by those invested with highest
authority in the Craft to be the truest exponent of its
secret teaching. In this journal an account is given
of a speech delivered in the Lodge of the Knights of
Malta by " Brother " de Branville (ex-officier du
Grand Orient de France), the principal points being
as follows :—

1. The religious tenets of Freemasonry are only a
continuation of the Egyptian doctrines transmitted
to successive generations by the priests of the temple
of Isis.

---

[1] On the title page of *Le Globe* we have a long list of the Masonic
titles and dignities of the editor, Juge. He himself tells us (*Le Globe*,
ii. 53, December 1839) that the principles of his journal were formally
approved by the French and foreign Lodges, and *Le Globe* was authorised as the official journal of Freemasonry in France. This paper is
also spoken of in the highest terms elsewhere (*Cf* "Le danger de
croire facilement aux prophéties," Berlin, 1872, p 67, &c)

2. Freemasonry received these tenets from the Knights-Templars, who, in order to escape persecution, assumed as a disguise the leather apron of the Craft.

3. The history of the Templars and the tragic end of Jacques Molay is embodied by the Masons in the twofold allegory of the Temple of Solomon and the story of Hiram; on this account secresy is most strictly enjoined.

4. It is an authenticated fact, that from Egypt come the religious rites secretly practised by the Templars, Grand Masters, and a certain number of the most fully initiated; and that the Craft reaches back to the mysteries of the beneficent goddess Isis.[1]

There is no occasion for us to discuss here the guilt or innocence of the Templars, nor have we anything to do with the genealogical fables of Freemasons;[2]

[1] The extracts we have just given from *Le Globe*, as well as those which follow, have been put together by Neut in "La Franc maçon-nerie au grand jour de la publicité à l'aide de documents authen-tiques," 2d Ed. Gand, 1867. As early as 1856-57, Neut published in his periodical *La Patrie* many of the transactions of the Lodge of the "Philanthropes" at Brussels, supported by documentary evidence, in consequence of which the then Brother Armand Tardieu was expelled from the Lodge in a meeting held January 11, 1858, for having divulged its secrets, and his name burnt between the two pillars (B & J.) *Cf.* the last document published in *Le Danger*, p. 70, note 1.

[2] Barruel ("Mémoires pour servir à l'histoire du Jacobinisme," Ham-burg, 1803, vol 11. p. 277), brings forward most interesting informa-tion respecting the connection of Freemasonry with the corrupt portion of the Order of Templars, and of the latter with the Manichees, who, as is well known, appeared in the Middle Ages under various forms. Even the secret name of Masons, "Children of the Widow," points to Manes, who was adopted by the widow of a Scythian, and constituted her heir (p. 290, note).

their own admission, that the religion they profess coincides with that of the ancient Egyptians, suffices for our purpose. Now Isis was the feminine deity, representing the moon, and emblematic of the fruitfulness of the earth ; her spouse Osiris (who is veiled in the myths of the Craft under the name of Busiris,[1] one of the earliest kings of Egypt) being the corresponding symbol of the sun, of masculine strength, and of the fertilising Nile. Thus, from their own lips, we have the Mason's Confession of Faith : it is a modern Pagan materialism, and has a system of morality to match. Of this more will be said later on. A struggle is now imminent between this modern Paganism and Christianity; it will be one for life and death. The facts speak for themselves, yet evidence shall be adduced from the above-named sources. An article by Brother Nash, which appeared in the English *Freemasons' Quarterly Review*, tracing back the origin of the Secret Society to the mysteries of Isis and Osiris, is commented on by Juge in his *Globe* under the following heads :—

1. Brother Nash explains most clearly how Freemasonry derives its origin from the mysteries of Isis and Osiris.

2. In a former treatise Brother de Branville proves the Order of Freemasons to be an offshoot from the Order of Templars.

---

[1] On this account the two pillars found in every Lodge are called respectively J. & B. Their Hebrew names, Jachin & Booz, as told to Apprentices, are a mere piece of ritualistic twaddle.

3. Nash demonstrates, in the work now before us, that the Templars borrowed their rules of faith and precepts of morality from the priests of Isis and Osiris.

4. "To speak in plain terms, we are, as Matter[1] has already observed, about to witness the last effort of ancient Paganism, which has rallied its forces for a supreme struggle with its successor" (Christianity) "before it finally abandons the field. In our opinion, it will not do to take our stand on any lower ground than this, if we would ascend to the source of those institutions which formed the materials out of which our so-called system of Freemasonry was in after-times constructed. From hence we shall have to witness a spectacle surpassing in importance anything that the human mind can conceive. We see unfolded before us not the history of institutions alone, but also that of centuries : the ancient heathenism of East and West is drawn up on one side ; on the other stands Christianity ; and of these combatants one must remain master of the field. We contemplate then — to borrow the words of Matter — the grandest speculative theories of Asia, Egypt, and Greece, successively attacked and overthrown by Christianity; which doctrines having risen up once more, are struggling desperately with their Conqueror, and, in order the more successfully to effect his ruin, have not scrupled to enter into an alliance with him.[2]

[1] "Histoire Critique du Gnosticisme," 2 vols , Paris, 1821.
[2] Hence it is easy to understand why so much is said about "mode-

Such is the grand drama . . . . for which the teaching of Zoroaster, imparted to the Jews, prepared the
way. . . . . The union of Judaism with the doctrines
of Plato gave birth to the Greek Philonic philosophy;
and finally, the disciples of this school make their
appearance in Christianity, carrying with them, in
part at least, their own language. If we pursue this
path, we cannot fail ere long to be convinced that we
shall soon witness the last effort of ancient Paganism,
which is once more rallȳing its forces for a supreme
struggle with its Conqueror, before abandoning the
field to Him." Our author goes on as follows:—" If
by this means we have been led to discover that the
old institutions, or at least the doctrines which were
embodied in their ceremonial, survived in the East
until the thirteenth century of the Christian era, notwithstanding the desperate conflict of which we have
been speaking, and if it be further proved that Gnosti-
cism was still flourishing up to the epoch of the first
Crusades, it will be easy to understand how the
Christians of the West, *i.e.*, the Crusaders, were
brought into contact with these Gnostic Christians,
and had the opportunity afforded them of adopting
some of their peculiar tenets and mysterious customs; amongst others, that of progressive initiation
into secret lore. The foregoing facts once clearly
established, our supposition will no longer lack

iation," "non-interference with the beliefs of others," " tolerance of
Christianity, in a modified form at least," and why the Bible has a place
on the " altar " of the lower Lodges in this country.

abundant proof, if it be further found that, amongst
the Western warriors, an association speedily formed
itself, which, in opposition to the creed of Rome and
the universal faith of Europe at that time, took upon
itself to recognise the existence only of a God whose
being is coeval with that of matter, who is incapable
of division into a plurality of persons, who is not
subject to human infirmities, and, consequently,
neither has died nor can die. . . . . And would
not our supposition be yet more triumphantly proved
if to this elementary doctrine another were added,
namely, that Christ could not have been God, but
was merely a being of superior intelligence, a Philosopher, a Sage, a Benefactor of humanity ; if it were
asserted that miracles must necessarily be rejected
as a violation of the eternal and immutable laws of
the universe, alike impossible and needless, God requiring no such means of enforcing the obedience of
His creatures ?   Are not these doctrines, which indisputably derive their origin immediately from Gnos-
ticism, the fundamental principles of Freemasonry ?
Does the Freemason divide into several persons the
incomprehensible Being whom he denominates the
Supreme Architect of all worlds ?   Does he believe
that death was, or ever could be, possible to this
Supreme Being, or that the exercise of His will alone
is not sufficient to form a law for mankind ?"   After
indulging in the violent onslaughts on ecclesiastical
hierarchies, dogma, and discipline, invariably found
in writings of this class, Juge finally refers to an

historical document preserved to this day by the
Templars of Paris, which he proves to be of incontestable authority, and to furnish incontrovertible
proofs of the correctness of his assertions.

Thus we find the most Holy Trinity, the divinity
of Christ, together with all that follows from that
doctrine, the possibility of miracles, in a word, the
whole scheme of Christianity, denied by the organ
of Freemasonry, in its name and with its approval,
whilst the lowest form of natural religion is set forth
as the only system recognised by the Secret Society,
and an irreconcilable war is further declared, with
the sanction of the same Society, against the Cross.
The foregoing, besides other documentary proofs, were
published by the Belgian Neut; at the same time he
challenged the League, in the most public manner possible, to contradict them. In spite of this challenge,
we find him about ten years later speaking in the
following terms at the Catholic Congress at Mech-
lin in 1867 :—"I have everywhere challenged Freemasons to prove the unauthenticity of my documents,
if it can be proved. I have sent my writings gratis
to the editors of Masonic periodicals, begging that
they would refute them, if this were possible, but they
have invariably kept silence. I am ready to guaran-
tee that everything I have printed is perfectly genuine,
and I defy any adversary to show me to be guilty of
inaccuracy in this respect. I have clamorously called
for some notice, even though it were of an unfavour-
able nature, but all in vain; I have never received an

answer" ("Assemblée Générale des Catholiques de Malines, 1867," Bruxelles, 1868, p. 340).

Members of the lower affiliated Lodges, Apprentices, Fellow-crafts, and Master-Masons, who are still groping in the twilight, will doubtless pronounce the testimony we have just brought forward (since they find it cannot be either contradicted or denied) to be the exaggerations of a few individual Freemasons. Therefore, if we wish to be clear on the matter, we must ascend to one of the higher grades of the Craft, where full daylight is admitted, to that of Rosicrucian, the 18th of the Scotch Grade, spoken of by the Prince of Orange in the Apology we mentioned above. The allegorical legend has for its subject the murder of the architect Adoniram, and the recovery of the password lost at his death, and believed to be the word Jehovah, which, with the secret meaning attached to it, is communicated to those who are initiated into the grade of a Master of the Scotch rite. In this manner the Scotch Master is made "High Priest." If we strip the legend of its fanciful dress, there remains pure Deism, in which every man is declared to be his own priest, perfectly independent of all revealed religion. But the adept must further be told who, in the character of Adoniram's murderer, buried the password, *i.e.*, Deism, and against whom on that account he must ever cherish a bitter and undying hatred, and wage war without intermission. For this purpose the grade of Rosicrucian is intended. However reluctant we are to enter upon the subject of the insane ceremonial of the Craft, it is impossible always to avoid doing so, especially as some knowledge of the rites attending upon initiation into the higher grades of Masonic science is indispensable to the elucidation of the matter we have in hand.[1] The walls of the Lodge are hung with black cloth. In the background is an altar, and over it a transparency on which are three crosses, the middle one bearing the usual inscription I.N.R.I. The Brethren sit round in deepest mourning, all clad in sacerdotal vestments, to signify that in natural religion to be a man and a priest means the same. Leaning their head upon their hand, they remain in profound silence, and betray sorrow and dejection. No one can fail to see the very obvious allusion to the day of our Lord's Crucifixion. After a while the President asks the Senior Warden what is the hour? The answer runs thus:—"It is the first hour of the day, the moment when the veil of the temple was rent, darkness and horror overspread the face of the earth, the light was extinguished, the tools of Masons were broken, the blazing sun disappeared from heaven, the cubical stone was shattered to pieces, the mystic word was lost!" In other words, the murderer of Adoniram, the deadly enemy of Masonic theory and practice, is He who on Good Friday died the death of the cross. The inscription on the cross also has its interpretation, namely this:—"The Jew of Nazareth led by

[1] *Cf.* " Les Grades des Maîtres Ecossais," Stockholm, 1784 ; Barruel, Mémoires, vol ıı pp 207-212.

the Jew Raphael to Jerusalem." Here, under the
designation of a common Jew, led up to Jerusalem
by another Jew, to receive the just penalty of his
crimes, we have Christ the Lord ; for the deadly foe
of Freemasonry is no other than He.[1]   As soon as
the candidate has shown by his answers that he
understands I.N.R.I. aright, the " Venerable " exclaims
joyfully, " My Brethren, the word is found again ! "
This exclamation is greeted by the initiated with
acclamation,[2] for another has been added to the
number of those who hate the Nazarean-malefactor
and withstand His work, who are even prepared, if
need be, to demonstrate openly the sentiments they

---

[1] The following is a literal translation of the passage, as taken from the
" Thuileur Portatif des 33 Degrés de l'Ecossisme," Paris, 1819, p. 64

" Freemasons consider the initial letters I.N.R.I. as standing for the
following words —Judea, Nazareth, Raphael, Judah.

   " Where do you come from ?—From Judea.
   Through what town have you passed ?—Through Nazareth.
   Who has been your guide ?—Raphael.
   Of what tribe are you ?—The tribe of Judah."

The last question appears to be interchangeable with the one to
which Jerusalem is the answer.   The difference is quite immaterial.

[2] I N R I. is also a shibboleth employed by Rosicrucians when they
exchange greetings (*Cf.* Barruel, p. 243).   The author there tells us
from his own experience that by no means all Rosicrucians are acquainted with the real meaning of the legend and its accompanying
ceremonies   They are in this case left in their good faith.   Even the
Prince of Orange, mentioned above, did not apprehend their full import.
This is not to be wondered at, for even in the grade of Rosicrucian
there are various lower degrees, the profoundest mysteries being reserved
for the select few (Barruel, p 215).   Thuileur Portatif—1. Chevalier de
Heredom ; 2. Chevalier ou Garde de la Tour ; 3. Rose croix, proprement
dit   Each of these subdivisions must have its own chamber in the
Lodge.

entertain by publicly partaking of flesh-meat on Good Friday.

As a matter of fact, the religious aims of Free-masonry lie at the bottom of all the collective efforts of Liberalism in the present day within the domain of the Church, although perhaps the majority of the easy-going members of the Lodges are ignorant of the fact. Refined prudence only lifts the veil for each one so far as to admit just as much light as his eyes are capable of bearing. In the "Disclosures of a Freemason on his Deathbed,"[1] the following cautions are published by Von Haller :—" The explanation of our moral system (*i.e.* religion) by means of allegories and of symbols must be suited to the varying capa-bilities of each individual aspirant; for this reason we must be very careful not to give them a meaning of such obvious ambiguity as thereby to make our inten-tions apparent, or in any way tend to diminish the good faith with which the candidate receives the interpretation given to him. It would be foolish to suppose that every Brother, immediately upon his admission, throws off once for all the prejudices which up to that time held him enslaved. The atmosphere

---

[1] "Révélations d'un Franc-maçon au lit de mort, pièce authentique, publiée par M. de Haller, &c ," Courtrai, 1826. The preface speaks thus —" I vouch for the fact that the document here submitted to the reader was made over by a dying Freemason to one of his friends, with permission to make of it whatever use he might see fit. The comments are intended as an antidote to the poison, and may serve to tear the veil from the eyes of more than one erring or misguided Brother." This little work is also translated into Dutch.

of the Lodge is not potent enough to impart to him instantaneously the spirit of the Order into which he has been admitted. The Catholic and the Protestant, the Jew and the Mohammedan, the members of every possible religious persuasion, must meet here under one banner, without appearing in any way to separate themselves from their own particular sect."

The following laws, binding on Masons in general, whatever their degree, may serve in further support of the point we have been endeavouring to prove :—

1. Every Brother who is received must propose to himself the object set forth in the catechism of the Lodges as the final aim of all the efforts of the Craft— namely, to build temples for virtue and prisons for vice, or to shed light upon the initiated ; that is, to dispel the darkness shrouding the whole world of the profane. Thus Freemasonry has a system of teaching peculiar to itself, whether called by the name of morality or of religion, in comparison to which all positive religions, even those that term themselves Christian, are but error and darkness.

2. The Masonic system of chronology differs from the Christian, the time of the "true light" being reckoned from the creation of the world, in proof that the light of Freemasonry is older than all positive religions—even than the Christian—and that it dates from the first man. Thus we see it can be none other than that system of natural religion under which complete unbelief seeks to screen itself.

3. In the language of the initiated, all Lodges are

"temples;" these represent the universe, and have accordingly their four quarters of north, south, east, and west. The Jew and the Christian, the Mussulman and the Fetish worshipper—in short, the adherents of every possible creed—have indiscriminate access to this temple, and are there admitted to the "light," that is, the knowledge of true virtue, pure faith, and unmixed happiness, retaining meanwhile the observances of their various sects. That which appears to the contented Freemason to be a philanthropic association, rising superior to all considerations of religious truth or error, all differences of Christian, heathen, and Jew, is, in point of fact, an habitual carrying out of religious indifferentism into daily life, until the conviction that all religions are equally worthless gradually dawns upon the mind of one individual after another, and qualifies for admission into higher grades of the Craft. Thus the time comes ever nearer when the mass of mankind will be prepared to receive that as their law which was formerly a secret known to a few only of the initiated.

4. Freemasonry communicates its "light" under the most awful and detestable oaths of secresy.[1] If virtue and truth tremble for their very existence because of some powerful oppressor, as was the case

---

[1] The candidate swears that, if ever he is found guilty of treachery, he will submit to have his head cut off, his heart and entrails torn out, his body burned, his ashes scattered to the winds. (*Cf.* Barruel, as already quoted, p. 197, who relates what he himself had seen and heard)

F

with Christianity in the time of the Roman emperors, one can readily understand that its teaching must be whispered in secret, not proclaimed amidst the throng of the market-place. But the disciples of truth and virtue are bound to stand forth boldly when occasion calls for public confession, and at such time concealment would be a crime on their part. If the teaching of Freemasonry is in harmony with the laws of Christianity and the peace of states, what has it to fear from Pope or king ? And if not, we can only say, it is impossible for that to be good to which concealment is habitual, and even indispensable.

5. What is it Freemasonry conceals with such scrupulous care ? Not its spirit of brotherly love and mutual assistance, a feature none can fail to praise, although it is reserved for the disciples of the Gospel to exhibit it in fullest perfection ; not its festive gatherings, although these are not always of an unexceptionable nature. On the contrary, the initiated appear most willing to speak of them, even in their printed publications. There must, therefore, be something at the bottom of the League which its members cannot and dare not mention.

6. We would remind any one who still shares the opinion of the First Napoleon, who pronounced Freemasonry to be " much ado about nothing," that this verdict in itself amounts to a criminal conviction, when we consider that, if it be true, mankind has for centuries been made the victim of a gigantic fraud, the sacredness of oaths has been systematically pro-

faned, and exalted persons who have joined the Society in all good faith have been made the laughing-stock of the populace.

Let us no longer deceive ourselves. The greatest service we can render to the initiated members of the Craft is to represent the whole affair as mere child's play, and describe the sound of the shells exploding in our midst as the harmless report of a drawing-room toy. The signs of the times are too plain to allow of this ; all must see that we have to encounter a precon-certed attack on Christianity. We are indeed con-fident that this is a citadel which can never be destroyed; but we ought, at the same time, to remem-ber the warning our Lord addressed to a careless and negligent people :—" The kingdom of God shall be taken from you, and given to a nation yielding the fruits thereof" (Matt. xxi. 43).

CHAPTER V.

THE COVERT WARFARE OF THE SECRET SOCIETY AGAINST MONARCHY.

THE further we penetrate into the real secrets of Freemasonry, the more careful must we be not to include in one sweeping censure all who belong to it. On the contrary, we distinctly assert that its three lowest grades, especially, include among their members many loyal subjects of authority—men [who . would not for a moment hesitate to abandon all connection with the Society if the scales which have grown over their eyes could only be removed. Such persons may be frequently heard to complain that the door leading to the higher grades of the Order is kept closed against them;[1] and not a few, grown weary of the perpetual delay, have quitted an association in which they expected to learn so much, and have in reality learnt so little. But our business, as we remarked before, is not with persons, but with things.

---

[1] It may be interesting to the reader to learn the names of the various grades, which we give according to the Scotch rite. They are taken from Thuileur :—" *Thuileur portatif* des trente-trois degrés de l'Écossisme du rit ancien et accepté, suivi du thuileur des trois grades symboliques écossais, tels qu'ils sont pratiqués dans la grande loge d'Écosse à Edimbourg   Paris, au magasin de Librairie Maçonnique, rue S Andre-des-Arcs, n 57, 1819—1. Apprenti ; 2. Compagnon ; 3 Maître ; 4. Maître

Three weapons are needed to enable the League to accomplish its ultimate designs: namely, Knowledge; Force, employed opportunely; and a Secret Propaganda, to permeate as widely as possible the most influential circles of society. Thus the Lodges may be divided into three classes—Lodges of Learning, of Action, and of Adoption.

The first comprises the learned world, as far as it belongs actually, or in spirit, to the Secret Society. Taking its stand upon freedom of academic instruction—one of the boasted strongholds of the present day—it is able to offer to mankind complete and perfect independence under the garb of science, and has been mainly instrumental in making our Universities and Schools of Art what they now are. The more entirely the Professor corresponds to the Masonic ideal, the more indispensable are his services to the Craft; he must occupy the most important posts, be frequently nominated to positions of prominence; give its tone to the educated world, above all, the

secret; 5. Maître paifait ; 6. Seciétaire intime ; 7. Pievôt et Juge ; 8. Intendant des Bâtimens; 9. Maître elu des Neuf; 10 Illustre élu des Quinze , 11 Sublime Chevalier elu ; 12 Grand-Maître-Architecte , 13. Royale-Arche ; 14 Grand Écossais de la voûte sacree ; 15 Chevalier d'Orient ; 16. Prince de Jérusalem ; 17. Chevalier d'Orient et d'Occident ; 18. Rose Croix d'Héredom de Kilwining ; 19. Giand-Pontife; 20. Vénérable Grand-Maître ad vitam ; 21 Noachite, ou Chevalier Prussien ; 22. Chevalier Royale Hache ; 23 Chef du Tabernacle ; 24. Prince du Tabernacle ; 25. Chevalier du Serpent d'airain ; 26 Écossáis, trinitaire, ou Prince du Liban ; 27 Grand-Commandeur du Temple, 28 Chevalier du Soleil , 29. Écossais de St André , 30. Chevalier Kadosch ; 31. Grand-Inspecteur, Inquisiteur-Commandeur ; 32 Sublime Piince du Royal Secret ; 33 Souverain Grand-Inspecteur-Géneral " The three last grades are meiely honorary.

casting-vote must ever be his in the assemblies of *savants* and *demi-savants*, as well as in the Parliament supposed to represent the popular mind. Should he be a Galen or a Justinian, care is taken that he shall be rich in honours and in gold. It is scarcely necessary to add, that the regulations of the Craft, binding on the common herd, are wonderfully relaxed in favour of such a man as this.

The Lodge of Action, or Red Lodge, is composed of the most determined Radicals, who, impatient of the slow process whereby their secret doctrines are to be gradually introduced into the world of science, of politics, and of society, deem the fruit already ripe, and want to tear it from the tree with one bold snatch. The earlier Carbonari, together with "Young Switzerland" and "Young Germany," were offshoots from this Lodge ; while the International itself may justly be termed its standing army.[1] In Italy it was, and still is, represented by Mazzini and Garibaldi ; in Spain, by Zorilla ; in France, by the Radicals ; whilst in Belgium it prevails almost exclusively, and is only held in check by the Catholic tone of a large majority of the population. Wherever it comes into unavoidable collision with Moderate or Blue Freemasonry, it is sure of careful handling, as was shown by the game carried on between the two Red leaders of Italy and the various Ministries of the United Monarchy. There is, indeed, no reason why these two parties should injure one another ; in their views and aims they are as closely allied as Orestes and Pylades, only a little

[1] *Cf* "Laacher Stimmen," year 1872, No. 2, p. 114.

brotherly strife goes on between them about the ways and means of carrying out these designs.

The Lodge of Adoption, or Blue Freemasonry, is a harbour of refuge for the Epicurean and the *Bourgeois-gentilhomme*, the commercial traveller and the rising artisan, as well as for the youthful aspirant to distinction in civil or military service. This Society is supposed to keep clear of politics. When a so-called reactionary Ministry is in power, it devotes itself to works of philanthropy and mutual benevolence, as well as to common participation in the pleasures of the table; when a Liberal Ministry is in office, it fawns upon it with abject servility, does the work of a secret police, and is never weary of lauding to the skies the wisdom of the rulers, and the prosperity of the people. This body of men compose the main force of the Liberals, and are, like the great mass of the people, at the disposition of their leaders, employed to secure success when anything important is at stake. For even the most unenlightened cannot fail to know that the real leaders keep in the background; they belong to higher grades, and on them it devolves to mark the pace at which the army under their command is to march. Should they start too early, or journey too far, brotherly love knows how to whisper in the ear of those in authority a word which shall effectually obviate all necessity of expelling them from the Craft. Anderson's "Book of Constitutions" expressly states, that "a Brother who has taken part in sedition against the State, without being guilty of any other crime, need not on that account be expelled from his Lodge." This proves, at the same time, that the rule forbidding all members of the three lower or symbolic grades to engage in politics is not to be taken in its most literal sense.

We are prepared to bring forward proofs that this division of the agents of the Secret Society into the three classes of thinkers, workers, and supernumeraries is no imaginary one. The following important instructions are found in the publication "Disclosures," &c. (*Révélations, &c.*, 11-14), already quoted above. We insert them *verbatim :*—" The teaching of Freemasonry is very influential, but let us bear in mind that it is never to be suddenly or explicitly unfolded before the eyes of aspirants, for an unfettered mind might draw from it conclusions highly prejudicial to our secret designs. We must know how, as soon as the sacred words Liberty and Equality have been uttered in the hearing of the candidate, to anticipate his thoughts, arrest their course in time, or change their current ; for this our symbols and hieroglyphics form a happy expedient, opportunely diverting his mind by directing attention to the manifold nature of the objects presented to his notice. This wise method of proceeding is the result of the sagacious policy of our founder, who was far too deeply versed in the knowledge of the human heart not to mix the mysterious and bewitching draught which we must continually hold to the lips, and instil into the soul, of every Brother with such consummate skill, that its true nature shall ever remain a secret, and its real properties be hidden under an innocent exterior.

Thus, in our truly illustrious Order, the amount of lore imparted must ever be proportioned to the capabilities of the recipient ; and in order to facilitate the spread of our doctrines, and to render their signification more or less apparent, we divide our neophytes into three different and distinct classes — the first comprising the inquiring minds, the second the impetuous and restless spirits, the third the superstitious and credulous souls. The doctrine to be expounded to each of these several classes is in itself one and the same, but the time and manner of imparting it must in each case be different. To the first-named class the true meaning appears at once as matter to be apprehended by mind and heart, and they take it in at a glance, as it is immediately and fully unveiled to them by their enlightened Brethren. In their case it is indispensable to employ at once every means, and bring into play all possible skill, in order to kindle their enthusiasm and keep it aflame, by representing to them that the light of the blazing star is the uniting bond and mainstay of our Association. With regard to the second class, composed of the turbulent and restless among our subjects, the duty devolves on us of leading them up by slow degrees to the lofty convictions we have mentioned. It is necessary to let them guess and grope their way amidst the symbols and parables presented to their notice, so that these may serve as a drag upon the wheel of their heated imagination, and prevent any troublesome aberrations. From the third class—the superstitious and credulous souls, amongst whom will invariably be found some of those dullards who seem created for the sole purpose of perpetuating a stupid ignorance—nothing more can be expected than that they should follow in a blind unreasoning manner the dictates of our teaching ; but this teaching must only be communicated to them according to the measure of their understanding, in order that they may receive it with avidity, practise it with care, and adhere to it with fidelity, fearful lest they violate the secret oath by which the loyalty of every fresh recruit is to be secured.[1] Thus by imperceptible degrees must that light be admitted by which, in the course of time, the whole globe is to be enlightened, and thus we shall at length behold fully developed that great and wondrous system which is to purify the earth and restore her primeval glory.[2] We must at all times take care not to reveal our real aim precipitately, since weak minds might be dazzled at first by so brilliant and searching a light. From time to time some few rays must be allowed to penetrate the gloom, in order gradually to accustom the eye to that resplendent light which is destined at some future

[1] In what an unfortunate position does this place the simple member of the Craft ! He swears by all he holds sacred that he has never heard the least word of harm in his "temple," and at once sets down the writings we quote from as the fabrication of a Belgian Ultramontane. If his social position entitles him to high rank in the Craft, he may possibly reach the highest grade of all, and still, especially if he seldom take part in active proceedings, remain in absolute ignorance of all that goes on. The Greek tragic poet said truly, that against folly even the gods themselves fight in vain.

[2] This view of the subject implies that the earth has been a great sufferer through the revelations of the Old and New Testament, and the social order built up upon them, so that it needs to be made a *tabula rasa*.

day to illuminate the whole earth; but we must moderate a glare which, if too piercing, might produce blindness—a result more fatal to them and to our Order than the darkness from which we seek to extricate them." Such are the instructions of the secret document; they afford abundant proof that Freemasons must be divided into the three classes we have named, and judged of accordingly if we would reconcile the many apparent contradictions with which we meet.

This distinction is especially necessary if we wish to comprehend the real and peculiar position of Freemasonry with regard to Monarchy. We here employ this word in its widest sense, as applicable not merely to the lawful wearer of the crown, but also to all civil authority, in as far as it represents supreme power on particular points, and requires obedience from its subjects in the name of God as a matter of conscience.

The "Word" plays a great part in Freemasonry, as in all Societies which are veiled from the gaze of the profane. The design is, to express the thing signified in the most concise form, and one by which the outside world may be led to suspect nothing, while nobler natures may have their interest aroused, the half-initiated and unsuspicious may not feel alarmed, and the initiated, when called upon to speak, may be enabled to make himself half or wholly understood by his hearers, according to their different degrees; the whole audience nevertheless enjoying the pleasing delusion that they have perfectly comprehended all that was said. The two sacramental words have already been mentioned; they are Liberty and Equality, and are contained in the name of Masonic *Free Brethren.* All speeches and songs of the Lodges revolve round these two centres. Formerly it was strictly forbidden to place them in juxtaposition, or in any way to couple the words together; in some parts, this rule may yet be in force, and may be the reason why we generally find one of the two treated of separately and magnified alone. But this veil of caution was to be torn away abruptly. On the 12th August 1792, the very day on which the unfortunate Louis XVI. was declared, after a trial which lasted forty-eight hours, to have forfeited his throne, and was led captive to the Temple, the legislative body passed a vote, deciding that from this time the date of Equality should be added to that of Liberty; in fact, the warrant for the King's capture bore this date, "4th year of Liberty, 1st year and 1st day of Equality." Barruel, an eyewitness of the events of that period, and also himself intimately acquainted with many Freemasons in Paris, relates that the Brethren, considering that the time had come when they were free to publish the secret they had sworn to keep, shouted aloud, " At last our goal is reached; from this day France will be one vast Lodge, and all Frenchmen Freemasons; the rest of the world will soon follow our example." He declares that he himself heard some of the most reticent of the Masons proclaiming publicly, " At last the object of our League has been attained, Equality and Freedom; all men are Brothers and

equals : 'all men are free,' was the whole purport of
law, the goal of our wishes, in fact, our great secret."
Long before these events took place, Barruel had
been received into the Order against his will, by dis-
pensation from the regular oath; he had once witnessed a reception, more in keeping with the rules
than his own had been, at the close of which the
"Worshipful" thus addressed the candidate, who had
just been sworn in and received as a Brother :—
"My dearest Brother, the secret of Freemasonry consists in these words, Equality and Liberty : all men
are free, all men are equal, all men are brethren."

Taken in their best acceptation, these words can
be repeated by any one. We are free, delivered from
the bondage of sin, free members of society, living
under the rule of law, not of arbitrary power. We
are equals, children of the same Heavenly Father ;
we ought therefore to love as brethren and relieve
one another in time of need. Hence we understand
how some of the best men are entrapped into joining
the Craft. Barruel himself testifies that, of his own
Lodge, during the Reign of Terror, the simple members showed a leaning towards Monarchy, whilst
the "Worshipful" remained what he was before,
a furious Jacobin.

Social intercourse with a circle of loyal Brothers
and apparently well-disposed friends is an agreeable
recreation even for a king, especially as he rarely
knows what it is to have a real friend, or to escape
from the shackles of court etiquette ; and since its

dark and terrible aspect is concealed from his view
with a fabulous dexterity, why should he suspect any
evil designs in this League? To Freemasons it is a
matter of still greater moment to have the head of
the State or one of his nearest relatives as their
Patron, to reckon his counsellors among their members, or to procure for one of the most deeply initiated of their Craft the nomination to some post of
importance. On page 18 of the "Disclosures,"
already often quoted, we read as follows:—"Liberty
and Equality, as figured by Solomon's Temple, form
the most powerful of auxiliaries in continually advancing our work, and drawing nearer to our great
and lofty end. For these we are indebted to our
illustrious Founder. It is of the utmost importance,
if we would bring our great designs to a happy conclusion, as well as render their execution a matter of
less difficulty and danger, that we spare no effort to
get into our power the most prominent members
of the clerical and military professions, the civic
authorities, the education of the young, kings themselves and princes, especially their children, their
counsellors and ministers; in a word, all whose interests might generally clash with our principles."

Here we have an explanation of the cringing submission exhibited by the Craft towards any existing
authority which they have not the power to overthrow. When, on the crash of the great Revolution,
Napoleon I. appeared as the heir to its fortunes, the
Brethren worshipped him in a manner that was abso-

lutely romantic; but no sooner had the conqueror fallen than they destroyed in hot haste all names and emblems that could recall him to mind, and the Grand Orient was no less ready to fall at the feet of Louis XVIII. than it had been at those of his predecessor. When Charles X. and his son were driven away, Brother Lafayette and the Citizen-King, who thought it an honour to belong to us, received the most extravagant ovations from the Lodges, as did also the Republic of the Blue Masons in 1848, and the subsequent author of the *coup-d'état*, their friend and brother, Napoleon.[1] Proofs of the greatest devotion to the civil authorities, and of a truly romantic patriotism, are also displayed, in the hope of enticing to their "temples" the chiefs of the corporation ; so that, this effected, the Freemasons may justly boast, "We wander amidst our adversaries, shrouded in threefold darkness. Their passions serve as wires, whereby, unknown to themselves, we set them in motion, and compel them unwittingly to work in union with us. Under the very shadow of authority Masonry carries on the great work entrusted to her."[2]

The loyal rejoicings of the Order are never to be accepted in good faith, but should be regarded as a mere cloak to cover the most extreme Radicalism. We find convincing proof of this given in the " Disclosures," &c. (p. 27), in the following words :—" Good

---

[1] *Cf* "Laacher Stimmen," 1872, No 2, p 115.
[2] *Cf. Vienna Freemasons' Journal*, MSS., for circulation in the Craft, 2d year of issue, No. 1, p. 66.

care must be taken not to express ourselves too
plainly concerning absolute liberty and equality before we have made ourselves thoroughly acquainted
with the mind of the aspirant, and the force of character he may possess. If we do not find him sufficiently firm, if we have reason to think the position
threatens to become critical, we must immediately
order to the front a new battery; adopt a milder
tone; with all possible skill and prudence soften down
the meaning of every phrase; and put our real views
quite out of sight. We interpret this Temple of
Solomon—that is, Liberty and Equality—as having
reference to our Society alone; there is no idea of
extending it beyond these limits; anything like rebellion, assertion of independence, casting off authority, are altogether out of the question. Quickly,
deftly, and at once, everything must be put in a fresh
light, and attention called to the fulfilment of duty,
the allegiance due to God, the practice of virtue, the
observance of unshaken loyalty to the powers that be.
Monsters, tyrants, scourges of humanity are suddenly
converted into fathers of their people, representatives
of God on earth, kings who deserve our esteem, our
homage, our veneration, on account of their sterling
personal worth and their exalted dignity and greatness.
In a word, to the eyes of such a neophyte, Freemasonry
must only aim at promoting the fear of Almighty
God, faithful obedience to rulers, humble deference to
authority, hatred of evil, love of all that is good and
virtuous. At given times, in order the more surely to

hurl from its car the Juggernaut which threatens us with destruction, it is necessary to feign to offer it incense and adoration."

It is not difficult for the student of history, the careful observer of the march of events, to see through the tissue of fraud wherewith Freemasonry seeks to undermine regular monarchy. One need only remember the fulsome and degrading flatteries heaped upon the Emperor Joseph II. of Austria, which proved as effectual in destroying his prestige as was the miscarriage of his own plans. Expressions such as these, " Dearest Joseph," " Beloved son," "Great, immortal Joseph," which abound in the pamphlets of the Craft, should never be uttered loud enough to reach the beetling heights where monarchs dwell. It matters not whether a Government has freely consented to be taken in tow by the Secret Society, or whether it is obliged to show its practical gratitude for services received ; in either case, the familiar path of "liberty and equality " must be trodden. The first step consists always of measures against the Church, for such strike with the force of a two-edged blade ; when once the altar, the main support of the throne, is attacked and robbed of its influence, the Christian part of the population, feeling that those placed over them have wounded them in their *sanctum sanctorum*, their religion, begin to waver in their confidence in the Government, and in their loyal affection to the hereditary dynasty. A 'mercenary press and the voices of the Brethren may indeed avail either to stifle the cry

G

which breaks from a suffering people, or to drown it altogether by vociferous praise of the new policy. They may succeed, by tale-bearing and calumny, in bringing into discredit the fidelity of the most true-hearted men ; but by these means the poison of dis-affection will be driven back into the very heart's blood of the population, there to produce a slow decline which will eat out the life of the State, and bring about the desired revolution.   The second blow is aimed at the aristocracy, those chivalrous defen-ders of the throne, and traditional champions of justice.   When a Government, becoming alive to its danger, seeks to free itself from the fatal embrace of such a foe, its struggles only serve to draw tighter the bonds which bind it.   Joseph II. brought down on himself a storm of abuse from all the European Lodges by his decree of December 16, 1785, which laid some restraint on the action of the "so-called Society of Freemasons," and attributed to them underhand proceedings.[1]   The war with the Turks was the work of the Secret Society, the plan being hatched by Herzberg and his dear friend Pitt ; one of the heads of the Craft, the Hungarian Count Nicholas Forgasch, personally carrying on an intrigue with Herzberg, in the hope of playing in the country of St Stephen a part similar to that enacted by

---

[1] The infamous political intrigues carried on by the Illuminati and by the Freemasons of North Germany were a special source of mischief ; the chief person concerned in them was the notorious Herzberg.   See an important document on the subject in Brunner, p. 516 *seq* , copied in the "Historische-Politische Blatter," p. 59 *seq*.

Orleans in France ; in fact, verses were printed in Hungary, openly giving him the title of King of the country. It was to revenge themselves on Joseph II. that the Freemasons all over Europe espoused the cause of Orleans in his attempt on the Regency ; and the same motive induced them to take part with the Emperor's sister in the notorious affair of the diamond necklace, in order through her to expose the monarch whom, at that time, they so cordially hated.[1]   Towards the end of his days, this well-meaning monarch recognised his error, and saw who had been his secret enemies ; but it was then too late, and the immense moral influence which he might have employed in support of the throne was irretrievably lost.   We will pass over the efforts of the Craft —unfortunately only too successful—to involve the Piedmontese King Charles Albert in its toils, and to undermine his dynasty, after having been instrumental in overthrowing the other thrones of Italy ; nor will we speak of the banishment of Isabella of Spain, just as she had succeeded in forming a better Ministry : for we do not intend to discuss in detail the events of the present day.

But what is of the greatest importance to our pur-

---

[1] See the references already given.   Rohan was a Mason of high grade, likewise Cagliostro, Orleans being Grand Master of the French Lodges.   Information respecting the influence of Freemasonry on the course of the Seven Years' War is found in "Historische-Politische Blatter," vol xvi. p. 477 *seq. ;* vol. xxix. p. 577 *seq*.   In regard to the political activity of the Order in more recent times, *Cf. idem,* vol. l. p 427 *seq.*

pose is the proof afforded by these events that Freemasonry is fundamentally opposed to regal and civic
authority. At the same time they show that intrigues
of an unmistakably revolutionary tendency are not
faux pas made by certain recalcitrant members, but a
necessary consequence of the fundamental principles
of the Society, and that only most imperfectly enlightened Brethren complain of violation of the rules
in those very circumstances where the strictest regular
observance has been practised.

1. From all that has been stated, it becomes apparent
that universal liberty and absolute equality is the object Freemasonry keeps ever in view. This liberty is
not the wise control exercised by the nobler and higher
part of man over all that is mean and vile in his fallen
nature, as inculcated by the Gospel, but it is, on the
contrary, a casting off of all restraints in religious,
political, and social life ; that emancipation of the
will and of the passions which never fails ultimately
to result in the enslavement of all that is best in man.
Liberty for all that is evil, bondage for all that is
good !—such is the motto of that Liberalism which
is the offspring of Freemasonry ; and the word
Equality is to be understood as meaning social democracy in its strictest sense. To sum up all, we have
before us in these two words, which express everything, an entire political system. In the "Disclosures"
(p. 14 *seq.*) we read as follows : — "Liberty and
Equality are the two main advantages towards which
our plans must ever tend, the employment of all pos-

sible cunning and powers of dissimulation being a
matter of course. Hypocris must lend us her able
assistance. We must continually search and probe
vacillating minds, and set them in motion so gently
that they may scarcely be aware of the slightest pressure. We must amuse them, carry them along with
us, deceive them at the opportune time, make them
in love with their own delusions, lull them to sleep in
the sweet sense of their new dignity " (of Freemasons),
" and only reveal our designs respecting them when the
goal is close at hand, and they, lost in the bewildering maze of an enticing and hopeless labyrinth, have
neither the power nor the will to strike out into
another path. In the end, clinging closely to the
guide who has led them thus far, they will be quite
prepared to regard the most startling and extravagant
revolution as the simple conclusion that must naturally be expected." It is only for the purpose of
duping weak or scrupulous persons that Freemasons
describe liberty and equality as merely the salt that
gives savour to the close bond of amity which unites
the Brethren. These principles are really intended
to have in due time a world-wide extension, and to
form the basis of a new structure of humanity. The
names of North, South, East, and West, given to the
four walls of the Lodges, sufficiently denote the cosmopolitan nature of the science taught within them. If
we remember the extraordinary activity of the propaganda of the Order in every land, it is simply
impossible to believe that brotherly intercourse with

a circle of friends could be the sole object of the
League. Besides, the larger the circle of friends, the
weaker grows the friendship. An Association boasting more than sixteen millions of members never is,
nor possibly can be, a circle of friends; and, whatever
solemn assurances are put forward to the contrary,
no one can view it otherwise than as a political union,
pledged in the name of Liberty and Equality to
acknowledge no monarch and no authority. We read
in the Vienna Journal (MSS. for the Brethren, 1st
year, No. 2, p. 163 *seq.*) :—" On being asked to give a
definition of the real object of the Society, the oracles
of the Order at length told us, in answer to the
strange request, that benevolence in its widest sense,
or, to speak more correctly, the promotion of the welfare of humanity by works of benevolence, was its
object. But let us examine the constitutions of our
Order, and find how this object is embodied there.
To understand this, we must glance at the heavy and
interminable chain of evil which humanity drags about
with it throughout every quarter of the globe, and on
examination we shall find that almost all this evil is
the effect of the pernicious influences working in the
world, whence arise the prejudices generally prevalent
as to foreign birth, inequality of rank, diversities of
religion. Let us contemplate this Order, dispersed
over the surface of the earth, and we shall see that its
main object can be none other than the good of mankind. It is a Society which proposes to itself, as its
primary and ultimate end, to banish completely from

amongst its members [1] those contemptible considerations of foreign birth, class distinctions, and religious differences, which have produced such lamentable results. Wherefore, one of its first principles is to regard the whole dignity of man as consisting in being what nature has called us to be—creatures of the same race, citizens of the same world, proprietors of the same earth, children of the same mother." The Sibylline veil in which these words are wrapt is in this instance a tolerably transparent one. With the prejudices of foreign birth the boundaries of States must also be swept away, and with class distinctions the kingly prerogative must likewise fall to the ground. The whole worth of man, besides his virtues (of course only natural ones), lies in the fact of his being a man like other men; and all men are equal, not in the Christian sense of all being children of one Heavenly Father, and fellow-heirs of redemption, but in a purely natural, human, and social sense.

We find the same thing expressed in other words in the "Disclosures" (p. 6 *seq*.): "The task of dispelling speedily and successfully the shades of night which enveloped humanity, of guiding the steps of mankind out of the region of darkness, and of opening men's eyes to the light of truth, so long obscured by clouds of error, required an intellect no less power-

---

[1] And not from amongst its members only, but in due course, and at the right moment, from the whole world, as is plainly to be gathered from the concluding sentence. Further information respecting the universality of these efforts of the League will be given under our fourth head.

ful than that of our Founder. Therefore, we must
ever hold in our hands the tools entrusted to us by
that great Master, labouring incessantly to keep them
in good condition, and to put them to a worthy use,
until the unexpected *dénouement* shall arrive to startle
the world with the most terrible, but at the same time
most felicitous, of all revolutions, and confer immortal glory upon that sagacious enemy of all crowned
heads. In order to achieve this, no effort must be
spared to attract, by the deceptive bait of Brotherhood, an immense multitude of persons, and unite
them in the same views, without allowing differences
of taste, character, and religion to offer any obstacle.
Our teaching must be regulated with consummate
skill, in order to animate and keep up this Association, and extend it beyond the limits of its own members to all the inhabitants of the world, so that even
the wildest and most primitive races of Central Africa
or America shall be included within our embrace.
This exalted doctrine, the soul of our Union and the
animating spirit of all its members, consists in that
radical instinct, the law engraved by nature in every
heart, which must ever be the basis of all our transactions—a thirst for liberty and equality."

Now, what is the King, in the Lodge and in the
eyes of the Craft? Simply "Brother So-and-so," no
more nor less than any other Freemason, or any other
man. His royal dignity appertains only to the profane world; it is the rough and unhewn stone, which
the blows of the Mason's hammer, the use of his

square and plumb-line, is to model into the form of a cube, *i.e.*, a stone of which all the sides are equal. The king takes his place in the Lodge as an equal amongst his equals, one in a circle formed of millions of friends. We are well aware that even to a Prince a real friend is an invaluable treasure, that the most exalted monarchs love to gather round them a small number of trusty companions. But that friendship alone can be termed real in which the Prince remains a Prince, in which his friendship bears the stamp of gracious condescension, and the individual honoured by it is ready to hazard life and limb to defend the rights of his royal friend. Now, according to the views of the Craft, the ruling Sovereign is an equal, a "Brother," on a level with all other initiated Brethren, soon to stand on the same footing with all the whole human race. However this bitter fruit of the secret teachings of Freemasonry may be concealed from him by intoxicating draughts of exultant adulation, the venomous serpent of treason ever lurks under the roses of loyalty. The Craft recognises no monarchy.

2. In his character of Brother and equal, the King has, according to Masonic teaching, no right of command. This follows as the logical consequence of what we have just stated; but as it has hitherto been our rule to prove everything step by step, we will make no exception in the present case. Brother Lamartine, by no means the reddest of the red, member and President of the Provisional French Government in 1848, expressed his conviction that "the

great ideas which were at the bottom of the popular risings in 1789, 1830, and 1848 were the offspring of Freemasonry." These so-called great ideas, however, denied the existence of monarchical rights. One of the organs of the League, a Jewish Brother named Weil, thus writes: "We exercise a mighty influence on the course of events and the progress of civilisation, in the work of spreading Republicanism amongst the people." [1] This means that the spread of Masonic principles will bring about the emancipation of nations, and at last teach them that no king possesses the right to command them. Brother Borne likewise says: "We have shaken the pillars on which the old building rests, with such force, that they must soon give way." This "old building" is the Christian State, the Throne, and the Altar. The "Disclosures" (p. 10) speak no less plainly on this point:—"By means of liberty and equality, our much-prized prerogatives, we must seek to dry up the tainted fountains whence flow all the ills of mankind ; we must obliterate every trace of the degrading differences of station, which obtrude themselves upon our notice ; we must restore man to his primeval rights, no longer recognising rank and dignity, two things the mere sight of which offends the eye of man and wounds his self-love. Obedience is a mere chimera, and has no place in the wise plans of Providence ; it rests upon the caprices

---

[1] *Cf* the above-named "Klageschrift eines Berliner Freimaurers" on the corruption of the League by means of the Jews, which appeared in the "Historische-Politische Blatter."

of fate" (royal birth), "and the exorbitant demands of a pride which is resolved that everything shall bend before it, and which regards the creatures inhabiting the world" (mankind) "as a low and despicable race of beings, created for the sole purpose of serving it as slaves." If every kind of authority is a violation of the hereditary rights of man, if to be born to the purple is only a freak of chance, and to wear it is an unpardonable exaltation of self at the expense of one's fellow-men, then every act of obedience is a folly and a degradation, and no king possesses the right to rule.[1]

3. According to these doctrines, it is criminal on the part of any ruler to persist in asserting his right to power. If complete political equality is an unalienable and primitive right peculiar to mankind, any encroachment on it is a glaring offence. Hence Brother Juge, in the treatise we have already quoted, speaks of "kingly greed;" hence, too, we so often meet with words such as "despot" and "tyrant," while the "Colossus" which is to be overthrown means just the same thing. The concluding sentences of the "Disclosures," p. 28, run as follows: —"Let us keep our eyes continually fixed upon the

---

[1] In explanation of what goes before, we quote a saying of the revolutionist Grégoire, from the *Moniteur*, Nov. 28, 1792, "Rapport sur la Savoie :"—"All Governments are our enemies, all nations are our friends ; either we shall be destroyed, or they emancipated : and emancipated they shall be. When the axe of freedom has struck down the throne, it will fall upon the head of any one who strives to piece together its fragments."

Temple of Solomon (the reconstruction of modern
society) and upon our emblems; but never let us
permit the real significance of our teaching to be
known, except in the Lodge of a few select Brethren !
. . . . Courage, Fraternity, Unity, Perseverance !
Let us arm ourselves with this invisible light, and
cherish within our hearts a courage worthy of the
loftiest souls.   My Brethren, let it be our firm conviction that we represent the lantern of Diogenes,
that we are fiery meteors of terrible omen to tyrants.
Unbroken transmission of our doctrine makes us
immortal, our unity renders us invincible; to our
blows is it reserved to fell this Colossus." These
blows, however, were represented publicly as virtuous
actions and heroic deeds, and the point at issue is
to do away with the produce of a criminal and unhealthy state of society, the plague of Monarchy.

4. Thus according to the express teaching of Freemasonry, kingly dominion, and indeed all authority
in general, is to be extirpated; in this way man will
see the dawn of a second Golden Age.   Let us listen
to the words of the Masons themselves: " At first this
independence, this casting off of all supremacy and
all power, must be represented, even among ourselves,
as only the restoration of the Golden Age, that
happy time of which poets sing, when à beneficent
Deity came and ruled the earth's first inhabitants with
a sceptre of flowers.   By this Golden Age we mean
those peaceful years when hearts, free from passions,
were strangers to the sting of jealousy; when pride,

covetousness, and other vices were unknown ; when
men were free and equal, ruling their conduct according to the laws of Nature alone, and recognising
no other differences amongst themselves than those
which wise Mother Nature had herself established.
But whereas nothing short of a miracle can work
so sudden a change, and any premature action can
only result in failure, we must set to work with skill
and the greatest caution, until men are freed from
those universal and ancient" (*i.e.,* religious) "prejudices
which, by robbing simple souls of their strength and
peace of mind, drag them into a deep abyss of error,
and bring them into subjection to the passions of
those imperious tyrants " (kings) " who are devoured
by ambition and avarice. . . . . Our policy must be
unfolded ever with vast skill and a certain amount of
mystery to the aspirant ; we must confine ourselves
to representing to him this freedom and equality as a
most delightful thing, a happiness reserved for our
Order alone : without losing sight of our real aim.
We must thoroughly imbue him with our spirit, until
habit becomes second nature to him, and the hour
arrives when our Society finds itself strong enough to
muster the whole world under its banner.   Up to
that time, we must depict our Society to him as an
elect family, free from those stormy passions and
gnawing cares of which mankind is the victim ; a
family which, rocked in the bosom of beauteous
nature, lives over again the Golden Age, and from its
safe harbour looks out with pitying eye over the

wide sea of error in which its hapless fellow-men are
struggling in the present hour.   We must hold fast
the fundamental principle of our Order, that all our
Brother Masons " (in the lower grades) " are only our
soldiers and workmen, whilst we are their generals
and the great architects commissioned by Freedom to
construct a vast edifice—*i.e.*, the reform of the human
race, through the destruction of kings, those scourges
of humanity."   After the secret document has coun-
selled that the Order be recruited as far as possible from
the youth of the upper classes, even of the aristocracy,
it thus proceeds :—" In education, we must gently
instil the essence of our teaching in its most attractive
form, and, without exciting the least suspicion, insen-
sibly prepare those in high places for the blow which will
annihilate them, endeavouring to weaken their prestige and destroy the power they have usurped over
their fellow-men by means of well-known writers,
whose views are in harmony with our plans.   We
must inspire inferiors with ambition, and with jealousy
of their superiors, teaching them to despise and hate
all whom chance has placed above them.   They must
thus be gradually led on to insubordination, by being
skilfully shown that to require loyalty and fidelity
proves an immoderate thirst for power, and is an
unwarrantable outrage on the rights of men. . . . .
Thus we shall induce young hearts who are incapable
of discerning our real end to help us in accomplishing
our great work, and in restoring to man the noble independence bestowed on him by his Creator as a pecu-

liar prerogative which alone distinguishes him from the rest of creation." From these words it may plainly be inferred how intimate is the connection existing between modern educational legislation and the designs of Freemasonry upon thrones and authorities. They may repeat over and over again a thousand times how they merely wish to lessen the influence of the Clergy and strengthen the power of the State; the more loudly their words proclaim fidelity to the State, the more firmly we believe a contrary feeling to exist in their hearts.

The abolition of monarchy and of authority in general is symbolised in the Masonic legends by Solomon's temple. This temple in Jerusalem, built at the command of God by the wisest of kings, remained standing for a long period, a pile of wondrous magnificence, dedicated to the worship of the true God. But after the lapse of centuries, a mighty host came from the East, and destroyed the building, carrying away into cruel captivity in Babylon the people of God. At length the hour of deliverance approached; a heathen king, divinely inspired, set free the captives, and gave them permission to re-build their temple, furnishing them besides with the means of accomplishing this undertaking. Let us now hearken to the interpretation of this scriptural history, as given by the Craft in its own words :— " The temple in its first glory is an image of the primeval condition of man, when he had been created out of nothing ; religion, and the ceremonial of re-

ligion, is simply the carrying out of that great law of
nature implanted in every heart, having its root in
those principles of mutual charity and toleration
which all men are bound to observe. The destruction of the temple and the thraldom of the servants
of the living God is emblematic of the pride, ambition, and greed which have brought into the world
dependence and slavery. The Assyrians and their
merciless host denote kings, princes, and governors,
whose power has laid a galling yoke on the neck of
so many oppressed peoples. Finally, the chosen
people entrusted with the rebuilding of the temple
represent our enlightened Brethren and Freemasons,
whose mission it is to reintroduce amongst mankind
that liberty and equality which is its distinctive prerogative, and thus restore to our planet her lost glory "
(" Revelations," p. 21 *seq*.).

Here, then, we see what the much-boasted philanthropy of Freemasonry—" benevolence in its widest
sense," as they call it—is driving at. In order to
throw dust into the eyes of the public, collections are
made in the Lodges on the occasion of any national
calamity, and the amount of the same ostentatiously
published. In some parts, as, for instance, in Holland,
schools are established for the orphans of Freemasons ; and a portion of the immense profits returned by the mercantile transactions carried on by
members of the Craft is devoted to objects professing
to be of general utility, but really confined to the
interests of Freemasonry. In this manner patronage

is gained, adversaries are silenced, and a favourable impression is made on the unreflecting portion of the upper classes. But their benevolent exertions always have been, and always will be, attempts to bring back the "golden age of universal liberty and equality" by means of the destruction of authority throughout the world. In a speech delivered at a celebration of the centenary of the Middleburgh Lodge, "La Compagnie durable," "Brother" Tiffle spoke thus:—"Our avowed object is the amelioration of the whole human race; not by making proselytes for ourselves, or for any religious persuasion or form of government whatsoever, but exclusively through benevolence, in the widest acceptation of the term. Our Lodges are schools, where we learn from one another the Royal Art of regulating our actions in such a manner that they may serve as a rule and example for every rational being. From the windows of our temples the eternal flame, burning upon our altars with a clear and vivid brightness, must shine forth upon the surface of the earth, so that all nations may walk by its light. Thus the partitions will not have to be thrown down ; they will gradually fall of themselves, rewarding the labours of Freemasonry, and enabling it to clasp all, —our sisters" (the female sex) "assuredly included— in its comprehensive embrace." The allusions made by Tiffle in this speech are fully explained by what has been said in a former part of this work. We can also now understand why Freemasonry is pleased to call itself the "Royal Art," since it claims to have dis-

H

covered the secret whereby all men can be happily governed—namely, by the abolition of monarchy and all manner of authority, and by the restoration of absolute liberty and equality.

V. In order to attain the end aimed at, Religion, the basis of authority, is to be uprooted.   The designs of the Secret Society are, as we have already shown, completely antagonistic to Christianity, and identical with those of Voltaire.   Several of the authorities we have quoted do not attempt to conceal that the Altar will be overturned at the same time as the Throne, if not before it, as being its principal bulwark.   The following sentences from the " Disclosures " (p. 23 *seq.*) are sufficiently explicit :—" Since it has been man's unhappy fate to survive the destruction of his distinctive rights" (liberty and equality!) " and to sink from the glorious position of the independence he once held ; since he is now in a state of subjection, is branded with ignominy, lies helpless in the abyss which the pride and ambition of his fellow-men have dug for him, and into which his indifference to his own real interests has enabled them to precipitate him—under these circumstances it becomes his bounden duty to rise up once more and wave aloft the standard of independence and equality wrested from him by the tyrant's hand, planting it upon the corpses of those pitiless monsters who were the original authors of man's fall.   But if, on the other hand, man is himself to blame for his misfortune" (by the free election of a king) ; " if his degradation is the work of his own arm, his eyes must be opened to see the fetters he has forged for himself. He must grasp the helping-hand we hold out to him, in order to burst his bonds and enable him to overcome in his turn the hated oppressor. For the Brethren of our Craft it is reserved to achieve this triumph—that is, to gather together in one vast corporation all the different families of nations who, originally all parts of one great whole, have become separated and scattered, and in proportion to their divergence from the common centre mutually estranged, to such a degree that they no longer have any desire to be reunited, and to compose once more the body of which they were formerly members. Let it be ours, my Brethren, to extinguish the torch of dissension which is consuming the world, and kindle in its stead that light by whose fructifying beams our race is to be created anew in vernal perfection and increased purity.[1] Soon, like a second Moses, shall we set these groaning nations free ; soon will all tyrants fall, and their power crumble at the sight of the wonders accomplished by our arm made strong in the justice of its cause. . . . . It has not been by means of force alone that man has been robbed of liberty and equality ; ignorance and superstition have also been

---

[1] We might imagine that one of the founders of the International had uttered these words ? And yet the document dates at the latest from 1820 At any rate, the Dutch translation, made from a second French edition, was printed in 1826.

brought to bear, in order to blind his eyes, and prevent
his claiming again the possessions so unjustly taken
from him.   Kings, those unfortunate tyrants, wishing
to plant on a sure foundation the throne they had
raised upon ruins, knew well how skilfully to instil
into the minds of their subjects the convenient doctrine that religion, the worship most pleasing to God,
consists in blind submission and loyal obedience to
earthly princes, and that the allegiance due to them
cannot be withheld without sacrilege.   This snare
was cunningly laid, and mankind was decoyed into it
by the novel bait of a dogma resting on an utterly
false basis ; which dogma early inculcated, prevented
every murmur, and rocked reason to sleep.   Thus
man became incapable of perceiving the rational distinction between divine and natural right, and viewed
any change of his" (social and political) " condition
not merely as a thing impossible, but as an outrage
on most sacred rights."   The advice is added that all
religious idols should be destroyed.   From such a
point of view no one can deny that, as the religion of
Jesus Christ is the true foundation of the throne, and
a Christian people is not easily induced to rise in
rebellion against its lawful rulers, it follows, therefore,
that in Europe every revolution must begin with the
Church ; for when once the altars are overthrown,
and the faithful thrust back into the gloom of the
catacombs, thrones will fall as a matter of course.
We have for years been called upon to witness in
Germany and Austria the furious battle of exoteric

Freemasonry, the Liberal party, against positive
Christianity, and all the blessed influences which its
external life exercises in the world. In the background stand the Liberal leaders; under their thin
disguise we recognise them to be the members of the
Craft. We know what the closing scene of the drama
will be. The concessions made at the expense of
the Church are only instalments paid off before the
final winding-up of affairs. They do not appease
the hungry creditor; they only incite him to make
fresh demands.

VI. An universal revolution is the first step on the
road leading to the world-wide republic of the future.
The old order of things, resting on religious prejudice
and political tyranny, must, says the Freemason, be
overthrown, in order that a new temple of humanity,
without kings and without authority, may be established on the groundwork of mutual liberty and
equality. In other words, an universal republic must
be founded. This republic can only be ushered in by
the spasmodic throes of an universal revolution, which,
although productive of a convulsion more terrible than
any the world has ever known, will be attended with
the most beneficial results. Innumerable speeches
made by Freemasons might be quoted, announcing its
near approach. One party amongst the Brethren holds
the belief that this end is to be attained by universal
extension of the Secret Society, and by getting the
education of the rising generation into the hands of
the Craft, so that at length monarchs will voluntarily

doff their crowns, and officials vacate their posts. The other party, on the contrary, does not dream of any such fools' paradise; and precisely those who belong to the higher grades know—as their ritual alone would suffice to teach them—that nothing short of a desperate revolution can usher in the golden age, along a path strewn with corpses and encumbered with ruins. In the "Astræa, Taschenbuch fur Frei-maurer von Bruder Sydow," 1845, p. 85, an orator speaks as follows :—"If the structure of humanity is to advance, the old scaffolding which has hindered the progress of the building must be pulled down, even though all the powers in the world cling to it to uphold it. That which is destined to destruction must in the course of things be destroyed ; and if human powers resist this law, at the behest of fate a stronger power" (query, the Chiefs of the Order ?) "will appear upon the scene to carry out the eternal decrees of Providence. The Reformation of the Church, as well as the French Revolution, proves the existence of this law. The old scaffoldings shall be forcibly torn away ; and if this demolition is punish-able by human law, it is nevertheless sanctioned by the Eternal law which presides over the destinies of the human race. Revolution is a crisis necessary to development."

The same idea is presented in a less didactic and abstract manner in the "Disclosures" (p. 25 *seq.*), where we read :—"Nothing is difficult to him who dares to undertake everything. The poison must be ueutralised by means of its antidote, revolution must

succeed to obedience, vengeance follow upon effemi-
nacy, power must grapple with power, and the reign
of superstition yield before that of the one true natural religion. . . . . The spell has to be broken which
has so long held mankind in an ignominious dependence, owing to blindness or false prejudice. The
idolatrous worship of tyrants, a degradation of the
worship due to the true Divinity, must be done away
with ; man, free by nature, must assist his fellow-men
in the recovery of their rights, the sacred heirloom of
them all. No means must be spared to regain liberty
and equality, so essential to man's happiness; with
unconquerable firmness and perseverance all must
strive to win them back. We may rest assured that
every crime committed in order to secure the good
of all is an act of generous virtue, which, sooner or
later, cannot fail to bring a rich reward." On this
account the candidate for initiation is required to
swear implicit obedience to his unknown Superiors in
the Order. Barruel states that the oath administered
to him on his admission was as follows :—"My
Brother, are you prepared to execute every command
you may receive from the Grand Master, even should
contrary orders be laid on you by King or Emperor,
or any other ruler whatsoever ? " [1]

Freemasonry has already on one occasion put forth
all its strength, with the object of kindling an universal conflagration ; we mean at the time of the French
Revolution, the waves of which swept far and wide

[1] Barruel, "Mémoires," &c., vol. 11 p. 193.

into other lands, threatening to devastate the whole
Continent of Europe. And even in our own day its
ignes fatui are viewed by an ambitious and tyrannical
Liberalism as beacons to warn us of danger, instead
of wandering lights to lure us to destruction. The
simultaneous action of two great influences contributed to bring about this state of things ; the pseudo-
philosophy of the Encyclopædists in the world of
letters, and the practical organisation of their principles in the Masonic Lodges, without which the
wished-for result could never have been attained.
We are fully aware that not all the Encyclopædists
were Freemasons. Voltaire himself only became a
member of the Craft when he was in his forty-eighth
year, on June 7th, 1778. One thing, however, is
certain, that their unaided efforts would no more
have been sufficient to bring about the Reign of
Terror than a swarm of gnats to darken the sun.
It is, moreover, equally certain that these doctrines
had for some long time past been known to, and
secretly disseminated by, Freemasons ; and when the
time for action came at last, they were openly proclaimed by them in the streets of Paris. The party-
leaders, Mirabeau, Sièyes, Grégoire, Robespierre,
Condorcet, Fauchet, Guillotin (of bloody memory),
Bonneville, Volney, Philippe Egalité, &c., had all
been initiated into the higher grades. The French
Revolution was nothing more than Freemasonry in
power ; its work was crowned on Jan. 21st, 1793,
by the death of Louis XVI, or, to borrow the lan-

guage of the time, " Citizen Capet, last of the race of
tyrants." Even Roltech and Welker, in their "Political
Lexicon," were constrained to acknowledge that Freemasonry had a share in the French Revolution, and
exercised considerable political influence during the
period of the Restoration in France, Spain, Italy, and
other countries. Wachsmuth also remarks, in his
" History of France during the Epoch of the Revolution," vol. i. p. 55, "that the literature of the time
immediately preceding that terrible event, the tendency of which was to subvert Church and State,
found in Freemasonry a zealous and useful ally."

Such opinions are, of course, always expressed with
reserve, the caution with which they are worded being
plainly discernible ; it will therefore be as well for
us to hear what the Craft, as the principal actor, has
to say about its own part in the drama enacted during
the last decade of the previous century.

Louis Blanc, a member of the Craft, gives us (in
his "Histoire de la Révolution Française," vol. ii. c.
3), an idea of the manner in which Freemasons
laboured at the work of revolutionising nations. He
says :—" It is necessary to conduct the reader to the
opening of the subterranean mine laid at that time
beneath thrones and altars by revolutionists differing
greatly, both in their theory and their practice, from
the Encyclopædists. An association had been formed
composed of men of every land, every religion, and
every class, bound together by mysterious signs
agreed upon amongst themselves, pledged by a

solemn oath to observe inviolable secresy as to the
existence of this hidden bond, and tested by proofs
of a terrible description. These men busied themselves with the performance of fantastic ceremonies
and the practice of works of benevolence, recognising
amongst themselves no differences of rank, except
the Masonic distinctions of Apprentice, Fellow-Craft,
and Master-Mason. Thus, we find Freemasonry to
have been widely diffused immediately before the
outbreak of the Revolution. Spreading over the
whole face of Europe, it poisoned the thinking minds
of Germany, and secretly stirred up rebellion in
France, showing itself everywhere in the light of an
association resting upon principles diametrically
opposed to those which govern civil society. The
very plan chosen for the construction of its edifice
(namely, its internal constitution) was, on the part of
Freemasonry, a virtual condemnation of the ideas
and arrangements of the world around. The ordinances of Freemasonry did indeed make great outward display of obedience to law, of respect to the
outward forms and usages of profane society, and
of reverence towards rulers; at their banquets the
Masons did indeed drink the health of kings in the
days of monarchy, and of presidents in the times of
republic; such prudent circumspection being indispensable on the part of an association which threatened the existence of the very Governments under
whose eyes it was compelled to work, and whose suspicion it had already aroused. This, nevertheless,

did not suffice to counteract the radically revolutionary influence continually exercised by the Craft,
even while it professed nothing but peaceful intentions."[1]

It was precisely these terrible revolutionary designs
of the Secret Society which induced its Provincial
Grand Master, the Prussian Minister Count von
Haugwitz, to leave it. In the memorial presented
by him to the Congress of Monarchs at Verona in
1830, which has since passed through many editions,
he bids the rulers of Europe to be on their guard
against the "Hydra." "I feel at this moment firmly
persuaded," writes the ex-Grand-Master, "that the
French Revolution, which had its first commencement
in 1788, and broke out soon after, attended with all the
horrors of regicide, existed Heaven knows how long
before, having been planned, and having had the way
prepared for it, by associations and secret oaths."

As a proof that Count Haugwitz did not take too
gloomy a view of things, we will proceed to quote
from two official manifestoes of the Craft. We know
well that such speeches, especially if delivered in the
presence of great persons, overflow with affected and
servile loyalty, and are worded in direct opposition to
the real character of their secret transactions; but when
the waves of political agitation rise high, the veil is
at times somewhat incautiously lifted, and orators are
apt to say what they subsequently regret. Thus
after the events of February 1848, the Craft sang

---

[1] "La Franc-maçonnerie dans l'Etat," p. 51 *seq.*

songs of triumph at the open success of its secret
endeavours.   A Belgian Brother, Van der Heym,
spoke thus :—" On the day following the revolution
of February a whole nation rose as one man, overturned the throne, and wrote over the frontal of
the royal palace the words 'Liberty, Fraternity,
Equality,' all the citizens having adopted as their
own this fundamental principle of Freemasonry.   The
combatants had not to battle long before the victory
over their oppressors was gained—that freedom won
which for centuries had formed the theme of Masonic
discourses.   We, the Apostles of Fraternity, laid the
foundation-stone of the Republic."[1]

Brother Peigné, Worshipful Master of the Lodge of
" The People's Friends," uttered similar words about
the same time :—" In our glorious Revolution of 1792
the Lodge of the Nine Sisters (*Neuf Sœurs*) gave
to the world men such as Garat, Brissot, Bailly,
Camille-Desmoulins, Condorcet, Champfort, Petion ;
the Lodge of the Iron-Mouth (*Bouche de Fer*) gave to
it Fouchet, Goupil de Prefeln, Sièyes ; the Lodge of
Candour (*De la Candeur*) Custine, the two Lameths,
and Lafayette.   So great is the fertility of Freemasonry, that she was able to produce all these great
minds, the lights of their age, without in any
way exhausting her vast resources.   The words
inscribed on her banner, 'Liberty, Fraternity, Equality,' ensured to France intellectual supremacy, and
were adopted as the national motto. . . . . To us,

[1] *Le Franc-maçon*, 1ere année, p. 39, July 1848.

Younger Brothers of the Craft, it belongs to show ourselves worthy sons of our illustrious ancestors."[1]

The Secret Society made itself very prominent as the party of Revolution, not in France alone, but also in Germany; and to it is to be ascribed the fact that the triumphant shouts of the " Mountain" on the left bank of the Rhine were " re-echoed by the noblest spirits of the Fatherland," to use their own phraseology. Only when blood began to flow like water did the Brethren in Weimar, Gotha, Brunswick, Berlin, and other places sober down. It was at that time (1794) that the Berlin Directory of the United Templars and Rosicrucians presented to the Government their celebrated manifesto : — "Almost before we were aware of the presence amongst us of this destructive teaching, it had become the idol of a great number of our Brethren. Here we have the source whence sprang the extravagant theories as to liberty and equality which are so thoughtlessly carried into practice in our own day. Associations within associations were formed, making strange and novel use of the newly-found (?) treasure. One great sect grew up well known to all, its exertions being no more of a secret than its name.[2] This sect it is which has honeycombed the ground beneath our feet, and prepared our ruin. . . . . We assert

---

[1] Discourse pronounced on January 1st, 1849.

[2] This odious sect is that of the Illuminati, acknowledged by the collective body of Freemasons in Germany, when assembled at the Congress of Wilhelmsbad, to be bone of their bone and flesh of their flesh. As one scapegoat at least must always be found, it appears they were pitched

boldly, in the hearing of princes and peoples, that the abuse of our ' League has given rise to all the political and moral disorder now universally prevailing. Apostate members of our Craft have originated the revolutions of the past, and they will be the authors of those of the future." Excellent, true-hearted men! You little knew your Order, although you were, or rather *because* you were, its ostensible chiefs. You believed it to be a club, where you met to enjoy your wine, discuss the topics of the day, and do one another a good turn—an opinion shared in by many thousands of your deluded Brethren, even in the present day.

Some materials for the tremendous conflagration which was destined to be kindled by the initiated members of the higher grades are to be found even in the lowest grade. Amongst other questions, the Apprentice is asked on his reception — " What sort of man should be admitted to the privileges of Masonry?" The answer is, "One who is freeborn." The ceremonial requires him to wear round his neck a rope—in the profane world an emblem of slavery. In order to call his attention again to the emphatic ·word, the question is repeated in somewhat different terms — " On what do you ground your hope of admission?" The correct answer to this is — "On my being free by

upon in the present instance to bear the blame of having kindled the infernal flame of revolution. We ask them to whom is it to be ascribed in France, Italy, Spain, and Portugal?

birth."[1] It often occurs that the aspirants to the
leathern apron are too much taken up with the
jugglery that goes on at the time to pay heed to
the principal word, and at a later period are quite
astonished at the Democratical intrigues of the
Lodge; but that does not matter in the least. It
has been said that all the children of Adam are
either nine-pins, or the balls that knock them down.
Those who are not the latter can be made very
useful as the former, and fill excellently their place
in creation. It is no good trying to give a thin
skin to the Pachydermata. The following directions
bear on this subject:—" In order to guard against
the disclosure of the designs of our Society through
dissatisfaction on the part of any member, we bind
every candidate by oath to the most inviolable
secresy, and enforce it by threats of mysterious
and terrible punishment; but independently of the
oath, and in addition to it, it is necessary to disguise the integral character of our teaching by means
of allegories, and deal out the amount of knowledge
to be imparted to each aspirant in a measure proportioned to his receptive powers. We must never

---

[1] Once for all, we give notice that the ritual of the lower or symbolical
grades, as quoted by us, is taken from " Instructions des trois degrés
symboliques écossais du rit ancien et accepté," Paris, à la librairie
maçonnique de Caillot, Rue St André-des-arcs, No. 57. The terminology,
about which so much fuss is made in popular writings, varies in the
higher grades, and is a matter of little moment, on which it is needless
for us to touch. It is best to regard these externals, as the Craft itself
regards them, as mere accessories and symbols, else the mask may be
mistaken for the real man.

admit him at random into any particular class, but only into a grade commensurate with such capabilities as he has already given satisfactory proof of possessing " (" Révélations," p. 17).

If we cast a glance at the map of the world, and pass in swift review its history since 1800, it is impossible to conceal from ourselves the fact that a large number of sovereigns have had their thrones, and even their lives, forcibly taken from them ; and that in more recent days ·the most ancient and sacred of all thrones—that of the Holy Father—has been completely overthrown. The thing most to be deplored is to see monarchy allowing Freemasonry to use it as a tool when attacking other potentates ; for the war is waged, not against any individual king, but against kings in general, and what is wanted is to establish an universal republic, in which God shall be ignored. In the blind folly of their hearts the persecutors of the Church have entered into a tacit league with Freemasonry ; it affords them ready help, places public opinion at their command, supplies them with an enthusiastic band of fellow-labourers. But let them not deceive themselves, the workman will expect his wages ; and for these he must wait until the last throne has fallen. We are forced to admit, with deep regret, that, unless appearances are altogether deceptive, the sun of monarchy must soon set, and the saying of Napoleon be fulfilled, that Europe would fall a prey to republicanism or to Cossack despotism.

Formerly rulers were, at least, not afraid of prohibiting that worst anomaly of political life — a Secret State within the State. In the year 1735 the States-General of Holland proscribed the Secret League, and Louis XVI. did the same in France two years later. The great Council of Berne proscribed it in 1748 ; Bavaria followed this example in 1799, and its total suppression took place in 1845. The Regency of Milan and the Governor of Venice issued commands to the same effect in 1814 ; John VI. of Portugal interdicted Freemasonry in the strictest manner in 1816. His prohibition was renewed in 1824, but did not long remain in force ; at any rate, since 1845 the Craft has been greatly on the increase in that country, and has become a powerful political agent. In 1820 several Lodges were closed in Prussia on account of political intrigues ; and in the same year Alexander V. banished the Order from the whole Russian Empire. A similar occurrence took place four years later in Modena and Spain. At the time of the Congress of Verona the existence of the Secret Society was menaced in almost all the states of Europe. But, after all, what has it become in our own day ?—the terrible *noli me tangere*, which neither statesmen nor authors dare to touch.

CHAPTER VI.

THE GREAT SECRET AND THE THIRTIETH SCOTCH DEGREE (KADOSCH).[1]

THE designs of the Secret Society in regard to the political reorganisation of humanity have, in the last chapter, come before the reader in all their terrible reality. But the more easy-going Masons frequently allege, in apology for these hellish plans, that the Society is not responsible for them collectively, since, originating in an abuse of its rules on the part of individual members, and only appearing under circumstances of extraordinary excitement, such plots cannot be laid to the charge of the whole body. We, on the other hand, are prepared to prove that these excuses will not hold water, because the frightful

---

[1] We draw our information from Barruel, "Mémoires du Jacobinisme," especially vol. ii. pp 199–226   The testimony of this author is the more valuable on account of his having, shortly before the French Revolution, been admitted to the grade of Master-Mason, although exempted from the customary oath, and on account of his having had intercourse with Masons of the higher grades at a time when the severity of the rule respecting secrecy was somewhat relaxed.   It is, moreover, in strict harmony with that of the *Thuileur*, to which we have access, and whence we also draw much of our information, although, as its circulation was limited, our author does not appear to have met with it.   The authority of this work, however, the title of

seeds of democracy are secretly sown broadcast, although with the knowledge of only the select few.

When the degree of Master-Mason is about to be conferred on any candidate, the Lodge is draped with black, the hangings are strewed with deaths'-heads and tears; in the centre of the hall is placed a coffin draped with black, and raised upon five steps; the Brethren stand around with tokens of grief and revenge. The Masonic legend in explanation of this runs as follows :—Solomon, the embodiment of human wisdom, gave the plan for the erection of the Temple , Hiram, of Phœnicia, furnished the materials ; Adon-iram, or Hiram Abif (Abiv = his father), superintended the building, and paid their wages to the Master-Masons, Fellow-Crafts, and Apprentices. One even-ing, when Hiram was about to close the Temple, a Fellow-Craft demanded of him the secrets of the Master-Mason. To each of the three classes a secret password had been communicated, for the purpose of mutual recognition, which they were never to divulge ; and now three of the Fellow-Crafts, determined to

which has been previously given in full, is indisputable, as it was issued by the Craft, although not given to the public   In the third place, we have made use of the Little Catechism of the three lowest grades of Freemasonry ("Instructions des trois degres symboliques ecossais," Paris). We may also remark that no substantial difference occurs in the rites of Freemasonry, or in its ulterior aims ; trifling variations only appearing with regard to formalities and unimportant regulations. Further information on this point may be found in Barruel, pp 227–247. We have carefully collated the Hebrew words with the original, and corrected them accordingly, as far as the various orthographic and vocalic errors allowed us to do this.

obtain possession of the secrets of the Master's degree, conspired on the evening in question to extort it from Hiram at any cost. Upon his refusal to betray his trust, he received from the Fellow-Craft a heavy blow upon his head; he rushed to the south door, where he was accosted by a second ruffian in a similar manner; he finally staggered to the east door, where the third conspirator was posted, who, on receiving a like reply to his demand, finished his victim. The three murderers buried the corpse beneath a heap of stones, marking the place by means of a sprig of cassia. Solomon, full of concern at the loss of Hiram, sent other Masters to search for him. The body was at length found, in an advanced stage of decomposition; whereupon one of the party exclaimed, Macbenac! that is, in the interpretation of the Craft, "The flesh is rotting from the bones;" or, more correctly, Mac-ben-akah, *i.e.*, "The son of sorrow is falling into corruption." For fear lest Hiram might have divulged the secret word of the Masters, it was agreed to abandon it, and adopt in its place Macbenac, which became the new word of the Masters' degree, and is still regarded by the Craft as sacred, being employed by Master-Masons only in their foolish ceremonies. The meaning of the fable is this. Every Master-Mason is entrusted with a twofold commission—First, to seek for the lost word, which he finds in the higher grades to be Jehovah, *i e*, natural religion ; and secondly, to revenge the death of Hiram, of which the Masters' sign is a constant

memorial; this consists in a feigned stab with the
thumb, the four fingers being stretched out meanwhile
horizontally, at a right angle. The candidate for the
Master's degree is extended on the ground, to represent the murdered man, and slowly raised up at the
sound of the above-named word.[1] The son of sorrow
(man) is falling into corruption (in the profane world);
but who is to blame for this? In the thirtieth degree
of Freemasonry, the most important of all, this question is clearly answered.

At first the new-made Mason is only allowed to
hear the words Liberty and Equality occasionally,
but when his ears have grown familiar with them,
at least in the Lodge, and he has learned secresy,
then he is raised to the grade of Master, and hears
for the first time of a Founder, whose murder has to
be revenged ; the succeeding grades, especially those
from the ninth to the tenth upwards, accustom him
to the idea of vengeance, so that it finally becomes
habitual with him. A thousand dreadful oaths
pledge him to preserve the secret at any cost ; and
by the time he is made a Rosicrucian, provided he
be fully initiated, he will have abandoned his belief
in Christ, and in all revealed religion. To sum up
all in a word, he will have become an out-and-out
materialist. If he gives proof of possessing the
needful qualifications, he may at length in the

---

[1] We are acquainted with the appointed ceremonial, but omit it as
immaterial. The letters M B. are also embroidered upon the Master's
apron.

thirtieth grade receive the titles of *Grand Inspecteur*, *Grand Elu*, Knight Kadosch (or Knight of the White and Black Eagle). The official manual, the *Thuileur*, states the required age for admission to be " a century and more," or that of a person " past reckoning." This fact amply proves that admission is only granted to a chosen few, who are dispensed with regard to age, whilst the rejected candidate is refused on the score of his being too young. This grade is frequently conferred on those who do not belong to the Scotch rite, as a merely honorary degree, persons whom it is considered advisable to dupe being admitted to it. It is divided into about six subdivisions, expressed with more or less intentional vagueness according to the end to be served. The grade, as adopted by most of the French Lodges, is very much softened down. In other words, many are received into this grade as an honorary distinction, and with a merely nominal admission, without being really initiated into it.

The word " Kadosch " means holy, sanctified, purified. However, let no man on this account entertain the idea that Knights of the Black and White Eagle aspire to peculiar sanctity ; the word is only intended to express that they are the elect, the privileged ones, who have been purified from every taint of prejudice. This grade is the *ne plus ultra* of the Scotch rite, the three following ones being merely honorary, intended for exalted personages, and being quite separated from the general machinery of the Ord

The ceremonies attending admission into the eighth
grade are terrific, and read like a preparation for the
scaffold. Barruel writes concerning them (p. 219),
" Several Masons initiated into the mysteries of the
grade in question have informed me that nö natural
or artificial horrors are left unemployed to test the
fortitude of the aspirant. Montjoie mentions a
ladder, which the Duke of Orleans had to ascend,
in order to cast himself headlong from the summit.
But that is not all. Let the reader imagine an under-
ground structure, from which a species of narrow
tower leads up into the Lodge. The candidate is
conducted to the bottom of this pit, through all sorts
of chambers, where everything is calculated to inspire
dread. Arrived below, he is locked in, bound and
throttled. Left alone in this condition, he presently
feels himself raised up by means of machinery, with
sounds which strike terror to the heart. Suspended
midway in this gloomy shaft, he rises slowly, the
process sometimes occupying several hours, only to
fall again, as if the lift had given way ; and he is
compelled thus alternately to rise and fall, enduring
the repetition of these horrors without uttering a cry,
or evincing the least sign of fear. Freemasons have
assured me that it was impossible to give an accurate
description of these ordeals, for the head grew dizzy
at the bare remembrance of them, and indeed at
the time it was found indispensable to administer
strengthening draughts to the unfortunate sufferer, to
keep up his physical forces at least, although it was

impossible to prevent the brain from reeling. Besides
this chamber of horrors, four apartments are necessary for the ceremony of the reception of a Kadosch.
The first is hung with black, a lamp within a triangle
is suspended over a trapdoor, casting its light on a
flight of steps leading down into a cellar, into which
the candidate is cast. There he finds a coffin, and
deciphers the inscription, ' The man who can overcome the terrors of death, shall arise from the
bosom of the earth, and claim to be initiated into the
great secrets.' The second apartment is hung with
white ; in the foreground are two urns, one filled
with burning incense, the other with flaming spirits
of wine, which latter lights up the chamber into
which only the high-priest may enter. The third
apartment is hung with blue, the canopy being
bespangled with stars, and the whole lighted up by
three yellow wax tapers. The hangings of the fourth
are red and white columns : in the east stands a
throne, and above it a crowned two-headed eagle,
holding a dagger in its talons, and wearing round its
neck a black ribband, to which a triple cross is suspended ; on its breast is a triangle containing the
words, *Nec proditor, nec proditur, innocens fovet.*
(Neither betraying nor betrayed, in innocence he
cherishes)—probably, his designs. From the wings
of the eagle hang down draperies of black and white
velvet strewed with red crosses, and forming a tent.
Behind the throne are two banners crossed ; one white,
with a green cross bearing the inscription, ' God wills

it ;' the other black, with on one side a red cross, on the reverse a double eagle holding a dagger, accompanied by the words, 'Conquer or die !' A double ladder is also placed in this apartment."

Only the most childish simplicity can regard these preparations, which we transcribe exactly as they are given in the *Thuileur*, as nothing more than a meaningless pageant, a much ado about nothing; indeed, such persistent blindness could not be otherwise than culpable. What an outcry there would be if but a fourth part of these heraldic emblems and strange devices boding murder and destruction were to be found within a convent ! What Religious Order demands of its subjects such blind obedience at all risks ?

If the candidate has stood the ordeals intended to test his implicit obedience and absolute secresy, and has proved his readiness, if need be, to persist in them until death, the mask is completely thrown aside. It is no longer Adoniram or Hiram whose death cries for vengeance ; the three Fellow-Craftsmen are not the real traitors against whom implacable hatred has been sworn. The two great institutions of the Christian world now stand out in terribly bold relief as the objects to be pursued and annihilated by the deadly hatred of the Craft, in order to inaugurate the return of the pretended Golden Age of Liberty and Equality, when man, long mouldering alive in the grave, shall be quickened as on the Easter morn of the Resurrection, and clothed once

more in full dignity and glory. Let us listen to the
Thuileur, which, though it tells us little, speaks in no
ambiguous terms.

"The grade of Kadosch commemorates the suppression of the Order of Templars by Pope Clement
V. and Philip the Fair, together with the murder of
the ` Grand Commander Jacques Molay, who was
burnt alive on March 11, 1314. On the final initiation of an Adept, the scene changes ; there is no
more talk of Hiram and his tragic end. For this
allegorical personage is substituted Jacobus Bur-
gundus Molay, whose death the Adept is to revenge,
either figuratively on the authors of the crime, or
implicitly on those who now deserve a like fate (*sur
qui de droit*)."

In that part of the Catechism of Freemasonry
which refers to a Knight Kadosch, we find the following questions and answers :—" *Q*. At what hour
was the Lodge opened ?—*A*. At nightfall. *Q*. Whom
do you recognise ?—*A*. Two persons worthy of
abhorrence. *Q*. Name them ?—*A*. Philip the Fair
and Bertrand de Goth (*sic*) Clement V." (evidently
Bertrand d'Agoust, Archbishop of Orleans, afterwards Pope Clement V.)

We cannot fail to perceive that Clement V. and
Philip the Fair—both directly or indirectly concerned
in the death of the Grand Commander Jacques
Molay, and now long since dead—cannot in reality
be the personages indicated as the object of the

sinister vengeance of the League; but they stand
for those who, in the present day, are vested with
the chief ecclesiastical and secular dignity, and
consequently for all their adherents, whether called
Jesuits or Ultramontanes, Legalists or Reactionaries :
all natural foes of the Craft. What clear light this
throws upon the shameful conduct of the Duke of
Orleans towards his royal cousin Louis XVI., and
upon the proceedings of Mazzini and Garibaldi!
How amply it explains many of the sad events in
recent times and in our own day!

According to the *Thuileur*, the thirtieth grade has
two subdivisions or points, that of the Knights of the
Black Eagle and that of the White, or *Kadosch*.
The passwords or signs of both these grades serve
to confirm what we have already said ; at the same
time, we must call the reader's attention to the
fact that the *Thuileur*—since some words might
prove dangerous, as hinting too plainly at bloody
vengeance—adds another rendering (preceded by
the word *écrivez*) which alters the meaning of the
first, or mitigates its force, giving to it, at any rate,
a false construction.

The password of a Knight of the Black Eagle,
Menachem (comforter) : *Answer*, Nechemiah (greater
consolation). Or sometimes Nika (Niccah, he
slaughters), Maka (Maccah, massacre), to be written
Nekam (he revenges), Makah (probably Maccah, as
above).

WORDS PECULIAR TO KNIGHTS OF THE WHITE
EAGLE, OR KADOSCH.

" At the reception of a Kadosch, a mystic ladder
comes into play, which the neophyte is required, to
ascend and descend.   The ladder is symbolic ; each
round represents some virtue (?).   Of these we will
give the several names, with their corrected meaning.

1st Round—Tesla Cades (probably Thisleh Ka-
desch, *i e.*, Thou shalt be silent, accursed one !)   Write
Tsedakah (Zedakah, justice).

2d Round—Charlaban (the white is burning, either
a reference to the dazzling whiteness of Molay's presumed innocence, or intended to convey a threat
against the Pope, who is clad in white).   Write, Schor
Laban (albus bos = the white ox), a metaphorical
expression for candour (!).

3d Round—Motech (motech, thy death).   Write,
Mathok (dulcedo, is sweet).

4th Round—Emmunac (emunah, truth, firmness).
Write, Emunach (veritas).

5th Round—Choemul Seal (ghemul scheal, schaal
—Retribution demands it).   Write, Hamal saghia
(labor magnus ; more probably Hamal seghiah, a
false and wearisome road) paraphrased in the following words, Progress in virtue (!).

6th Round—Sabael (if this spelling be correct, this
word is a blasphemy with which we will not disgrace
our pages ; if written Zeba El, it signifies a Band of

Warriors, or the Hosts of the Lord). Write, Sabbal (onus), betokening Patience (!).

7th Round—Choemul Binem Rabira (probably Their retribution is fourfold). Write, Ghemul, Binah, Thebunah (Retributio, Intelligentia, Prudentia = Retribution, Sagacity, Prudence).

The Shafts of the Column—On the north side, Oseb Eloah (he who apostatises from the highest). Write, Oheb Eloah (Deum amans, He who loves the highest), love of one's neighbour.[1] On the south side, Oseb Scherabal (Oseb sar abel, *i e*, he who falls away from the Prince of Misery). Write, Oheb Kerobo (Propinquum ei amans, Brotherly love). Properly Oheb Rerobo, *i e*., a Friend to his neighbour.[2]

The sacred word is Nekam Adonai (the revenge of the Lord); this word is common to the Knights Kadosch of every land, whether Sweden, Germany, Prussia, England, or France.

Password on Entrance—Nekam (to revenge). *Answer*, Menakem (revenger.) On going out, Phaal Col. *Answer*, Pharas Col. These two mottoes are likewise incorrectly interpreted by the *Thuileur* as meaning *operatum est omne, explicatum est omne—i.e*., All is done, all is explained. They signify rather, He does everything, he destroys everything.

[1] According to the opinions of Freemasonry, to be developed later on, man has taken the place of God.

[2] The names of the Pillars were probably intended to form a phrase. If this supposition be a right one, the northern one would signify, He who forsakes the Highest loves him who is really highest—*i e* man, and the southern pillar, He who forsakes the promise of misery is a true friend to his fellow-men.

The working-hours of this grade are from nightfall
—*i.e.*, nine hours after noon—until daybreak.   In the
vestments of a Kadosch we constantly meet with
the eagle holding a poniard in his talons, the motto
" Conquer or die," the crossed swords, the sash of
crimson and gold with a dagger, or the dagger
attached to a riband and purple rosette.

These hieroglyphics, transcribed literally from
the official manual, have intentionally been given at
length, and we leave the reader to draw his own
inference from them.   Barruel had not access to this
source, but from other writings, and from personal
intercourse with Masons of the higher grades, he was
led to form for himself this conclusion, namely, that
" the grade of Kadosch is the soul of Freemasonry,
and the final object of its plots is the reintroduction
of absolute Liberty and Equality through the destruction of all royalty, and the abrogation of all
religious worship " (p. 222).   He tells us, moreover,
that when a friend of his boasted of being, as a
Rosicrucian, in possession of the entire secret of Freemasonry, he drew the man's attention to the fact
that, in spite of having reached that exalted grade,
he was far from having attained the highest point,
proving this by laying before him the hieroglyphics
of the Craft, and thereby forcing from him the confession that he was ignorant of their meaning, and

had asked in vain to be made acquainted with it, but believed them to be of much the same nature as the Square, the Trowel, &c. "I know," Barruel proceeds to say, "that my friend had only to take one step more in order to see his mistake, and I therefore gave him the instructions necessary for reaching that grade, in which all attempts at deception are once and for ever abandoned, and no self-delusion is possible as to the ulterior object of the grades which are still more advanced. He himself was far too anxious for thorough enlightenment not to employ at once the means I pointed out to him, especially as he wished to dispel my supposed prejudices against the higher grades. A few days later he entered my room in a state of which his own words will give the best idea. 'O my dear friend!' he exclaimed, 'what you said was indeed true—only too true. What was I thinking of? Good heavens! what was I thinking of?' He could say no more, but kept on reiterating his former exclamation, 'What you said was indeed true; but do not press me further, that is all that I can tell you.' . . . . 'O my poor friend!' I replied, 'it is I who ought to beg your pardon; you have just bound yourself by a terrible oath, and I am really to blame for it. But I assure you, when I advised you as I did, I forgot all about the oath, or I should have spoken differently.' . . . . That man had lost all his fortune in the Revolution, and he admitted to me that full compensation had been offered to him, but only on certain terms. 'If I

consent,' he said, ' to go to London, Brussels, Con-
stantinople, or any other town I please, my own
wants, and those of my wife and children, will be
amply provided for.' 'Well and good,' I remarked,
' but probably under the express stipulation that you
preach Liberty, Equality, and red-hot revolution.'
' Exactly so,' he answered, ' but that is all I dare tell
you. Good heavens ! what was I thinking of ? For
goodness' sake, ask me no more questions ! ' ' That
was quite enough for me,'" says Barruel in conclusion :
and he evidently remained firmly persuaded that in
their secret heart many members of the higher
grades detest bitterly the occult designs to which, in
spite of their good intentions, they have fallen
victims, and would be even more willing than was
his friend in question to disclose them, if the solemn
obligation laid upon them did not render their doing
so a matter of serious risk to themselves.

The fanatical advocate of Freemasonry and of the
rights of man, Condorcet, so notorious at the time
of the French Revolution, lays down very fully in
his chief work, " Esquisse des Progrès," &c. (especially
époque 7 and 8), the principles with which a Kadosch
is supposed to be imbued   He endeavours to make
his readers see how grateful they ought to be to the
ancient secret societies, especially towards the
Order of Templars, "whose peaceful and inoffensive
miṣsion it was to preserve intact in a small circle of
initiated a few primitive truths to serve as a sure
antidote to the dominant prejudices of the day."   In

the terrible revolution he beholds the long-prepared and long-looked-for triumph of the Secret Society; the death of Molay he regards as a brutal act of barbarism. According to his ideas, the members of the Craft may be compared to sages "standing by, full of virtuous indignation at the sight of suffering nations, the very sanctuary of whose conscience is not safe from the oppression of kings; of kings, too, who are themselves the superstitious slaves or political tools of an encroaching priesthood. . . . . These Secret Societies are composed of noble-minded men, who make bold to investigate the foundation on which power and authority rest; who unveil to the people the important truth that freedom is their inalienable inheritance; that there exists in favour of tyranny (*i e.*, royalty) no pre-scriptive title, no contract whereby a nation is irre-vocably bound to any one family; that those placed in authority, whatever their function or jurisdiction, are the official servants, not the governors of the people; that the nation must ever retain in its own hands the right of withdrawing the authority it alone has conferred, should abuse be made of it, or should it be no longer found conducive to the public in-terests; in a word, that with the nation rests the power to depose or punish its appointed officials." The mind of the *Kadosch* may be still more plainly gathered from the wild appeals to the swords of the Brethren made by Bonneville ("Esprit des Religions," i. 156 *seq*) "Traverse with one bound the cen-

K

turies of the past, incite the nations to pursue Philip
the Fair (*i e.* kings) with their vengeance ! All of
you, whether Templars or no, help a free people to
build in three days an immortal temple to Truth !
Down with the tyrants ! Earth must be freed from
them !"[1]

However often we may be assured that the ritual
of the thirtieth grade, as practised at present in
France and elsewhere, has been greatly softened
down,—*i.e.*, that there is no longer any question of
bloodshed,[2]—we find it nevertheless impossible to
abandon our opinion that the real and essential
character of the secret teaching remains unaltered,
and that the best we can hope for is, that humanity
may be spared a repetition of such sanguinary
spectacles as the death of Louis XVI. But besides
the material act, there is, so to speak, a moral de-
capitation possible for kings and priests, if religion
be trodden down into the mire, and hereditary
monarchs either chased from their own dominions,
or made the slaves of an imperial convention, the
decrees of which they must perforce obey, if the
continuance of their own existence is to be a thing
possible.[3]

---

[1] Barruel, pp. 274, 275.

[2] The same is said in the *Thuileur*, p. 104—"Celui (le but) qu'ont
adopté la plupart des loges de France, est entièrement mitige."

[3] The following expression of " Brother " Louis Blanc's sentiments
respecting the years immediately preceding the first French Revolution
may be interesting in this place —" Thanks to its clever system of

mechanism, Freemasonry found in princes and aristocrats patrons rather than enemies. Even monarchs, as for instance Frederic II. of Prussia, have condescended to handle the trowel and tie on the apron. And why not? As the existence of the higher grades was carefully concealed from them, they only knew as much of Freemasonry as could be revealed to them without danger."—"Lettres à un Franc-maçon, extraites du *Bien Publie*," Brussels, 1855, p. 74. Also "La Franc-maçonnerie dans l'Etât," p. 37.

CHAPTER VII.

THE project of a future and universal Red Republic
lies at the heart of Freemasonry, it is its legitimate
offspring, not a bastard child sprung from the heated
brains of a few individuals, who have misapplied the
rules of their Craft, rules pretending to be of the
most lamblike innocence. If the worthy Brothers
forming the Party of the Blues do not see things as
we do, they have only themselves to blame.

The deductions of logic and the experience of
history combine to teach us that political radicalism
infallibly leads to socialism ; nor does Freemasonry
tell a different tale. A democratic republic is its
ideal, and the socialist agitation of our own day is
from beginning to end a fruit out of its garden, a
weapon out of its armoury. We will now bring forward the principles, the ceremonies, the utterances,
and the proceedings of the Craft, in order to establish the truth of this proposition.

1. If we examine the fundamental principles of
Freemasonry, we shall find socialism, and to a certain
extent communism, are both secretly and openly

taught, and proclaimed to be the normal and legitimate condition of society, in comparison with which
the existing social order is an abuse of power, and a
fruit of rapacious violence. Liberty is the first idol
worshipped by the Craft, but this liberty can never
be anything more than a dream so long as differences of rank, and the bulwarks that support them,
—that is, the property of individuals—remain intact.
Although the inhabitants of a State may be represented a thousand times over as possessed of equal
rights in the eyes of the law, the projects of emanci-
pators will always prove illusory, so long as the few
are rich and the many poor. Those who adopt as
their motto the word "Freedom," in the naturalistic
sense in which it is used by the Craft, must, if they
would be consistent, regard inequalities of rank and
social position, especially those of property, with as
much abhorrence as they would a hostile garrison in
the heart of their own country. A long series of
initiated Masons had, in 1790, already discovered
this ; we mean the Society of Equals of the Pantheon,
led by Babeuf, Darthe, and Sylvan Marechal, the two
former of these chiefs being called upon to show
their fidelity to their principles by suffering the
penalty of the guillotine (1796). Therefore Freemasonry recognises no diversities of rank, or, to use
its own words, "the design of the League is to
reunite that which social convulsions have severed."
It desires to remove the inequalities of rank as one
of the "original causes of the grievous and innu-

merable evils which afflict mankind." The abolition
of royalty, of the aristocracy, of the priesthood, and
of every form of worship, are only the first steps
on the path of this psuedo-freedom. If, as another
primary condition of his personal emancipation, man
be required further to cast off the fear of God—if he
be viewed in the light of a citizen of this world alone,
he has every right to claim his share in the common
Mother, and poverty thus becomes a disgraceful
bondage, and the wealth of the "upper ten thousand" a glaring injustice. The second idol of the
League is Equality, likewise understood in a purely
naturalistic sense, not merely equal participation in
rights and duties, but also in the enjoyments of life,
as those are bound to admit whose highest officials
lay down maxims such as the following :—" Freemasonry regards all mankind as creatures of the
same race, citizens of the same world, proprietors
of the same earth, children of the same Mother."
The principles of Christianity teach us that riches, if
lawfully acquired, may be rightfully retained, nobody
having a better right to contest their possession
than that of any other gifts and superiorities,
mental or physical; only they lay upon their proprietor the obligation of a more large-hearted benevolence towards his needy fellow-creatures. Very
different are the views of the true Mason. He
regards the possession of riches as nothing more nor
less than criminal covetousness; for ought not the
good things of the world to be common to all?

Let us give their own words—" It is for Equality to
produce that delightful peace and mutual confidence
which is so intensely to be desired, but at the same
time so utterly incompatible with avarice ; for does
it not tend to paralyse its rapacious efforts, and
restore to man the common use of all those good
things, the possession of which is a source of so much
anxiety, and their loss the cause of so much grief?"
Even the inequality arising from difference of intellectual endowments is objected to, and the following
proposition laid down :—" In earlier times the absurd
opinion prevailed that the intellectual superiority
and greater mental acuteness of a portion of mankind entitled them to claim a tribute of esteem and
veneration at the hands of other and inferior men.
But the fact that his fellow-man is more gifted than
himself cannot justify any one in an act of idolatry.
The jealous God who created man will allow no one
to usurp a share of the worship due to Himself, and
He rejects as impure the incense of adoration offered
to Him if the least grain finds its way to the altar
of a frail and perishable idol, utterly unworthy of so
exalted a tribute. In a word, to recognise in a
fellow-man anything more than an equal is a degradation of human nature, a violation of human rights,
a trampling upon the dignity of mankind" (" Réve-
lations," pp. 11, 12). Thus what is wanted is a complete levelling of mankind : we are to have no more
varieties of rank, of rich and poor, of learned or unlearned. The coward and the hero, the king and the

beggar, the fool and the philosopher, the saint and the sinner,—all are equal, and it is an act of profanity to pay more respect to the one than to the other! Those who work in the same shop must all enjoy the same position, and receive the same wages; the most skilled artisan does not deserve a single word more praise nor a morsel more bread than any of the others. This last principle has already made its way down to the lowest strata of society; for instance, the Paris *ouvrier* watches with Argus' eyes lest any inequality of wages should creep in, lest a more skilful hand receive a *sou* over and above the earnings dealt out to his slovenly and ignorant comrade; and this state of things is justly deplored as boding the imminent ruin of real and useful industry. What would become of virtue, of scientific research, of all that ennobles man, if this Liberty and Equality were transferred from the dark recesses of the gloomy Lodges into the broad daylight of the market-place, and the glare of the crowded thoroughfare? If this our condemnation be thought somewhat too severe; if it be objected that the maxims we have been discussing may be, after all, the ravings of a few misguided Brethren, for which they alone should be held responsible, we answer that Liberty and Equality, as they are understood by Freemasonry in the sense just explained, are the sacred Palladium of the Association; they constitute its very soul and spirit. But our assertions rest upon more convincing proofs than any brought forward as yet, and we now proceed to examine—

2. The ritual common to the Craft. Every accepted candidate is called a "Brother," and treated
as such, his position in the "profane" world being no
longer recognised.

> " We men are all Brethren, all kinsfolk are we,
> We know no distinctions of rank or degree ;
> And the Brother adorned with riband and lace
> Owns as Sister the maiden of lowliest race."

This Brotherhood is not merely an image of the
friendship supposed to prevail amongst members of
the Craft (a friendship well known not to be of a
very ardent description), or of the equality of rights
to which they are admitted.   It is also an appropriate
expression of social equality, as it can only exist
amongst the members of a family, and of the equal
claim possessed by all men to enjoy the pleasures of
this life and the produce of the earth.   Practised, in
the first instance, within the Lodge, of which the four
walls represent the four quarters of the globe, its true
aim is to reform and regenerate the whole world
Some may perhaps allege as an objection that the
various grades of Apprentice, Fellow-Craft, and
Master-Mason betoken disparity of rank.   This is not
so ; these only show a difference in the degree of
initiation in the exoteric teaching, and correspond to
differences of age in the outside world.   The Apprentice is the "Brother" of the Master ; he sits at
the same table with him, and partakes of the so-called
love-feast, whilst passing, perhaps unconsciously,
through his noviciate in the Order of Democracy.

Every Freemason wears an apron, square, &c.—in
short, the implements of his Craft—for only fellow-
workers can be Fellow-Craftsmen. Social democracy
has adopted the Scripture maxim, " He that will not
work, neither let him eat."   The apron, as a token of
obligatory labour, is met with in every grade ; even
the "Sovereign Prince of the Royal Secret," in the
thirty-second Scotch grade has his apron of white,
doubled and decorated with crimson. Thus the world
is to become one great city of workmen : this cherished
idea of the "International" apparently comes from
the same source as that association itself.

But the most unequivocal testimony is that afforded
by the ceremony of reception,   The candidate is
deprived of all metal, and stripped of all clothing
except his shirt, drawers, shoes, and stockings; his
left breast and left knee are made bare ; his right
heel is slipshod.[1]   This absurd figure then enters the
Lodge, a fitting type of the class of worthies which
we have the opportunity of admiring on the occasion
of every street-fight.   Here he receives the apron,
with which every Brother is invested ; all stand
around attired in the same costume, as labourers all
doing the same work, eating at the same table, receiving the same reward.   In the ritual peculiar to
the great Lodge in Berlin (Sarsena, 93) we read—

[1] To these ceremonies the questions addressed to the Apprentice
refer —" *Q.* How were you prepared for admission ?—*A.* I was
neither naked nor clothed, I was deprived of all metal, a cable-tow
put round my neck, and thus I was conducted to the temple."—
V. *Instructions des trois degrés,* p 8.

"*Q.* Why had you to appear neither naked nor clothed?—*A.* In order to intimate to me that splendid apparel dazzles the populace, but the truly virtuous man rises above such vulgar prejudices. *Q.* Why were you deprived of all metal?—*A.* Because money is an emblem of vice, and the true Mason should possess nothing of his own."[1] What more could any one want to prove beyond a doubt that Freemasons esteem the possession of personal property as being no better than theft?

When one of the softer sex appears in the Lodge, she is greeted by all Masons as their Sister. We will not inquire whether this universal sisterhood could be tolerable to any modest woman in a purely naturalistic bond such as this; but the fact remains that Lodges for women have existed for years, and that their members are treated as Sisters in the Lodges of men.

[1] These instructions were considered too outspoken for later times, especially after the failure of Babeuf's attempt. Thus, we find a different version given in the "Instructions," p. 13, which affords an amusing specimen of the mummery practised in the Lodge —"*Q.* Why were you deprived of all metal?—*A.* Because on the building of the Temple at Jerusalem no sound was heard of axe, hammer, or other metal tool *Q.* What was the reason of this?—*A. In order that the sanctity of the temple might not be polluted. Q* How was it possible to complete that structure without the aid of such implements?—*A.* The materials were prepared in the forest of Lebanon, conveyed on carriages, and set up by means of mauls prepared for the purpose. *Q.* Why were you slipshod?—*A.* Because the place of my admission was holy ground, of which God said to Moses, ' Put off the shoes from thy feet, for the place whereon thou standest is holy ground.'" In his version the gist of the whole lies in the answer given in italics; the rest is all by play. He who has a true vocation apprehends its real meaning; the well meaning simpleton, duly impressed with the sacred character of the Lodge, looks no lower than the surface.

Let the reader reflect on what would be the probable
effect on the institution of marriage of a consistent
carrying out of this idea of Sisterhood.   Can there
be any doubt that the decree issued by the Paris
Commune of incendiary memory, abolishing wedlock
and authorising free love, originated in these laws of
licence?   And the dissolution of family ties, known
to be the avowed object of the efforts of Socialism
in the present day, is not this, too, the final development of a long-laid scheme?   If so, we need not
wonder when we hear children claimed as being the
property of the State, nor will it surprise us to find,
on occasion of the laws regulating school inspection
passing through the Berlin Parliament in 1872, how
certain journals asserted, with brazen effrontery, that
school supervision belongs exclusively to the State,
without being at the pains to support this axiom by
any proofs.

In the following questions and answers we meet in
the Apprentice degree with the same idea as to the
equal right of all men to the enjoyments of the
earth :—" *Q*. Where is the Senior Warden placed ?—
A. In the west.   *Q*. Why so ?—*A*. As the sun sets
in the west, so the Senior Warden is placed there to
close the Lodge, to pay the workmen their hire, and
dismiss them to their homes with feelings of content
and satisfaction " (" Instructions," p. 5).   And at the
close of the Lodge the question addressed by the
Worshipful Master to the above-named dignitary has
a similar import :—" *Q*. My Brother, are the workmen

content?" The answer runs thus :—"They declare
it at both of the pillars, Worshipful Master." A
similar idea breathes in other clauses of the same
chapter:—"*Q*. Why does the Junior Warden represent Beauty?—*A*. Because he is placed in the south,
where the sun reaches its meridian, in order to call
the Brethren from labour to refreshment, and from
refreshment to labour, and to give glory and honour
to the Worshipful Master (who represents the sun)."
These hints are of course veiled in flowery disguise,
as is invariably the case in the lower grades; and
indeed this circumspection cannot be safely dispensed
with even in regard to actual Members, since, on their
admission, they are unable to cast off all at once the
prejudices they bring with them from the "profane"
world. Moreover, any premature disclosures would
serve to keep at a distance members of the wealthy
and influential classes, for whose sake concealment
has been judged especially desirable. In spite of all
caution, nevertheless, it appears that many get an
inkling of what goes on behind the scenes. Whilst
the petty tradesman is in hot haste to enter himself
as a candidate, the merchant prince, whose fortune is
made, seeks an opportunity of withdrawing from the
Brotherhood, or, if his prospects seem from the first
to be good, deems it his most prudent course not to
enter it at all. It is of still more moment not to let
the slightest whisper of their designs upon the
Government get wind—above all, in districts where
the new schemes of universal prosperity and happiness

for mankind are likely to meet with considerable opposition. In this case the Craft resorts to its old expedient of making scapegoats of others, and, by skilfully taking the aggressive, contrives to spare itself the wearisome and perhaps impossible task of successfully standing on the defensive. And since it seemed too daring a thing, immediately after the Franco-German War, to tell the Liberal despots in Germany that the ascendancy of the International was to be imputed to the follies they had committed, a ready alternative was found in accusing the Ultra-montane of a secret understanding with that League ; *black* as well as *red* Internationals were spoken of. And yet no one was more thoroughly convinced of the radical falsity of this accusation than Freemasons themselves ; the Brethren of Italy, France, and Bel-gium especially, appeared more in their true colours. In the last-named country they appeared as Atheists and Radicals of the most extreme description, and the dregs of the populace, tools ready to their hands in making any disturbance, showed plainly what their views were in regard to our various social in-stitutions.

3. Our proofs of the warfare waged in secret by Freemasonry against Society are, in the third place, taken from the declarations of some of its leaders and principal orators. Its own especial moralist, Brother Helvetius, as early as 1758, in his work entitled "Sur l'Esprit," preached what were essentially the doctrines of Socialism, though he was careful to re-

strict equality to the realm of intellect. The following is a brief abstract of his propositions:—"As in the material world everything depends on the faculty of perception, there exists no original difference between mind and mind; all capacity, all talent, the moral character of individuals and of nations, depends purely upon chance circumstances, on their opportunities of receiving impressions, on their education and form of government. If any mental incapacity at all exists, it arises from the fact that all are not equally disposed to receive impressions." The conclusion is simple. If all minds—*i.e.*, men—are equally noble and equally good, if they all possess the same capacities and desires for enjoyment, it follows that the good things of the earth ought to be equally portioned out to all, in order that the equality of mankind may be practically proved.

The theory of Fourier, the well-known Communist and Freemason, asserted the possibility of effecting an equal distribution of property without resorting to violence, by proposing to provide common dwellings, called "Phalansteries," calculated to accommodate a fixed number of persons. De Lamartine, in reference to this idea, remarks most justly (*v.* " Histoire de la Révolution de 1848," i. 7):—" Fourierism is a mere day-dream; community of goods, which he would introduce by means of his 'Phalansteries' (a kind of industrial and agricultural cloister), presupposes angels for their tenants, gods for their directors, mysteries for their daily bread." Modern Freemasonry, on the contrary, aims at nothing short of a complete transformation of society, as was proved by the doings of the Paris 'Commune in May 1871. As far back as the year 1508, a Masonic Professor at the Liberal University of Brussels expressed himself thus:—"When the Reformation and the French Revolution have borne their full fruits, by striking off the fetters which shackle society, and by developing the individuality of each one of its members, then it will be time to set about the reconstruction of society on a new plan" (*Bien Public de Gaud*, May 14, 1858).

Not a few similar voices, precursors of the International, made themselves heard about the same time. A New York paper, *Le Libertaire*, in the interests of Freemasonry, published the following declaration:— " The *libertaire* (one who enjoys absolute personal freedom) knows no country but that which is common to all. He is a sworn foe to restraints of every kind: he hates the boundaries of countries (international); he hates the boundaries of fields, houses, workshops (behold the end of all private property); he hates the boundaries of family (marriage is to be done away with). In his eyes the whole human race forms one vast corporation, each member of which has one and the same right to full emancipation and perfect development, whichever the hemisphere they inhabit, whatever the race whence they spring, whichever the sex to which they belong. . . . As far as religion is concerned, the *libertaire* has none at all, he protests against every creed ; he is an Atheist

and Materialist, openly denying the existence of God
and of the soul. He believes, however, in boundless
Unity (the Universal Substance of Pantheism), and
in perpetual Progress; and as this Unity, either
in the individual or in the mass, is not possible as
long as matter continues the slave of mind, and mind
the tyrant of matter, so progress is not capable of
indefinite perfection as long as it remains hampered
by any of those barriers on which the murderers of
their kind have scrawled the name of God in charac-
ters of blood."[1] The notorious Eugène Sue was not
far wrong in saying, as he did as early as the year
1845, that "Freemasonry is in the van of the Liberal-
democratic party."[2]

Every person of any intelligence has by this time
become aware that these socialistic schemes have
their root in the very centre of Freemasonry, and
that all its boasting about philanthropy and benevolence tends in the direction of democracy. Our
readers may be interested in hearing the following
testimony from the lips of an orator of the Lodge
at Rouen :—"If we wish for a clear and concise
definition of the real aim of Freemasonry, let us not
endeavour to find it in popular opinion; it must be
sought for in our own institutions. We see the Craft
put tools into the hands of its members, calling on
them to reconstruct a temple which was the proto-

[1] *Emancipation Belge*, June 28, 1858.
[2] "Lettre du 13 Janv. 1845, à MM. les membres de la Loge de la
Persévérance d'Anvers. La Franc-maçonnerie dans l'état," p 83.

type of perfection. Freemasonry belongs to the socialistic school; the defective condition of society creates the necessity for its existence; it believes reform to be possible, otherwise the mission it has undertaken would be a hopeless one. . . . . Freemasonry has heard the groans of the sufferers who are trodden down by a defective social order of things, and whose cause a celebrated philosopher advocates in saying these words—' All things in this world are not as they ought to be.' . . . Freemasonry believes in progress; it calls loudly for reform, that reform whose final object has been eloquently expressed by the same author as follows—' Would you hear what your mission is? I will tell you; it is a vast one—to unite all men in one great cosmopolitan family.'" [1] The designs given here in rough draft have, since 1864, been worked out by the International with terrible minuteness, and recent times have proved this sect itself to be the offspring of Freemasonry (*Laacher Stimmen*, 1872, No. 2).

We have already remarked that a complete convulsion of our social organisation is contemplated by those who have been really initiated into the higher grades. This is admitted by a member of the Lodge at Metz. " Freemasonry is socialistic in the highest degree ; it has outrun the disciples of Fourier in organising a new order of things. We must not imagine that these socialistic ideas are nowadays only beginning to strike root in our temples ; they

[1] *Le Globe*, vol. iv. p. 166. " La Franc-maçonnerie dans l'état," p. 81.

have thriven there ever since the time when the first-fruits of Liberalism appeared. If you would convince yourselves of this, look through the higher grades, and you will find that in them man is led up by gradual steps to those advanced views which have only been embraced by a few select spirits. ' As an example " (of these advanced views): "moral and religious errors, and above all the fatal belief in the natural depravity of man, have been the cause of almost all human failings. The nature of man is good, his surroundings alone are evil. . . . . The disciple of Fourier must feel that the time has come for him to betake himself to our temple, where to his surprise he will find himself as much at home as if it were a dwelling prepared expressly for him. He may perhaps gaze with tender emotion on the spot where the first cradle of his infancy stands. We would tell him that subjection to maternal authority " (*i e.*, the Craft) "is an admirable preparation for achieving future success, and one of the best tests of his own readiness to sacrifice himself for mankind. The Grand Orient has long since unrolled the plan of operations for the coming social agitation; let each individual Brother study it in detail, and act in accordance with the impulses imparted to him."

But it may be objected that all our evidence is taken from the Lodges of France and Belgium, in which countries Radicalism is known to be rampant. It may therefore be well to turn our attention to Germany, where similar testimony is not lacking.

The following extracts are taken from the *Latomia*, an organ of the Craft (vol. xii. p. 237):—"Communists point out to us two axioms on which the whole theory of Communism rests; axioms which, if apprehended correctly, and carried out in moderation, cannot be regarded otherwise than as incontrovertibly true. First and foremost are the principles establishing the equality of all men in the eternal order of things, and in the second place those liberal views which would make the few subordinate to the many, private and individual interests subservient to the general good. It is impossible to do otherwise than welcome Socialism as being a valuable ally of Freemasonry in its work of ennobling mankind, a fellow-helper in its efforts to promote their welfare. For Freemasons cannot refuse to acknowledge that Socialism practically treats the above-mentioned principles, in so far as they aim at promoting the happiness of the human race, in a less extreme manner than Communism—indeed, in much the same way as their own Order does. Moreover, need we do more than glance at the fact that from the legend of Solomon's material temple the first idea of our spiritual structure was derived—need we do more than observe the sign of recognition exchanged between Apprentices, in order to convince ourselves of the close affinity existing between the rules of our Royal Craft and the principle that the work of every man should be proportioned to his capacity, and the wages he receives to the amount he has performed. Thus Socialism, Freemasonry, and Communism have, after all, a common origin."[1] Although this explanation is most carefully worded, and the bitter pill of socialistic theories is sugared over to deceive the palate of the well-to-do citizen belonging to the lower grades, it fully recognises nevertheless, the kinship existing between Socialism and Freemasonry—an admission made with evident reluctance, but which is of infinite value to ourselves.

In the annual for Freemasons published by Bechstein (1849, p. 270), we read as follows:—"The nature of the intercourse between nations, and their mutual relations to one another, must be dependent on the practical realisation of the fact that all men are brethren, that all mankind constitute but one great family. All strive after happiness; every man has a right to enjoy life, but in the exercise of this right he is sadly straightened by the stress of existing circumstances."

4. The action of Freemasonry is in strict harmony with those flowers of rhetoric of which we have just presented our readers with a small selection. Somewhere between 1840–50, Eugène Sue published his infamous "Mystères de Paris," a work intended solely to spread moral corruption, and intensify the class-hatred with which the lower orders regarded the upper strata of society. The enormous sale of this work was not due to its literary worth, but to the efforts of the 40,000 Brethren which the Grand Orient

[1] Cf Eckert, "Die Frage," &c., p 62 *seq.*

could boast of possessing on the banks of the Seine;
and its design of stirring up the mud at the bottom
of the river was completely fulfilled before many years
had elapsed. In May 1847, when the crop of revolution was already in the ear, and ripening for the
sickle of the Reds, a Congress of European Freemasons was held at Strasbourg, at which the leaders
of the Socialist party, Caussidière, Rollin, Blanc,
Proudhon, Pyat, and others, were present in their
character of Members of the Craft.[1] That the so-
called *work* then accomplished was not merely political, but also socialistic in its tendency, is abundantly
proved, as well by the sentiments of those who were
present as by the colouring imparted to the revolution
which broke out nine months later, *i.e.*, in February
1848. The excited workmen of Paris set the ball
rolling with their horny hands; the timid *bourgeoisie*,
as represented by the National Guard, assented to it
with throbbing hearts; and when success crowned the
work, the Craft did not dare, of course, to withhold its
homage. The Grand Orient hastened to burn incense
before the idols recently set up, and the speech
delivered by the head of the deputation was unmistakably socialistic. We will give the account of
it which appeared in the *Univers* of that date (1848,
No. 449):—" Paris, May 8, 1848. A deputation of

---

[1] We owe this information to Eckert, whose labours have been of so
much service to us ; he states that it was obtained from a most reliable
source in Berlin, which he was prepared to name, if necessary —Cf.
Laacher Stimmen.

Freemasons, belonging to the Grand Orient of France, wearing their insignia, waited on the Provisionary Government, in order to present an address giving in their adhesion to the Republic. This deputation was received by MM. Cremieux, Garnier-Pagès, and Secretary-General Pagnerre, who also wore the insignia of the Craft. M. Bertrand, as the representative of the Grand Master, began his speech with these words:—'All glory to the Supreme Architect of the Universe. The Orient of France to the Provisionary Government. Although the Freemasons of France are by the constitutions of their Order removed far from the sphere of any political disturbance and crisis (!), they cannot forbear to express the pleasurable feelings with which they regard the social changes of recent occurrence. The words Liberty, Equality, Fraternity, have ever been inscribed on the banner of Freemasons; and now that they read the same motto on the national standard of France, they welcome the triumph of their principles, and joyfully congratulate you on having been the means of extending the privileges of Freemasonry to the whole country.[1] Forty thousand Freemasons, divided into five hundred Lodges, promise you their help." The answer of the Minister Cremieux, himself a Mason, is of a very similar description:—" The great Architect has given to the world the sun to enlighten it and

---

[1] This language is identical with that employed on the occasion of the first French Revolution, and particularly on the day which saw Louis XVI. made prisoner.

liberty to uphold it ; it is His will that all men should
be free. He has given them the earth as their portion, that they may make it bear fruit. . . . . From the
first, Freemasonry has contained within itself the
elements of Republicanism ; and this has been the
reason why it has been successful in finding adherents
at all times and in all places.   There is not one single
Lodge but can proudly boast of having invariably
furthered the cause of Liberty and Fraternity.   From
henceforward it will be the task of the Republic to
carry on the work of Freemasonry, and to exhibit
itself to all nations as a glorious pledge of the union
which at some future time is to prevail over the whole
face of the globe.'   We do well to note these words,
as they afford undeniable evidence that a social republic realises all a Freemason believes in and hopes
for."

     During the reign of Napoleon III. the process of
democratic fermentation went on in the French
Lodges with ever-increasing speed.   On the other
hand, the more moderate *blue* Masons complained, as
they were ever wont to do, of the extravagant proceedings of some of their Brethren ; nevertheless it was
precisely these latter who of all others most clearly
apprehended the real spirit of their Order, and who
applied themselves with bold energy to carry it out
practically in daily life.   But in May 1861, a regular
revolt broke out in the Grand Orient ; a tiny spark,
insignificant enough in itself, having sufficed to make
the smouldering ashes blaze out into a glowing

flame. Prince Murat, the then Grand Master, had
voted in the Senate for the temporal power of the
Pope, and a large majority of the two hundred and
sixty-nine Lodges of the Orient refused to allow such
a crime as this to go unpunished. The Prince of the
Reds naturally sided with the rebels; however, from
the camp of Murat there issued a pamphlet entitled
" Sédition au sein de la Maçonnerie," which placed
the conduct of the opposition party in a most un-
favourable light. In fact the Grand Master himself
designated the majority of his subjects as revolutionary and socialist agitators of the worst kind,
adding that even Blanqui and his followers, in 1848,
had not gone to greater lengths than these misguided
Brethren. All this justified a Legitimist paper of the
day in saying, " Rub off the shining varnish of philanthropy and brotherly love, and beneath the brilliant
exterior you will find political intrigue, unbelief, and
revolution." In accordance with the principles of
extreme democracy, religion, Christianity, and the
property of individuals were successively attacked.
Whilst one voice exclaimed, " Religion, whatever it
be, enslaves the conscience," another asserted that
" Catholic education destroys all moral sense," and
Brother Fauvety wound up by denouncing as canni-
bals all holders of property, saying, " Every man who
consumes without producing, flays and devours his
neighbour." The party of Reds wanted to appoint
Prince Jerome Bonaparte as Grand Master; but
although they formed nine-tenths of the body of

Freemasonry, they were nevertheless unable to carry out their design, as the Emperor forbade his amiable cousin to accept the proposed honour, nominating in his stead to the Grand Mastership a Protestant, Marshal Magnan, who was not even a Mason, and had therefore in the course of one day to be initiated into the whole series of thirty-three grades.   Occurrences such as these excited at that time much attention in other countries, and might have been productive of much that was disagreeable for the Craft.   On this account the *Allgemeine Zeitung* of May 26, 1861, felt bound to speak in behalf of its friends (such of them, at least, as were to be found on German soil), in the following paragraph :—" Are we not justified in concluding, from recent events in France, that Revolution, and especially organised Democracy, when unable to subsist under any other form, joined the ranks of Freemasonry ; so that its most active militia are now formed of members of the Craft, and it stands in close connection with the Italian Lodges, over which Cavour is said to exercise so powerful an influence ?"   By these words public opinion. is doubly deceived, whether intentionally or unintentionally, we are not in a position to decide. In the first place, there was no question of an organised democracy in the French Lodges, but of Socialism of a very dangerous description.   Furthermore, this revolutionary agitation is falsely laid at the door of the so-called *Saviours of Society*, who, being then in power, by their measures of repression are said to have forced the movement into the shade of the Lodges. But the truth is, that Socialism had been at home there for centuries ; it is, in fact, no foundling adopted out of compassion, but the legitimate offspring of the Craft.[1]

But the apple of discord, thrown among the labouring portion of the community, had not proved influential enough to bring the designs of the Socialists to maturity. The malcontents had yet to be disciplined, and formed into a compact cosmopolitan body. This was done when the League of the International was founded in St Martin's Hall, London, September 28, 1864.[2] It is notorious that on this occasion the adepts of Freemasonry took a leading share in the transac-

---

[1] One of the writers in the *Historisch Politische Blätter* (p 421) fell into the same error, as is proved by the following extract :—" We opine that the struggle of Socialism against capital and landed property in France, being forcibly repressed in its external manifestations, has taken refuge in the Lodges, making them a very hell for the unfortunate *bourgeoisie*, who formerly took the lead there. While political Liberalism alone was in question, this *bourgeoisie* held unlimited sway in the Ministry and in the Chambers, no less than in the Lodges Times will soon change, if they have not already changed. The existence of the *bourgeoisie* is now only possible under the ægis of imperial despotism, and even in the Lodges it is only upheld by force. Things have not as yet gone so far in Germany ; this constitutes the difference in the state of Freemasonry in the two countries." We think that sufficient evidence has now been forthcoming from Germany to prove the essentially socialistic nature of Freemasonry. It is, however, true that on the right bank of the Rhine the external life of the Church has yet to be stifled, to effect which the Craft has just made a compact with the Liberal Government. When this point has been reached, we need not doubt that the Secret Society will push on further. But we must let it run the length of its tether ; it lacks neither patience nor perseverance, although it has to pass through many stages of existence.

[2] Cf. Pachtler, *Die Internationale Arbeiterverbindung.* Essen, 1871.

tions, and that the ultimate aims of the Craft plainly
showed themselves beneath the *blouse* of the workman.

And when, during the terrible seventy-two days
which elapsed between March 18th and May 29th
1871, the International held its first passage of arms
within the walls of Paris, Freemasonry exhibited a
truly maternal tenderness towards this her own peculiar child.   A procession, composed of at least five
thousand persons, in which members of all the grades,
not excepting those of women, took part, wearing their insignia, and in which 150 Lodges of
France were represented, wended its way to the
town hall of Paris.   Maillet, bearing the red flag as
a token of universal peace,[1] headed the band, and
openly proclaimed, in a speech which met with the
approval of all present, that the new Commune was
the antitype of Solomon's temple, and the corner-
stone of the social fabric about to be raised by the
efforts of the Craft.   The negotiations carried on by
Freemasons with the Government of Versailles on
behalf of the Socialists, and the way in which they
planted the banners of the Craft on the walls of the
Capital, accompanying this action with a threat of
instantly joining the ranks of the combatants if a
single shot were fired at one of those banners, was all
of a piece with the sentiments they expressed.   Elie

---

[1] It must not be forgotten that Freemasonry contemplates a final and
social revolution, the most terrible, but at the same time most salutaiy,
of all, which is to be the forerunner of universal peace.

Reclus, a man of letters, one of the principal writers in the *Revue des Deux Mondes,* the great journal of Freemasonry, distinguished himself as a furious champion of the Communist cause.

Hitherto we have mainly laid before the reader the transactions of French Masons, in order to illustrate the socialist theories as they appear when put in practice. We know well what the children of darkness will reply to us. They will have recourse to their usual subterfuge, namely this—" Such things do occur in some lands, and injudicious Brethren are to blame for them. But with us the case is quite different; nowhere are more loyal subjects to be found than in the Lodges of this country." On this account we have, at the risk of exhausting our reader's patience, endeavoured as far as possible to let Freemasons speak for themselves, by bringing forward witnesses of various nationalities, and constantly referring to the rules and ritual of the Craft. All has pointed in the same direction, namely, of proving that Socialism was born and bred in the lap of Freemasonry. But the descent of the ladder must be a gradual process; to spring at one leap from the highest round to the lowest, and incur the obvious risk of breaking one's neck, would be an act of sheer madness. First must come a liberal revolution, brought about by the storming of a Bastille, or, in a slower and more constitutional way, with the forced concurrence of a Prime Minister, who has long been deprived of his liberty of action; and when the

poison has had time to circulate freely, then the
moment comes to speak of a social revolution. In
France the liberal convulsion took place long ago ; it
has even passed already through several fresh stages,
and the curtain will soon rise on the second act of
the drama. Hence in that country, more than in
any other, can the Freemason venture to enunciate
boldly his schemes of universal happiness. In Germany, on the contrary, Liberalism has been left a
long way behind, and the Craft has plenty of work
on its hands, that is to say, the work of advancing
Liberalism at the expense of ecclesiastical liberty, of
Christian marriage, Christian education, Christian
faith and practice. When this business has been
duly despatched, the work of Socialism will begin,
as surely as two and two make four. In Belgium, a
country which in 1830 accepted Liberalism as a
christening gift, Freemasonry has already shown its
socialistic proclivities by the recognition of such
plebeian hangers-on as the *Solidaires* and Free-
thinkers, themselves most zealous partisans of the
International. In September 1871, Zorilla, the Grand
Master of Spain, threatened, unless his wishes were
complied with, to let loose the International in that
country. Plain proof enough of the intimate relations
existing between the two. In Italy we meet with
the very same thing. Since the year 1848, Piedmont
has thrown herself into the arms of the Craft, and has
found in it her greatest ally in spreading the liberal
revolution throughout the Peninsula. But as the

last stage has long since been reached by the occupation of Rome, Freemasonry is now beginning to show
a fresh side of its character, and betraying, in the
person of its most active members, those socialistic
tendencies which threaten to deal with the liberal
monarchy in much the same way as it dealt with the
petty sovereigns of former days.   The next social
earthquake in this unhappy country will shake to its
very foundations, if it does not completely overthrow,
the old order of things.

   From among the most recent events in Italy we
select the following as specially calculated to
manifest the socialist tendencies of Freemasonry.
Garibaldi and Mazzini, the well-known revolutionary
leaders, and at the same time high dignitaries of
the Secret Society, agreed, at the Socialist Congress
held in Rome, November 1871, upon a common
course of action, namely, the establishment of a
national social and democratic republic in Italy.
And when, eight days after the death of Mazzini,
on the 10th March 1872, the socialist party in Rome
made a solemn funeral procession to the Capitol in his
honour, their ranks were swelled by a great number
of Freemasons with bands of music, and 150 banners.
But still more significant were the preparations made
for the great blow which the social democrats of Italy
proposed to strike on occasion of a contemplated
popular gathering to be held in the Roman Coliseum
on November 24, 1872.   With this end in view, the
Freemasons met in Congress some weeks previously

(1st–3d Nov.) at a villa near the village of Locarno, in the district of Novara.[1] On October 29th, the representatives of several Italian Lodges had already met in Genoa. These were Philippo Cordova (from the parent Lodge in Rome), Antonio de Franchi (Naples), Benedetto Maria La Vaccara (Palermo), Andrea Giovanelli (Florence), Alberto Mario (Turin), and Quadrio (Genoa). On the following day, they continued their journey by way of Alexandria and Arona to Locarno, where, on their arrival, they found Felix Pyat[2] (France), Kossuth (Hungary), Klapka (Switzerland), and General Etzel (Prussia). The sittings in the villa lasted from 4 P.M until midnight, and during that time not one of the " Brethren " was allowed to leave the house under any pretext whatsoever, with the exception of one young Prussian, who filled the post of Secretary to Etzel and shorthand writer to the Assembly. The Congress was opened by Etzel, with a speech delivered in French, upon these three points—1. Would a war between France, such as it is under Thiers, and Italy, such as it is under the *consorteria* (the Conservative party in the Government), be a suitable means of furthering the

---

[1] These details are taken from the *Univers* of 12th and 19th November 1872. Our informant professes himself a secret convert fiom Freemasonry ; we leave him to vouch for the accuracy of the details he gives. That he is in the main coirect will be made apparent fiom facts we shall presently adduce.

[2] One of the most zealous promoters of the International and of Socialism in France, and the exciter of seditions amongst the workmen in Le Creuzot, at the commencement of the year 1870.

cause of Democracy ?[1] 2. What are the principles which ought to form the basis of a new provisionary Government, under the dictatorship of Gambetta in France, and under that of Garibaldi in Italy ? 3. What new form of worship is to supersede Catholicism ? These questions were answered as follows by the votes of the majority :—1. As the use of any means by which the cause of Democracy may be furthered is justifiable, war is a suitable means to be employed. ` 2. Communist principles with a new religious ideal. 3. The new Gospel of Democracy according to Brother Renan (Part IV. chap. xli), published in the form of question and answer (*ridotta a catechismo*). After this the following resolutions were passed :—

1. To support the insurrectionary committees in the issue of notes of the value of five francs.

2. To lay in a store of arms and ammunition.

3. To establish a secret corps for the discovery, notification, and surveillance of the principal Catholic writers, and of the most influential members of the clergy and aristocracy, in order that every possible means may be employed to overcome the existing opposition to the civil and religious changes which it is desirable to introduce. The object of the proposed popular meeting was stated to be the

---

[1] We are well aware what sort of people those are who consider that " the end justifies the means " The world at large is made to believe that these are the Jesuits, in order that no possible imputation may be cast on the real culprits.

M

following: To gauge the power of social democracy, to help it to give free expression to its opinions, to feel the pulse of national enthusiasm, and see what can be done with the masses.

The projected demonstration of November 24 was prevented by the vigilance of the Government, large forces of the military and of the police being called out. Nevertheless, on November 22, the conspirators agreed upon their plan of action, the *Patto Fomano*, forming it after the model of the Paris Commune, and determined forthwith to enter upon the path of secret conspiracy. Twenty-three Italian Lodges immediately gave in their adhesion to the scheme, a proceeding which made no small stir. On this account the *Perseveranza*, a Milanese journal, in the number published December 6, 1872, sought to justify the Craft, on the score of only twenty-three Lodges having taken part in the plan. But this article, intended as a defence, only served as an accusation. We will give it word for word—" It cannot be denied that twenty-three Lodges were a party to these trans-actions ; six belonging to the Orient of Leghorn, five to that of Palermo, the other twelve being the Lodges of Regalbuto, Genoa, Ravenna, Alessandria, Messina, Rome, Cagliari, Parma, Marola, Spezia, Massa, and Pietra-Santa. In case any one should be anxious to know the names of each, we will subjoin them here. The Lodges of the Orient of Leghorn, the Virtuous Leaders (*i virtuosi anziani*), Garibaldi and the Future, the Modern Pelican, the Reappear-

ing Dawn, Unitaria, Modern Revolution.[1] I give
the names of the Lodges of the Orient of Palermo,
also word for word. The Freemasons doubtless have
their own reasons for selecting these names, and
who knows what influence they may have on our
future; one far greater, perhaps, than we at present
suspect. The names are as follows:—

" 1. Liberty, Fraternity, Equality. Universal Freemasonry, Family, Italy. Lodge George Washing-
ton of the Orient of Palermo. The only known
delegate (of November 24) of this Lodge was Luigi
Castellazzo, who also represented Leghorn.

" 2. Lodge Mount Lebanon, of the ancient and
recognised Scotch rite, of the Orient of Palermo.
Ignazio Catalani, Worshipful Master; Vincenzo Cuc-
chiara, Senior Warden; Giovanni Rosa, Speaker;
deputy sent to the Committee (November 24) Ulysse
Bacci, living at Rome, the director of the Masonic
Review (*Rivista Massonica*).

" 4. Lodge Il Rene, of the Orient of Palermo.
Officials unknown; deputy, Napoleon Parboni, of
Rome, a strong partisan and promoter of the Social
Congress, and Vice-President of the Preparatory
Committee.

---

[1] These significant names are in themselves enough to prove how
far one ought to believe the old fiction put forward by Freemasonry,
that it never interferes in political or religious questions. Unfortunately the *Perseveranza* forgot to give the names of the " Worshipful,"
the " Warden," and the " Speaker." However, we know that Brothers
Mauro Macchi and Luigi Castellazzo formed the deputation sent from
the Lodge of Leghorn to the Socialist Congress in the Coliseum.

"The remaining Lodges are,—Queretaro [1] (of the
Orient of Capizzi,[2]) which recognised the Committee,
but sent no deputation. Lodge Mazzini and the
Future (Orient of Regalbuto [3]). Lodge L. Caffaro
(Orient of Genoa). Lodge of the Virtuous (Orient
of Leghorn). Lodge Gagliando (Orient of Ales-
sandria). Lodge Rome and the Constituency (Orient
of Rome). Lodge Liberty and Progress (Orient of
Cagtiari), represented by Ulysses Bacci, who was at
the same time the representative of the Lodge Unity
and Garibaldi, of the Orient of Palermo. Lodge
Joseph Mazzini (Orient of Parma), represented by
Luigi Aresi. Lodge La Castellana (Orient of
Marola). Lodge The Future (Orient of Spezia).
Universal Freemasonry, Family of Italy. Lodge
The Zenith (Orient of Spezia). Lodge Unity and
Progress (Orient of Massa). Lodge Versaliese
(Orient of Pietra-Santa[4]).

"Here," continues the *Perseveranza*, "we have
the aggregate of the Lodges which voted with

---

[1] This name, that of the fortress Queretaro, where the unfortunate
Emperor Maximilian was shot, tells well for the loyal feelings of Freemasons towards rulers

[2] Capizzi, a little town in Sicily, cannot number more than 4000
inhabitants   From the fact that it has its own Orient, and consequently independent Lodges, one can judge of the extension of the
Society in that island. This need not, however, surprise us, as almost
all *employés* and Government officials on the island feel bound to
become Freemasons.

[3] Another small town in Sicily, in the province of Catania, numbering only 8500 inhabitants.

[4] In Tuscany, in the province of Lucca. Population, 11,000

the Committee. Not a single one out of Apulia, where, nevertheless, there is a Lodge in every village and an Orient in every town; not one out of Naples, where they may be counted by dozens, and where, I believe, they are divided into three orthodox Orients, not to speak of the unorthodox ones; only a few of Sicily and Tuscany; scarcely any of Emilia and Liguria; none of either Romagna or Venice; only one of Rome. Of all the Sicilian Lodges, only six made common cause with the Committee. The sum total of the Lodges in agreement with it is merely twenty-three, a very small proportion of the whole body of Italian Freemasons."

Thus far the *Perseveranza.* This article places two points beyond a doubt: 1. That Freemasonry has spread far and wide in Italy, a fact which plainly bodes no little danger to the throne and to society; 2. That in spite of the vigorous measures taken by the Government, twenty-three Lodges ventured to declare openly for the socialist republic; a number which, under existing circumstances, is no trifling one, and affords convincing proof of the socialist tendencies of the whole Order. How many more Lodges were restrained by prudential motives, deeming it the wiser course to keep in the background for a time, because they reckoned amongst their members many Government officials? And not one of the professedly loyal Lodges entered a protest against the procedure of the twenty-three democratic ones. On the contrary, we find the Italian Masons of the Scotch rite issuing a circular, which was printed at Rome and published in the *Unità Catholica* of December 17, 1872,[1] in which, without any circumlocution, they boldly proclaimed the new duties devolving on Freemasons, to fight against the Church and the Government established in Rome; and, furthermore, enjoined on every man the duty of all possible exertion, in order to train up the people to the exercise of true liberty, and thus prepare for the advent of that happy day when both religion and idolatry will have ceased to exist, when there will be neither tyrants nor slaves, neither fortunate nor unfortunate, but one great corporation of well-instructed families, independent and free, active and happy.[2]

In the present day, both in Italy and elsewhere, religion forms the centre round which all parties

[1] This publication bore the signatures of the Worshipful Master Benmielli 18 ∴ (ι ε, of the Eighteenth Grade, that of Rosicrucian), of the Speaker, Ant. Petrocchi, and the Secretary, Luigi Martoglio.

[2] One important accessory must not be lost sight of here. As long as Italian Freemasonry required the services of the Piedmontese army, in order to dethrone the remaining sovereigns of the Peninsula, it was profuse in expressions of loyalty to the Savoy dynasty. Since its first object, Italian unity and centralisation, has been attained by the sacrilegious occupation of Rome, the Secret Society has been engaged in gradually undermining a throne, already somewhat weakened by preceding events, in order to make way for a social democratic republic. The introduction of this latter would be impossible, were the six or seven independent States of Italy still existing, and able to render each other mutual assistance. From 1848 to 1870 nothing was heard but unlimited enthusiasm for Victor Emmanuel; but now all is entirely changed. Let the same rule be applied to the present situation in Germany, and its true import will at once be plain.

revolve ; even political opinions take their colouring from religious views. All real and thorough Christians declare themselves loyal subjects of the lawful and established Government ; all those half-hearted, timid warriors, who are Christians only in name, profess liberal views, whilst atheists wave on high the banner of Democracy. Therefore the Secret Society, charging its members with the mission of spreading unbelief amongst the nations of Europe, makes them at the same time apostles of Democracy ; and every state which purchases for itself immunity from covert attack, by consenting to the secularisation of marriage, of education, and of social institutions, hastens the triumph of Republicanism. The Secret Society knows this better than do any of those who tremble before it ; on this account, true to its old system of deceit, it casts the blame of all civil disturbances on the small party of united and uncompromising Christians, reproaching them with being dangerous to the State, and repeating the accusation so often, that at length all simpletons believe it. What is called " public opinion " nowadays is nothing but the voice of a corrupt and mercenary press, under the influence of Freemasonry. When will men rouse themselves ? How much longer is the fate of nations to be abandoned to the tender mercies of the " Brethren ? " We know not, but one thing at least is certain, that heaven has decreed that as the sin of each man, so shall be his punishment.

A similar fate is in store for Germany, unless we
can be wise in time. The contented Freemason, who
is far from dreaming that anything lurks behind the
Liberalism of the day, will, when the witched dance
of Socialism and Fraternity-proper opens, stare in
blank amazement, especially as he finds his hands
fettered and his tongue tied by a thousand oaths;
but he cannot escape eating the fruit of what he has
sown, and his teeth will be all the more set on edge
the more honestly he has laboured in cultivating the
noxious tree. As far back as 1849, the unhappy De
Lamennais gave in the *Réforme* the following truth-
ful sketch of the impending disasters :—" In virtue of
his sovereign prerogative, man rises up against God
and declares himself to be free and equal to Him. In
the name of Freedom, all political and social institutions are overthrown, in the name of Equality all
hierarchies are destroyed, all religious and political
ascendancy is abolished. . . . . Then the reign of
violence, of hatred, and of terror begins over the
corpse of priest and king, a fearful fulfilment of the
prophecy : a whole nation shall rise up, man against
man, neighbour against neighbour ; amidst terrible
confusion the child will rise up against the old man,
and the people against their great ones. In order
to depict these terrific scenes of horror and crime,
of licence and butchery, this carnival of error, this
chaos of outlawry and debauchery, these blasphemous shouts and devilish songs, the dull and unceasing
sounds of the destroyer's hammer and the execu-

tioner's sword, the explosion of bursting mines and the yells of exultant joy which hail the widespread carnage;—in order, I say, to depict scenes such as these, it were necessary to borrow the language of demons, as some monsters appear to have rivalled them in their fury. (Cf. *Journal de Bruxelles*, December 3, 1849).

CHAPTER VIII.

OPEN hatred of God has been stated to be the most
striking characteristic of the present day, and, certainly, it cannot be denied that a terrible stream of
impiety pervades the whole of the atmosphere by
which we are surrounded. Whilst it is, on the one
hand, a cheering sight to see the Children of the
Cross cling all the more closely to the symbol of our
salvation now that danger threatens it, and to behold
them evince so marvellous a spirit of self-sacrifice,
and an enthusiasm which recalls the earliest days of
Christianity; on the other hand, it is lamentable to
witness the unblushing audacity with which society
at large publicly parades in politics, in science, in
the press, and in daily life, the fact of its apostasy
from God and from His Anointed. It is of course
indisputably true that in all times and in most
places some have been found to deny the God who
created them; but this deplorable fall to the last
and lowest depth to which human nature can sink
has invariably been the mournful result of intellectual error or moral depravity, and the few who
have fallen thus low have been contented with

toleration at the hands of their fellowmen. But since the commencement of the last century unbelief has advanced with rapid strides; it has come not only to be regarded as on a level with orthodox belief, but even to claim precedence over it. Those countries and peoples which have given such corrupting opinions free admittance into their midst, and allowed them to make good their footing in society, proudly boast of superior cultivation and refinement, and dignify their `unbelief with the name of intelligence. Furthermore, in order to cope with the overwhelming superiority of numbers on the side of belief, they strive, by secularising all education, from the village school up to the University, to make themselves masters of the rising generation, and consequently, of the future.[1] Thus mankind is being gradually dragged on to a pre-determined goal. De Camille has depicted the true state of things as follows:—" No one can prognosticate what terrible secrets may be hid for us in the womb of the future, but all must acknowledge that recent times have given birth to a hideous offspring; pseudo-refinement, falsified public opinion, spurious science, sophistical principles, untrue ideas, false desires, a perverted conscience, and corrupt morals—all these meet us at every turn, and nothing escapes their infection. They spread to the royal palace and to the lowly hut; they influence both the highest minister of the Crown and the ragged urchin

[1] See *Laacher Stimmen,* 1872, No. 7, "*Kultu, rein modernes Schlagwort.*"

who shouts in the rear of a popular demonstration; they have distorted, enfeebled, and in some instances done away with the homage paid by Governments to truth, justice, and morality; or at least they have so far stunned and intimidated those in power as to destroy in them that strongest instinct alike of the individual and of the nation, the instinct of self-preservation.[1] And in the face of these menacing clouds, liberal Christians can still reconcile it with their conscience to make concessions to the spirit of darkness under cover of modern ideas, to enter into an agreement with it, and consent to carry grist to Beelzebub's mill, on condition that he should refrain from interfering in their own private oratory.

The spirit of hostility to God could never have attained its present proportions, and its actual power, if the forces at its command had not been thoroughly disciplined and organised. For individual unbelievers can only corrupt individuals, and even numbers without concerted action have no power to turn the current of social life into fresh channels. Especially in opposition to the serried ranks of the Church, an undisciplined army, however numerous, can effect next to nothing. But of late, apostasy from God has shown itself to be a persecutor of the people of God; and this new phase of its character becomes daily more apparent. . Already it has succeeded in making itself the almost absolute master of what is erroneously

[1] De Camille, "Storia della setta Antichristiana" (Florence, 1872). Compare *Civltà Cattolica*, quad. 524, 20th April 1872, p. 190 *seq.*

called " public opinion," and in rendering legislature
so difficult in those States which remain true to their
historical traditions and established rights, that the
Government has sometimes suspended its action
altogether, or, in other cases, despairing of being able
to cope with the enemy who batters so loudly at
the gates, has delivered over to him the keys of the
citadel.

In Freemasonry we find the power which organises
the terrible and occult forces that are at work
amongst us.   In the following pages it will be our
endeavour briefly to review the principal forms which
this enmity to God has successively assumed, and in
this way to expose the true and ultimate aim of
them all.

It is, of course, self-evident that the League could
only attain to its final antitheistic goal by passing
through various stages.   And here we may distinguish
four different streams, which often intersect one
another, and often run parallel ; a revival of Judaism,
Deism, Pantheism, and that lowest and worst of all,
the Antitheism of humanity, which would have man
occupy the throne of the Most High, declaring God
an usurper, and man himself the true Deity ! We will
now proceed to examine these four external manifestations in detail.   With regard to the two first, it
will not be necessary to go into great detail, as we
have already had occasion to say much that bears
directly on the subject in the second and fourth divisions of this work.

I. A shallow Judaism was the first form of religion which the Secret Society substituted for revealed faith ; and this explains the frequent reference
made in its official documents to the esoteric teaching of the East, transmitted to it by means of the
Templars. These Jewish doctrines, which are chiefly
directed against the New Testament revelation, often
recall the Sadducees and Samaritans of our Lord's
time, since, like these, they acknowledge no divine
revelation subsequent to that of Moses, have a strong
element of Epicureanism, and recognise no sacred
writings but their Pentateuch, which, moreover, differs considerably from our own. What Freemasonry
asserts concerning its connection with Gnostic teaching may to a certain extent be true, in so far as it
limited to a shallow morality the diluted Judaism it
taught, and amalgamated at pleasure any dogmatic
theories it might chance to possess, with either Pantheistic, Gnostic, or Manichean elements.[1] But it is
well known that the Brotherhood does not trouble
itself much about such trifles. Inasmuch as the
existence of a God is matter of belief at all, He is the
"Supreme Architect of the Universe," and One in
person, the doctrine of the Most Holy Trinity being
a Papal invention. Redemption by Jesus Christ is
rejected as a heretical belief originated by the Druses

---

[1] The Freemason Condorcet, who took so active a part in the first
French Revolution, goes so far as to claim as belonging to Freemasonry
the various sects of Manichean tendency in the Middle Ages.—See
Barruel, as above, p. 308.

of Lebanon, which spread to the West, and became the basis of the Papal power. The real Saviour, *i.e.,* the political and social liberator, is rather the Jesus or Josue of the Old Testament, the son of Nun, and related to Moses and Aaron, who introduced relaxations of those unduly severe religious laws which were founded on abuses in external life. Here we have teaching plainly opposed to the doctrine of the Trinity, harmonising in the main · with the tenets of the Monarchians, the Arians, and the Socinians, and offering naturally many points of attraction to those who deny the divinity of Christ. Perhaps the modern Judaism of the present day is derived from this source. And as the adoption of views such as these pledges the Freemason to a lifelong enmity to the Saviour in whom Christians believe, it is easy to understand that the strict Jew, inspired with the same zeal which animated Saul, is with no great difficulty prevailed on to join the Craft. Long experience teaches us that the contingent contributed by Judaism to the ranks of Freemasonry is comparatively larger than that of any other religious body; it is said that the descendants of Abraham compose two-thirds of the Grand Orient of Paris.

This judaising tendency is very apparent in a document now before us, published by the Orient of Brussels, "to the greater glory of the Supreme Architect of the world, in the year of true light 5838 (1838), with the object of commending a work by the Freemason Marziale Reghelini (de

Schio), in the interests of Masonry, entitled,
"Histoire du vrai Jésus Christ Nazaréen.'" As
this publication supplies all the information necessary to give us a nearer acquaintance with the
subject before us, the reader will permit us to make
a somewhat lengthy extract from it, which, in spite
of its serious nature, cannot fail to provoke an
occasional smile :—

"The instruction imparted to every Freemason,
and the emblems wherewith our temples are adorned,
combine to teach him that our Order or Brotherhood
is descended from the Knights-Templar, and their
illustrious Grand Master, Jacques Molay.   Every
Brother who possesses the least acquaintance with
the history of the Crusaders, knows that they were
driven out of Palestine by Saladin the Great at the
end of the twelfth century.   Although that province
was then in the hands of the Mohammedans, the
Templars, thanks to their honourable conduct, were
allowed to retain possession of some hospices, where
such of their Brethren could find shelter as came
from the West on a pilgrimage to the grave of Jesus
Christ, the liberator of mankind.   In the times of
truce between the Mohammedans and the Crusaders,
a continuous stream of Templars flowed into Jerusalem ; and the hospitable and friendly terms on which
they lived with the inhabitants of the country, enabled
them easily to obtain an intimate·acquaintance with
the old traditions of Arabia, of which country Palestine
forms a part.   In this manner their eyes were opened

to the delusive nature of that false fame, attracted by
which, for more than two centuries, the misguided
nations of the West had been led to seek a grave
in the deserts of Asia and Egypt.   They plainly
saw, moreover, that fanaticism had been the means
of involving Europe in an unjust war, and that
the belief in the grave of Jesus of Bethlehem, as
that of the liberator of mankind, was a mere fable,
on which the Popes built up their power;[1] for
when Omar, on the conquest of Jerusalem, in the
year 636, according to the ordinary calendar, discovered that the temple of Solomon had been long
since destroyed, he rebuilt it on the former site,
dedicating it to the Incomprehensible and Eternal
One ; for, doing this, he received the name of San-
cratius.   Furthermore, with the intention of honour-
ing Jesus (Josue), the son of Mary Amram, and
nephew of Aaron and Moses, he removed into this
temple the grave which the Arabic Christians belonging to the army of Mohammed and Omar venerated and made pilgrimages to, in remembrance of
their own Saviour and Lawgiver.   Thus the Templars
arrived at the conviction that the belief in Jesus of
Bethlehem, as a Being both human and divine, equal
to God His Father, and like Him eternal, was nothing
but the old heresy of unorthodox Christians, or an

[1] We do not, of course, dream of attempting to refute such fables of
the Craft ; the reader must take these false statements, and others
which follow, for what they are worth.

imitation of the heresy of the Druses of Lebanon, who, a century before the commencement of the Crusades, *i.e.*, in 996, believed, as they now believe, that in the Caliph Hakim, the Eternal Creator had become incarnate. No sooner had the Templars become aware of this error, than they embraced the faith of Jesus, the son of Mary Amram, whose life had been spent in proclaiming the mercy of the Eternal God, and preaching the hope of a future existence. This code of mercy they adopted as their own.

" By means of some fragments of the real Pentateuch, the Templars at the same time learnt that this Jesus, son of Mary Amram, had, under the mysterious name of Osee, been chosen chief Captain, and consecrated High Priest by the lawgiver Moses (Deut. xxxi. 7, 8, 14, 23 ; xxxii. 44; xxxiv. 9), and that on the death of this latter, Jesus announced a new law of justice and equality, and abolished the priesthood of Juda, who, during the latter years of Moses' lifetime, had got all power into his own hands, and employed it to bring the Israelites into a disgraceful bondage, called the Nazarean. All this our Brethren of former times found recorded in the Pentateuch, the Koran, the Arabic traditions, and popular beliefs. The dogmatic truths and liberal doctrines of Jesus, the son of Mary Amram, were brought to Europe by the Templars ; the Order increased in numbers and influence, and the spread of these doctrines caused great uneasiness to despots and priests, who gave themselves out for the heirs and representatives of the priesthood of Juda, abrogated by the liberator Jesus."

Next follows an account of the execution of Jacques Molay, plainly designed to cast odium on the authors of the deed, upon the king, and especially—here the Belgian origin of the whole thing is betrayed—upon bishops and upon the Pope. Those Templars who escaped the general massacre (so runs the tale) carried on in Europe the building of the temple to the Great Architect of the Universe with untiring energy, combating feudal oppression under the cloak of the freedom which a corporation enjoyed, and of the useful calling they followed. In this work the principles of Liberty and Humanity, learnt in the East, were of no small service to them. In France, Germany, England, Italy, and elsewhere, they became the terror of landed proprietors, and of the higher clergy. In order to render their position secure, they formed themselves into a body of stone-cutters and Free masons, and established a noviciate for the purpose of testing the courage, perseverance, and discretion of candidates. But through the ill-advised reception of some prominent members of the aristocracy and clergy, the old spirit of the Order became deteriorated, and by imprudent interference in politics, its members exposed themselves anew to the danger of persecution. Finally, however, the true doctrine was revived, and the

right course of conduct returned to. The document
we quote from proceeds as follows :—

"The traditions preserved throughout the whole
Order show that our ancestors admitted no other
doctrines than those of Jesus, the son of Mary Amram.
In order that these might not be lost, a sealed copy
has been handed down by the first Superiors of the
Order, the genuineness of which is evident and undeniable. It ordains—

"1. That at the head of every document issued
by the Brethren, in an individual or corporate
capacity, should stand a profession of faith in our
Lawgiver Jesus, the son of Mary Amram, the in-
variable formula to be employed being, 'To the
glory of the Great Architect of the Universe,' expressed by the nine initial letters, A. L. G. D. G.
A. D. L. U. (*A la Gloire du Grand Architecte de
l'Univers*), to expose and oppose the errors of Pope
and priest, who commence everything in the name
of their Trinity."

"2. That all proceedings at the opening or at the
closing of our Lodges, as well as all documents either
of individual members or of the Brotherhood in
general, should be dated from the Creation of the
World, or the Era of Light, in opposition to the modern system of chronology invented in the end of the
eleventh century by a Pope, who introduced the use
of a later era ; a pitiful and cowardly artifice by which
to obtain universal recognition of the event from
which he dated."

" 3. That in remembrance of the Last Supper or Christian Lovefeast of Jesus the Son of Mary Amram, an account of which is given in the Arabic traditions and in the Koran, a solemn festival should be held, accompanied by a distribution of bread, in commemoration of an ancient custom observed by the slaves of eating bread together, and of their deliverance by means of the liberator (Josue). The distribution is to be accompanied by these memorable words—' This is the bread of misery and oppression which our fathers were forced to eat under the Pharaos, the priests of Juda ; whosoever hungers let him come and eat; this is the Pascal sacrifice (of the liberator Josue); come unto us, all you who are oppressed; yet this one year more in Babylon, and the next year shall see us free men.' This instructive, and at the same time commemorative, supper of the Rosicrucians, is the counterpart of the Supper of the Papists."

" 4. That in honour of our Jesus, spoken of in the Pentateuch under the name of Osee, all our work should begin and end with a threefold and joyous huzza for him ; and this salutation is to be repeated every time that a guest or a deputation is brought into the temple, as well as at the opening of a lovefeast, and after every toast drunk on festive occasions. This huzza consists in the thrice-repeated exclamation, Osee, Osee, Osee, *i.e.*, Long live the memory of Jesus, son of Mary Amram ! . . . ."

" Such are the ordinances of our masters ; the

traditional interpretation of them has always been preserved in the Orient of Venice.[1]   This is consequently the creed of Freemasonry ; it rests upon the system of Jesus, the Christ, the Liberator of Israel, who instituted a liberal and moderate code of laws, and abrogated the priesthood of Juda ; a creed laid down in Arabic traditions, in the Koran and Pentateuch, and by those historical writers commonly known under the name of the prophets.   All this proves to a demonstration the real object of papal anathemas, now no longer hurled against monarchs, or those amongst their subjects who adopt reformed views.   Priestly dread of the disclosure of the truth is the real cause of the persecutions constantly renewed against Freemasonry ; for the Western Popes are well aware that we alone possess in our traditions and sacramental words evidence that must sooner or later bring about the destruction of the spiritual ascendency and chimerical dominion of Rome."

Even here, in this earliest stage, the antitheistic strain which runs through all the higher grades of Freemasonry already becomes apparent.[2]   We have not to do with theoretical unbelief, nor with a simple denial of the positive beliefs of others, but with an

[1] The Scotch rite likewise professes that many of its mysterious ceremonies came to it by way of Venice.   See Barruel, as above, p 295.

[2] The document we have quoted from is, in fact, the work of a Rosicrucian, and is apparently addressed to the Brethren of the Eighteenth Grade alone.

element of active aggression which strikes at the
root of Christianity, and is determined to gain the
mastery over it. We deal with a foe prepared
for a hand-to-hand fight with the God of revelation, and ready to run an equal race with Christianity, in seeking proselytes amongst all classes
of society. On the authority of a wild fiction,
alleged to rest upon the incontrovertible testimony of ancient records and testimony never
forthcoming, the unwary candidate is persuaded
into rejecting the books of Holy Scripture and into
looking upon the Pentateuch itself—our version of
it, at least—as spurious. The Saviour adored by
Christians is represented as being a common Jew
of Bethlehem, who was confounded with the ancient
Josue, the son of Nun, by the credulous and barbarous
Druses of Lebanon, and afterwards exalted to
be the God of Christendom by the Western Popes,
for the furtherance of their own selfish aims.[1] As
a matter of fact, Freemasonry refuses to acknowledge any Redeemer except a democratic liberator
of society, the Josue (Jesus) of the Old Testament,
the champion of religious enlightenment. His religion, the only true one, is limited to two tenets ;

---

[1] In fact, according to Barruel (vol ii. p. 270), any candidate admitted
by the corrupt portion of the Order of Templars was obliged to swear
belief in " a Creator who neither had died nor could die." "Receptores
dicebant illis, quos recipiebant, Christum non esse verum Deum, et
ipsum fuisse falsum ; non fuisse passum pro redemptione humani generis,
sed pro sceleribus suis."—*Dupuy,* " *Traité sur la Condemnation des
Templiers,*" p 38.

belief in an eternal and merciful God, and in a future existence. The fact of having a priesthood which is a class apart involves the slavery of the rest of mankind; on this account it must be done away with, and he who overthrows it is a true philanthropist and faithful follower of Josue, who did so much in his day, besides conferring on his people the blessing of a liberal and moderate code of laws. Thus, according to these views, Liberty and Equality constitute the only real and practical religion, and to struggle against despots, aristocrats, and the clergy, is the lifelong vocation of a true son of the Craft. The opening formula of even the most unimportant document is a tacit protest against the " absurd popish invention of a Trinity." Finally, the most sacred mystery of the Christian religion, the Holy Eucharist, is shamelessly travestied and made to figure in a socialistic comedy, as " the bread of misery and oppression," that oppression under which the world at large lies groaning, and on its distribution in the Lodges, is accompanied by the portentous words, " This year you still sigh in the Babylon of political, social, and religious slavery, but next year you shall be free men," free from the yoke of religion above all.[1]   Therefore war with Rome, war with the knavish Pope, war against his spiritual ascendency and fantastic dominion; and

---

[1] The banquet of the Rosicrucians is indeed called the Mystic Supper, their glasses being termed chalices, instead of " cannons," as is usual in the three lower and less important grades.—*Thuileur*, p. 68.   For a description of the Mystic Supper, see " La Franc-maçonnerie dans l'état,"

war, too, with all whose beliefs are not limited to faith
in the Josue of Masonic legends, the social and religious liberator of mankind.

II. To England appertains the honour of giving
birth to Deism, and bestowing it as a birthday gift on
the Secret Society, to celebrate its entrance, in 1717,
upon a new stage of its existence, the three persons
chiefly concerned in the transaction being out-and-out
Deists. This shallowest of all so-called systems of
philosophy only recognises the existence of such objects
as can be seen and handled; it is a fungus growing upon
the decaying trunk of Protestantism, and refuses absolutely to acknowledge whatever is supernatural and
immaterial. This threadbare natural religion, out of
which every man is at liberty to fashion garments
according to his own pattern, recognises at most a
higher Being, who has made the visible world, or who,
as Architect of the universe, has constructed the things
we see around us out of pre-existing matter ; who, His
work once finished, troubles Himself no more about
man and his doings ; who least of all has given to the
world a positive revelation of His being and His will.
Here, in short, we have the " Jehovah " of the Rosicrucians, the " Great Architect " of all lower grades.
It is notorious with what avidity these notions were
caught up by empty heads in England, France, and

p. 24. The author, however, appears not to have had access to any
very lengthy accounts, so that he failed to discover the socialist bearing
of the whole affair. He also gives the words of distribution in an
incomplete form.

Germany, and with what astounding rapidity they spread, both within and without the Lodges, assuming importance, finally, under the pretentious name of Rationalism. This was for many years the weapon employed by the Secret Society in its war against the God of revelation, one which, even in the present day, it continues to turn against all who see in the truths of the faith anything more than a mass of wax which every man may mould according to his own particular fancy. We have already brought so much evidence to bear on this subject in the former part of this work, that we may content ourselves here with showing how the Secret Society has made use of Deism in its antitheistic warfare, and how it still continues to do so. For this purpose we shall give copious extracts from a publication originally written in High German, of which a Dutch translation appeared in Amsterdam in 1792; a work which is all the more worthy of credence, as it is supported by documentary evidence.[1] It asserts that the whole plan of the enemy may be summed up in the following propositions:—

"1. Superstition (*i e.*, Christianity and the law of

---

[1] The title in full is as follows ⌐—"*Ernstige en trouwhartige Waar-schuwing aan de Grooten dezer wereld, voor het gevaar van eenen geheelen ondergang, waarmede de troonen, de staten en het Christendom bedreigd worden; met bewijzen en oorkonden. Amsterdam. W Brave*, 1792. Reprinted at the Hague in 1826." According to the opinion expressed by the Dutch translator, the author of this work, which at the time created a great sensation, was a Professor Hoffmann, of Vienna, editor of the *Wiener Zeitschrift.*

Moses) has hitherto been the mainstay of the tyranny and deception by means of which princes and priests have drawn mankind into their net. Fear of a future life, of an eternity of punishment, had been a motive powerful enough to hold weak minds bowed down under the load of prejudices sucked in with their mother's milk, and to enervate the boldest spirits, rendering them incapable of any great action. This is the evil of Christianity, that it enslaves minds to such a point that they are willing to endure any present suffering, with the consoling hope of a life to come. On this account it becomes indispensable to undermine the pillar which bears up such a structure of superstition; but as the number of those who yet fondly cling to the pious fictions of their childhood is very large, and the roots of political and civil institutions strike deep in the national soil, it is necessary to go cautiously to work. Here philosophy may take a useful hint from Nature. As man is chiefly worked on through his passions, these must be excited, and Christianity must be made ridiculous, ere the dominion of Faith can be overthrown in the heart.

"2. To effect this, a literary association must be formed, to promote the circulation of our writings, and suppress, as far as possible, those of our opponents.

"3. For this end we must contrive to have in our pay the publishers of the leading literary journals of the day, in order that they may turn into ridicule and heap contempt on everything written in a contrary interest to our own.

" 4. ' He that is not with us, is against us.'   Therefore we may persecute, calumniate, and tread down such a one without scruple ; individuals like this are noxious insects, which one shakes from the blossoming tree, and crushes beneath one's foot.

" 5. Very few can bear to be made to look ridiculous ; let ridicule, therefore, be the weapon employed against persons who, though by no means devoid of sense, show themselves hostile to our schemes.

" 6. In order the more quickly to attain our end, the middle classes of society must be thoroughly imbued with our principles ; the lower orders and the mass of the population are of little importance, as they may easily be moulded to our will.   The middle classes are the principal supporters of the Government ; to gain them we must work on their passions, and, above all, bring up the rising generation in our ideas, as in a few years they will be in their turn masters of the situation.

" 7. Licence in morals will be the best means of enabling us to provide ourselves with patrons at court, persons who are nevertheless totally ignorant of the importance of our cause.   It will suffice for our purpose if we make them absolutely indifferent to the Christian religion.   They are for the most part careless enough without us.

" 8. If our aims are to be pursued with vigour, it is of absolute necessity to regard as enemies of enlightenment and of philosophy all those who cling in any way to religious or civil prejudices, and exhibit this attachment in their writings. They must be viewed as beings whose influence is highly prejudicial to the human race, and a great obstacle to its well-being and progress. On this account it becomes the duty of each one of us to impede their action in all matters of consequence, and to seize the first suitable opportunity which may present itself of putting them entirely *hors du combat.*

"9. We must ever be on the watch to make all changes in the State serve our own ends; political parties, cabals, brotherhoods, and unions—in short, everything that affords an opportunity of creating disturbances must be an instrument in our hands. For it is only on the ruins of society as it exists at present that we can hope to erect a solid structure on the natural system, and ensure to the worshippers of nature the free exercise of their rights."

It is easy to see that this plan is a *facsimile* of the work which the Secret Society had not merely sketched out, but actually begùn, in concert with the so-called "philosophers" of France. Animated by a like spirit, and employing the same tools as these latter, Freemasons had for some time past been actively at work at the Courts of Berlin, Weimar, and Vienna, on the banks of the Rhine and the Iser, and they had succeeded in undermining the Christianity of the influential classes. Their efforts were, indeed, attended with less success on the right bank of the

Rhine than had been the case on the left; but for
this the Brethren themselves were not to blame,
the tenacious conservation of the German mind, and
the dread excited by the recent horrors enacted in
France, proving formidable opponents to struggle
against. Another plan was therefore adopted, that
of employing science as a means—slower, it is true,
but not less sure—of combating revelation, whereby,
through the strong materialistic and naturalistic
tone imparted to education, a race of men should
be trained up whose sight would be strong enough
to stand the broad daylight of religious Nihilism.
Now hatred of Ultramontanes and of orthodox
Catholics is openly preached on the housetops,
and the faithful are even expected to be grateful for
the exhibition of such pious zeal. But it is all very
well to proclaim a thousand times over on the
public stage "liberty of conscience and freedom for
every shade of opinion and religious persuasion, for
every upward tendency and higher aspiration of the
human heart." Behind the scenes there lurks the
persecuting Nero, armed with exceptional laws, with
outlawry and exile, determined to know no rest until
the very name of Nazarean is obliterated. Liberalism, the exoteric teaching of this dark league, is, in
its very essence, persecuting and intolerant; any
union with it is a preposterous idea, a thing impossible. For forty years the Catholics of Belgium
have had to expiate bitterly their ill-advised "Union"
of the year 1830; and they daily gain a stronger

practical conviction of the truth of the assertion we have just made.

The keynote of Freemasonry is, War to the death against all revelation. As far back as the end of the preceding century it expressed itself in these terms:[1]—" Belief in revelation is a malady to which weak and pious minds are very subject; it is an infectious epidemic, employed ever since the world began, to effect the destruction of human liberty; it is alike incompatible with sound reason and true freedom; it is the parent of fanaticism and supersti-tion." " The laws of the Mosaic and Christian religions are the contemptible inventions of petty minds bent on deceiving others; they are the most extravagant aberrations of the human intellect." " The selfishness of priests, and the despotism of the great, have for centuries upheld this system (of Christianity), since it enabled them to rule mankind with a rod of iron by means of its rigid code of morality, and to confirm their power over weak minds by means of certain oracular utterances, in reality the product of their own invention, but palmed off on the world as the words of revelation."

In reading these strange effusions of the Deistic mind, we must not overlook the fact that political re-volution is the object ever kept in view by those who uttered them, an object to the attainment of which the overthrow of religion is nothing but a necessary preliminary. In the present day Freemasons pursue

[1] *Waarschuwing,* vol. xi., Nos. 1, 2, 8.

precisely similar aims; now, however, the Brethren are cautious and prudent, as they were in the early years of the reign of the Emperor Joseph II.; that is to say, they speak only of the future triumph of an odious unbelief, and wisely abstain from all mention of political intentions.

The following remarks are taken from the *Latomia*, vol. iv., and form the introduction to a review of the "Kirchenlehre und Ketzerglaube" of Dr A. Drechsler, a work favourably commented on and recommended to the perusal of Freemasons :—" Considered in its religious aspect, Freemasonry forms a whole of which Protestantism is but the half; this latter regards the substance of religion as a direct communication from God to man, and permits a partial use of reason, in so far as it is necessary to mould this extravagant compound into some sort of shape. According to Freemasonry, on the other hand, it belongs to reason to create not the form alone, but also the substance, of religion. Protestantism must either return to Catholicism and proceed onward till it reaches the domain of Freemasonry, or voluntarily continue to occupy a half-way position between the two; because reason will not for ever content itself with labouring to give an appearance of reason to facts which are above reason: it must seek in different ways to bring the material supplied to it into union with its own spirit, until, as the final result of these efforts, it arrive at the clear and full conviction of the utter futility of all such attempts at union. At this point it asserts another right indisputably its own ; it rejects the stubborn material forced upon its acceptance, and boldly claims to choose for itself, and if need be, to create what is most suitable to its purpose. This gives a clue to the phenomena at present exhibited by Protestant religious life, especially in England, to the allegorical meaning attached to Christian history, to the vague apprehension of Christian dogma. The last efforts made to uphold ecclesiastical Christianity occasioned its complete expulsion from the realm of reason, for they proved but too plainly that all negotiations of peace must result in failure. Human reason became aware of the irreconcilable enmity existing between its own teachings and the dogmas of the Church. . . . Finally, all educated minds felt the need of a brief summary of that which mankind possesses in the Church, and that which is on the other hand offered to it by natural religion."

The upshot of these quotations is exactly the same as that of preceding ones. Christianity, being absolutely incompatible with reason, may perhaps be tolerated for a while as a toy for fools to play with, but it must on no account be allowed to lay down laws for the regulation of public life ; this would be an outrage on human reason, which occupies a position of irreconcilable hostility to the teaching of the Church. This course of action does, it is true, involve the setting aside of a positive right ; for the safety of the Christian Church is guaranteed by most solemn treaties; but above the positive right stands the natural one, *i.e.*, the right of mankind to unlimited progress; and to this Christianity opposes an obstacle. It remains then to reduce this latter to a condition in which it must be content to live on sufferance. This is the path in which all modern ideas move, both of writers and politicians, exactly as they did at the time of the first French Revolution, and the period which preceded it. The upholders of Christianity form nowadays a mere party in the State—the minority, in fact, although the great mass of the people still clings with tenacity to the Christian faith.

Deism, as professed by Freemasonry, recognises no eternity. In order to defend itself against the attacks of Dr Eckert, a pamphlet was published at Leipzic in 1865, entitled, " The Attitude of Freemasonry in the Present Day, a history and disclosure of the aims of the Craft, together with an answer to the most recent charges brought against it, by E. G. Eckert, D.D.L., Dresden." Notwithstanding all his prudence, the following admission escaped the pen of the advocate :—" Freemasonry teaches nothing impossible; its secret consists in teaching man to discern realities. It instructs him in the art of being good without reference to heaven or hell, independent of the motives of hope and fear. The Mason does not await a future life to receive his reward ; he has it here, and is content."

What then can be said to the decree of the Grand

Orient of Paris, which, in 1865, after due revision of its statutes, acknowledged the existence of a God, and of an endless life ? It must be pronounced a disgusting piece of hypocrisy, intended to beguile the world of the "profane." That social chaos inevitably follows on the denial of a future life, is testified by the declarations made in the Paris Convention of 1795, immediately after the fall of Robespierre, by Deputy Lecointre. "A people," he says, "which is without religion, without form of worship, without churches, or any public divine service, is also without country and without national customs, and prepares future slavery for itself. Contempt for religion has been the agent in bringing ruin upon this great empire; and a similar fate is in store for every nation whose code of laws is not based on the immutable foundation of morality and religion."

III. We are, however, very far from intending to imply that Freemasons have any religious tenets peculiarly their own, for what they desire to accomplish is rather the overthrow of all religion, and every form of positive belief. In this war of extermination they make use of any destructive theory which may present itself, not excepting Pantheism ; in fact, this latter is an auxiliary all the more welcome, because it of all others is the farthest removed from revealed Christianity. Besides, the Craft recognises in Pantheism an old and valued friend, to whom both history and natural religion show her to be nearly related. She ʰᵉrself asserts her connection with the pantheistic Manicheism of the East ; and it was from the study of Arabian disciples of Aristotle that Amalrich of Bena learnt his Pantheism. Much the same thing, too, may be said of the Cathari, the Brethren and Sisters of the Free Spirit, the Albigenses, and even the corrupt portion of the Order of Templars. Almost all the sects of the Middle Ages had a strong pantheistic colouring, and developed into religious and democratic agitators of the very worst description ; and it is precisely from these that the Craft claims genealogical descent, as with these it is historically connected.

It is, moreover, a fact worthy of notice, that Spinoza, the father of modern Pantheism, stood in secret relation to many " Friends," and that all his literary efforts were directed to the end of obtaining acceptance for the opinions of Freemasons throughout the educated world. A few words respecting this remarkable man may well find a place here. Baruch or Benedict Spinoza was born on November 23, 1632, at Amsterdam. His parents were Portuguese Jews, and destined their son to become a Rabbi. He applied himself early to the study of the Bible and the Talmud ; his intellectual gifts, añd the remarkable progress he made, excited the admiration of his teachers, although his critical remarks, and the sceptical turn of his mind, aroused their worst misgivings, and led them to threaten him with expulsion from the Synagogue. The ambitious young man then took up

with Calvinism, and although at heart an unbeliever
in everything supernatural, he made outward profession of belief in the gospel, by frequenting Calvinist
and Arminian places of worship. He received instruction in Latin and Greek from a German physi-
cian named Van den Ende, an avowed atheist, who
met his death in 1674, at the hands of the common
hangman, for having taken part in a conspiracy.
The Jews, fearing Spinoza might prove a dangerous antagonist, sought to win him back to their
Synagogue by means of bribery ; and when this
attempt failed, they endeavoured to rid themselves
of him altogether, one of his own nation actually
stabbing him with a knife as he was in the act
of leaving the theatre. Through the influence of
the Rabbis, he was, in 1655, formally expelled from
the Synagogue, and at the same time banished
from Amsterdam. From that time he lived mostly
in the country ; and when, in 1670, he removed to
the Hague, he rarely during the remainder of his
life appeared out of doors. On February 21, 1677, he
died of consumption, at the age of forty-five years.
His "Friends" were numerous, and ever ready to
give him a helping-hand. Only four years before
his death, the Elector-Palatine Charles Louis nominated him to the Professor's Chair of Philosophy at
Heidelberg ; but this post he declined, on the plea
of inability to comply with the condition imposed,
namely, "that he should never make any use of
philosophy which might lead to the overthrow of

existing systems of religion." This little man, of
dark and sallow countenance and repulsive features,
chiefly confined his studies to theology, mathe-
matics, physics, and philosophy. The whole gist of
his teaching may be stated in these propositions:—
All that exists, God and the world, forms but one
substance, which is God, possessed of two attributes,
thought (spirit) and extension (matter); from the
Universal Substance of producing nature (*natura natu-
rans*) spring the various forms of existence, individual
things, or produced nature (*natura naturata*). Consequently, he denied the personality of God, His
spiritual and supernatural being, the creation of the
world,[1] human freedom, the distinction between good
and evil. Miracles, according to Spinoza's theory, are
an absolute impossibility, since he proposes as the
object of religion, no other than the one proposed in
all ages by Freemasonry—the introduction of a code
of morality regulated by reason. His views of history
are as materialistic as his whole system; they all
hinge upon fatalism, and may be considered as having set the fashion for the realistic mode of writing
history so prevalent at the present day. In regard to
persecution, Spinoza was not a whit behind the Craft,
of whose teaching he was the principal advocate in
modern times. The design of all his studies was to
bring about the overthrow of revealed religion by

---

[1] The incarnation of God appeared to him a thing as repugnant to
common sense as to say that the circle has assumed the nature of a
square.

means of science, the persecution of dogmatic religion being his idea of religious liberty. His "Tractatus theologico-politicus"[1] contains the following proposi-tions, so thoroughly in harmony with the spirit of Free-masonry. The aim of religion, he avers, is obedience (avoiding as yet the use of the word "tyranny"); that of philosophy is truth: between these two there can exist, once and for ever, no connection and no relation-ship; true philosophical religion contains everything which would be left of positive religion, were it stripped altogether of the supernatural element; it needs no faith in history and in miracles for its support, no ceremonies and no future reward, since it is its own reward. Hence it follows that religion is intended for the great mass of mankind, as it is undeniable that the number must always be small of those who, directed by reason, practise virtue for its own sake. At the end of his treatise Spinoza expresses an idea of the Church's rights, which recalls the times of Nero. "Those invested with supreme command in the State have the right to do all which they have the power to do." In other words, "might before right." Here

---

[1] This was written as far back as the year 1663, and was at first privately circulated amongst his friends; but later on, in 1670, it was published anonymously, Hamburg being given as the place where it was printed, instead of Amsterdam. Immediately on its appearance, the work was proscribed by the Dutch Government, but it reappeared, and was widely circulated under an altered title in Holland, England, Germany, France, Switzerland, and elsewhere—proof enough that other agencies were at work in the matter. For Spinoza's life, doctrines, and writings, see Feller, "Biographie universelle. Wetzer-Welte, Kirchen-lexicon," under *Spinoza*.

we have the terrible imperial doctrine of State supremacy, which, originating with the Cæsars, was later on dressed up by Hegel in a scientific garb, and has for the last two centuries made the life of the Church more and more to resemble a lingering martyrdom, while now it fills anew the hearts of all true Christians with anxious apprehension. These doctrines are the more closely followed by members of the Craft as they find the influence they possess gradually increasing. To these propositions Spinoza appends the following conclusions :—Those who are invested with authority in the State are also empowered to determine what is good and right for the State, to expound Holy Scripture according to their own discretion, and, above all, to order and arrange the externals of divine worship, and the observances of religion, in the way they shall deem most conducive to the public good. For the philosopher, on the contrary, Spinoza claims liberty " to hold what opinions he pleases, and to express those opinions, provided always that he does not assume a hostile attitude towards anything established by law, or encourage political insubordination." This is as much as to say, " Freedom for ourselves ; slavery for our opponents."

Thus, with the assistance of his allies, this Jew of Amsterdam became the father of popular philosophic Rationalism, and especially of modern Pantheism, down to the time of Ed. V. Hartmann, the philosopher of the Unknown. The inevitable consequence of this line of argument is to give the foremost place amongst all classes of human knowledge to natural science, and at the same time to supply a formidable weapon for the attack on positive religion. His theories of Church policy constitute the ideal of all religious persecutors, whether secret or open ; the amicable relation formerly existing between Church and State, which was the bulwark of society and of good manners, is now no more, and the powers of darkness are incessantly at their work of devastation, striving to bring about that last and most terrible convulsion which, like a second deluge, is to overwhelm the whole human race.

In its true nature, Freemasonry has ever been pantheistic.[1] The so-called Natural Religion and Worship of Nature which it professes prove this, and numerous documents may be found to bear testimony to the fact. We will quote a few of these.

The *Latomia*, a Masonic periodical published quarterly at Leipsic, speaks as follows (vol. v., p. 35) :— " Egypt is to be regarded as the cradle of all our learning, especially as being the land where Craftsmen were first initiated into the Secret Society as it then existed, into the Corporation or Fraternity of Masons. Throughout the whole of Asia Busiris the sun-god was adored under the name of Mythras and the

---

[1] We would remind the reader of the opinions expressed by Juge, already cited in our fourth division, under No 4, which bear a close affinity to those of Spinoza, and met with the approval of the whole body of Freemasons. See p 65 *seq*.

emblem of fire ; the temples of the Freemason are likewise enlightened by the presence of that life-giving symbol !" Thus, among the Freemasons, Heliogabalus, one of the maddest of the Roman emperors, might find a large number of pious scholars, like himself, priests and servants of the sun.

In the *Freemasons' Journal* of Vienna, "for private circulation amongst the Brethren" (vol. xi. 3, p. 21), the Speaker of the Lodge thus addresses his hearers— "In early times the Samothracians worshipped only the heaven and the earth, since Nature was to them father and mother, and there were then no priests and despots, who by means of craft and force, super-stition and oppression, mental and physical coercion, led them to disown, and even to hate, their Divine Creator." In harmony with this pantheistic wor-ship of Nature is the Masonic practice of not merely dating from the Creation of the World, but making the year begin on June 24th, the summer solstice.

In the *Astræa*, the Freemasons' Pocket-book, 1837, by Sydow, we read—" The ancient peoples of the East worshipped the sun under the figure of some deity ; its arrival at the end of its annual course, the winter solstice, was bewailed by the Egyptians as the death of Busiris ; amongst the Ethiopians it was represented by Memnon, amongst the Persians by Mythras, amongst the Greeks by Bacchus, amongst the Babylonians by Adonis, amongst other nations by Atis. . . . . In this manner all the various nations

celebrated the death and resurrection of their respec-
tive deities, who were, in fact, nothing else but imper-
sonifications of the sun. The myth of Adon-Hiram
must be regarded as one of the oldest representations
of the history of the sun-god, as introduced into the
temples of the Masons, and ever since preserved by
them in the original form." Here we once more
find the Pantheism of the Manicheans under a new
aspect.

But even this heathenish worship of Nature is
impiously dressed up in, and disguised by names
borrowed from, Christianity. When the Brethren dedicated their Lodge in Vienna to St Joseph, no one was
further from their mind than the holy foster-father of
the Saviour. They probably thought of the Spring
Equinox, or, possibly, of their first patron, the
Emperor Joseph II. For them the festival of St John
the Baptist means the time when the sun reaches its
meridian, the full plenitude of its power to enlighten
and fructify. It is therefore a joyous festival for the
Craft, as all the dwellers on the Rhine between
Cologne and Coblentz can testify, when, on the re-
currence of this day, the Freemasons' steamboat
glides gaily by, with colours flying. The day of St
John the Evangelist, December 27, is for them, on
the contrary, a day of mourning, on account of the
diminution of the sun's light and productive power,
as it formerly was for the Phœnicians, who then com-
memorated the death and resurrection of their god
Adonis. If the Brethren in bygone times called

themselves Knights of St John, they did not know which of the two saints was their patron, but merely employed this holy name to screen themselves from the espionage and persecution of the outside world.[1]

The Leipzic Freemasons' paper, "for private circulation" (year 1850, No. 18, p. 137), gives a sketch of the proceedings on occasion of the winter solstice and new birth of light (Dec. 29, 1849) in the Lodge of True Friends of Unity at Brussels. The orator spoke as follows:—

"Freemasonry recognises only four principal feasts, the two equinoxes and the summer and winter solstices, *i.e.*, the days which mark the divisions of time, and portion out the year into four almost equal periods. This determination is the result of long thought and deliberate conviction ; for our festivals are not arbitrarily fixed by man, nor therefore liable to be altered and moved by him at his pleasure. No, my Brethren, our festivals are marked out in the heavens, they are indicated to us by the changing position of our earth in regard to the sun. The time has now come round when the brilliant orb which quickens all things is about to enter once more on his

---

[1] See Eckert, "Die Frage," &c , p 35. Tertullian writes thus of the ancient pagans ("De Præscript ," c 40).—"Diabolus ipsas quoque res divinorum Sacramentorum in idolorum mysteriis æmulatur. Tingit et ipse quosdam utique credentes. Expiationem delictorum repromittit et sic adhuc initiat. . . . . Signat illic in frontibus milites suos. ˙Celebrat panis oblationem. Quid? Quod et summum pontificem in unis nuptiis statuit."

resplendent and royal course. It is Christmas-time! Glory to the great Architect of the Universe!· All that lives, all that breathes, is bestirring itself anew, and preparing to shake off its temporary lethargy, its icebound sleep. Ought not grateful emotions to fill every heart at such a season, for, of all the festivals we celebrate, this is the greatest. On this day light is born again into the world!" . . . . In conclusion, I would point out to you that the striking allegory of the two-headed Janus,[1] represented to us by the two Johns, whose festivals coincide exactly with the times of the summer and winter solstice, with the birth and the victory of heaven's light—that this allegory, I say, offers to the philosopher, even more than to the *savant*, an inexhaustible field for diligent research." The writer adds in his report that this piece of magnificent rhetoric was received with repeated out-bursts of applause, and that the orator was warmly complimented upon it by the Most Worshipful Master in person.

We find the Apostle St Paul, in his Epistle to the Romans, severely rebuking the heathens of old, and declaring them to be inexcusable, because, notwith-standing the many natural aids they possessed to attain to the knowledge of God, they turned aside from Him, their supreme and only Lord, choosing rather to worship creatures. And from this fact we may form some conception of what must be the immense weight of guilt attaching to an association

---

[1] This name of Janus has also been employed by a modern heretic.

which, standing as it does in the broad noonday of
Christian revelation, voluntarily closes its eyes to the
truth, strives, moreover, to involve the whole world in
its conscious and deliberate apostasy from the faith
of the only-begotten Son of God, and spares no effort
of human cunning to beguile the minds of men and
gain multitudes of adherents. This system of modern
Paganism must of necessity contain within itself a
neverfailing spring of hatred to Christian truth.[1]   A
certain vague agitation may be remarked stirring in
all classes of society, which portends a future and
frightful struggle between Ormuzd and Ariman, between light and darkness. The worst of it is, that
those in whose hands power rests are either miserably
enslaved and bound with a thousand chains, or are in
abject fear of a monster far less formidable in reality
than in appearance. So the one bold stroke which
alone could promise deliverance is never dealt, and
nations, good and honest at heart, go like sheep to
the slaughter.   Held in an iron grasp from which
they cannot escape, they writhe in a long and painful
death-struggle, one revolutionary paroxysm succeeding another while they wearily and anxiously look
for a second deliverer who shall break the magic`
spell, and reinstate Christendom in the possession of
her rights.

---

[1] The sacred mysteries of Christianity were termed "pagan phan-
tasmagoria" by the Freemason Faider, speaking in the Lodge of
Fidelity at Ghent, on July 2, 1846.   See "La Franc-maçonnerie dans
l'état," p. 26.

IV. From the doctrines of Pantheism and the external ceremonies of an Oriental worship of the sun and of nature, Freemasonry enters upon the fourth and worst stage of its conflict with God, *i.e.*, the antitheistic Worship of Humanity, which places man himself upon the throne of God. For if God be nature, and nature God, the highest thing in nature, Man, must consequently be the most perfect embodiment of the Divinity, must be himself God.

Every one of the above-named anti-religious systems has its own motto. Jewish Antitheism speaks incessantly of "Toleration," which is the watchword of the Craft while in its infancy; Deism of "Enlightenment," the watchword of the Craft when it has obtained open recognition; Pantheism of "Perpetual progress," the watchword of the Craft when it begins to rule; Humanism of the "Worship of humanity," the watchword of the Craft when it wields the rod of the tyrant. All these words are in their general meaning unexceptionable, and are therefore repeated by a simple-minded and unsuspecting public, which looks on them as something sacred. To the initiated only is revealed their true and full import. The pleasing word "Humanism," forms no exception. By the word *humanitas* the old Romans understood human nature at its best, advanced civilisation, polish and refinement of mind and heart; more particularly that general cultivation which every man ought to acquire before entering upon any course of professional study. Where can the nation or individual be found

that would not fain be considered civilised? In the
word itself no harm can be found; but thanks to the
second meaning attached to it by Masonic ingenuity,
the innocent exterior conceals a deadly poison,
which, when circulating in the veins, stimulates man
to open rebellion against God, and incites him to
utter with his mouth the arrogant words of Lucifer—
" I will ascend into heaven, I will exalt my throne
above the stars of God: I will sit in the mountain
of the covenant, I will ascend above the height of
the clouds; I will be like the Most High " (Isa. xiv.
13, 14); or rather, I will myself be the Most High.
The following lines are in the same strain:—

> " When corrupted creeds decay
>   And sunken nations pass away,
>   Arise, mankind, now dawns the day."

In the pantheistic sense, man is the highest development of the all-pervading Divinity; in him that
stage is reached in which matter becomes spiritual in
its nature, and is elevated to a consciousness of its
personal identity. Man, then, is a sovereign monarch; he is responsible to no one but himself for his
actions; he is himself his own master. At most, as
member of a body politic, he is bound to conform to
those laws which are the expression of the general
will, and in case of any infringement of them, to bear
in silence the punishment due to him. As the highest
embodiment of the divine element, he contains within
himself the germ of boundless progress.

But the God of Christianity is, on the other hand, exalted far above Nature, and infinitely removed from the sphere of things created; by one word of His mouth He called all things into being; He created us men, and breathed into our bodies an immortal soul. He is our supreme Lord, Lord of body and soul, Lord in time and eternity. As our great Lawgiver, He lays upon us laws which cannot be transgressed with impunity, whilst leaving us at liberty to exercise free-will; by a good use of this free-will man may merit an eternal reward, but for him whose will rebels against that of his Maker an eternity of punishment is reserved. Furthermore, He has given us revelation to be an infallible judge in matters of faith, and upon our obedience to the decisions of this judge, He has made our eternal happiness to depend.

Against this God of Christianity the occult teaching of the Craft, acknowledging as it does no higher being than man himself, rises up in the bitterest animosity, and declaims against Him as an usurper from whose yoke man must free himself. This enables us to understand how a Freemason could utter words so unspeakably blasphemous as these—"Dieu c'est le mal;" how it was possible for the *Libertaire* to make use of the terms we have already quoted, and say that humanity must not allow itself to be checked in its career of endless progress by those barriers "on which the murderers of their kind have scrawled the name of God in letters of blood and mud."

P

This last phase of antitheism made a dramatic and legalised *début* on the public stage in the days when Freemasonry celebrated its triumph.   In 1793 belief in God was a crime prohibited in France under pain of death, and the worship of reason was set up as the national *cultus*.   On November 10th of the same year a prostitute might be seen in Paris exalted upon a triumphal car, a crucifix placed beneath her feet, conducted by an escort of statesmen and philosophers to the Cathedral of Notre Dame, there to be raised upon an altar, while incense was burnt and songs were sung in her honour.   A like disgraceful scene was also enacted in other French towns.   This deification of man with all that oppresses and degrades those who are unregenerate ; this blasphemous social apostasy from God and from virtue; this recalling of the wildest times of Paganism, in which man is his own deity, was not an act perpetrated in a moment of passing intoxication, but a work planned long ago, and carried into execution when a suitable moment came.   Freemasonry, the antipodes of Christianity, will give itself no rest until its theories have been once more put into practice, and spread over the face of the whole earth.

Here, then, we have the meaning of the terms " Humanitas," the " Worship of humanity," " Social civilisation," " Political progress," " Ennobled human nature," " Intellectual culture ;" expressions daily made use of by the assailants of the Church as their war cry, when opposing the cross of Jesus Christ.   We have

already quoted so many passages from 'Masonic publications, exposing their sinister designs, that a few
only can be introduced here; they will, however,
amply suffice to prove the truth of our allegation.[1]

In the Freemasons' periodical, " for circulation
amongst the Brethren " (Altenburg, 1823, vol. i. No. 1,
p. 95 *seq.*), we find the following passage treating of
the true object of the worship of the Craft:—" The
idea of religion indirectly includes all men as men,
but in order to comprehend this aright, a certain
degree of cultivation is necessary, and unfortunately
the over-weening egoism of the educated classes
prevents their taking in so sublime a conception of
mankind. For this reason our temples consecrated
to the worship of humanity" (*i.e.*, the Lodges of the
higher grades) " can as yet be opened to only a few.
We should indeed expose ourselves to a charge of
idolatry were we to attempt to personify the moral
idea of humanity in the way in which the Divinity is
usually personified (!) . . . . On this account, therefore, it is advisable not to reveal the *cultus* of humanity to the eyes of the uninitiated, until at length the
time shall come, when from east to west, from north
to south, this lofty conception of humanity shall find a
place in every breast, this worship alone shall prevail,
and all mankind be gathered into one fold and one
family."

Since man is God, it follows that all which is

[1] We refer any one desirous of making himself acquainted with the
whole heathenish scheme to Eckert, " Die Frage," &c., pp. 22, 62.

human is divine, and the more intrinsically human the more essentially divine. This maxim is the Very soul of Masonic teaching, the "eritis sicut Dii" of the serpent in paradise, the *ignis fatuus* appearing under a thousand varying hues in the mythology of the ancients, in the mysterious rites of Secret Societies, in the Lodges of the Craft, and leading astray many who are made to believe that it is the brightest flame of heavenly wisdom. This is what self-knowledge, a word so suggestive of virtue, is intended to signify when uttered in the hearing of the Apprentice on his first "admission to the light." Brother N. J. Mouthaan says plainly, "We must live as gods. Is this a highflown hyperbole, a poetical exaggeration utterly devoid of truth? . . . . The spirit which animates us is an eternal spirit; it knows no division of time or individual existence. A sacred unity per-vades and governs the wide firmament of heaven; it is our one calling, our one duty, our one God. Yes we are God! we ourselves are God. My brethren, do we understand this aright? Man is akin to God; in man dwells the same spirit as in God, this spirit is indivisible. Looking upon our spiritual nature, we men may be said to form part of the great whole, the great Being of God. The myths and legends, the beliefs of benighted nations, will all one day disappear before the consciousness that man himself is God. And why is mankind so slow to receive this truth? why are so many impediments placed in its way, so many pitfalls dug in its path? Simply because man,

a creature of sense, has no desire, no ambition, to
subdue his human nature, and obtain the mastery
over his body. He who is conscious of his own
divinity cannot breathe in this lower and stifling
atmosphere, which is death to the soul. The man
who feels himself to be God must live a life to which
death cannot have access."[1]

According to these views Christianity and the
Christian state are outposts of the enemy which are
already carried. The collective voice of the State
must henceforth decide all questions of truth, since
in it alone all power rests. But it is needful to advance cautiously, and step by step, because premature
action might rouse the confessors of Christianity to
a desperate conflict, and inaugurate a most undesir-
able series of martyrdoms. Hence the first thing is to
erect *a godless state*, separation between Church and
State being already presupposed, or, what is worst of
all, the voice of the Church being completely silenced.
Thus Humanism remains master of the situation, and
can legislate as it pleases ; and it will not fail to create
a state hostile to God. Any one who appeals to a
superior divine authority is guilty of treason against
all that is highest and most God-like on earth, for *the*

[1] *"Naa een werknur in 't Middenvertrek, Losse Bladzijde, Zaarboekje
voor Nederlandsche Vrijmetselaren,"* 5872, p. 187 *seq.* Innumerable
passages of a similar description might be quoted from German poetic
literature. One finds traces of these opinions everywhere, from 1790
to the first years of the present century. In 1800 the fruit appears to
have been considered ripe for gathering, as is shown by the almanacs
which were then published in Weimar, Berlin, and Leipzic.

State itself is God. Of course, where this system prevails, no time-honoured historical rights, if obnoxious to the public taste of the moment, have any chance of holding their ground ; they are swept away without scruple, one single vote being sufficient to turn the scale against them. That which the State decrees is alone the highest morality. "Law is the public conscience." Of natural rights there can be no question, as these presuppose a universal code of laws binding upon mankind, and a supernatural lawgiver. Moreover, such would inconveniently limit the absolute sovereignty of man in the State; that is, the sovereignty of the nation, the will of the people forming an irresponsible tribunal before whose decisions the most ancient charters are nothing more than waste-paper.

The moral law of this system is limited to the precept, "Follow the dictates of nature," *sequere naturam.* Here again we meet with a principle to all appearance completely harmless, for certain ancient teachers of morality made the highest virtue of man to consist in following his nobler impulses ; and even the Christian is ready to own that grace does not destroy nature, but rather purifies, strengthens, and elevates it. But the Masonic worship of humanity, based as it is upon Pantheism, recognises no fundamental distinction between good and evil, regarding the practice of mortification and self-denial as contemptible folly on the part of the Christian ; for if man himself is divine, the impulses of his heart must also be divine, and what usurper shall dare to control the exercise of his prerogative in this respect? All that is human is good: so the vices and misdeeds of Jupiter, Juno, Venus, Hercules, and Mars, are to be commended !

The humanistic morality of Freemasonry is nowhere more honestly exposed than by Brother Helvetius in his two works "On Mind" ("De l'Esprit," Paris, 1793), and "On Man" ("De l'Homme," Paris, 1797).[1] Born in 1715, he showed himself throughout his whole life, and in all his writings, a worthy member of the Craft. He died at Paris in 1771, where two years later the Freemasons honoured his memory with much ceremony and solemnity. [2] We must give a short extract from the first-named of his works, in order that the reader may form some idea of the dark abyss of moral depravity into which he would allow mankind to sink.

According to Helvetius, the motive by which our

[1] His first work, "De l'Esprit," was published in 1758, and gained for its author great applause in the allied courts ; Frederick II. of Prussia, the Empress Catherine of Russia, the Duke of Brunswick, George III. of England, and others, being amongst his admirers. His second, and posthumous work, "De l'Homme," also written in the interests of the Craft, is directed from first to last against religion and the Catholic Church. According to him, the Catholic Church is a purely human institution, an instrument in the hands of those who love tyranny and seek after gain. The only true worship is that of reason, the worship of humanity ; every other is a worship of lies. The Church is prejudicial to the prosperity of nations, destructive to virtue, &c. See "Kirchen-Lexicon, Wetzer-Welte."

[2] *Jaarboekje*, 53, years 5771 and 5773.

conduct is to be regulated is one which appeals to
nature and the senses. He makes the moral character of the individual, as of the nation, to depend on
chance impressions, on education, and the forms of
government. He denies the existence of abstract
virtue and vice. What is beneficial to all in general
may be called virtue ; what is prejudicial, vice and sin.
Here the voice of Interest alone has to speak ; each
one of us falls in most promptly with those ideas
which harmonise best with his own inclination and
advantage ; errors and faults arise only from our
inability to perceive in what our true interest consists.
Individual self-sacrifice promotes the common good,
and therefore the exploits of warriors meet with
universal praise ; narrow self-seeking is injurious to
the community, and therefore cowardice is a disgrace.
In regard to mankind at large, no action can be
exclusively good or evil; the wish to benefit the whole
world is one which can never be fulfilled, because the
interest of one nation is always at variance with that of
another. Passions are only the intensified expression
of self-interest in the individual, therefore they are
never pernicious, but, on the contrary, necessary ; to
destroy them is to injure the interests of the community. The strongest passions inspire the noblest
deeds ; witness the Dutch people, who, when hatred
and revenge urged them to action, achieved great
triumphs, and made their country a powerful and
glorious name. And as sensual love is universally
acknowledged to afford happiness, purity must be

condemned as pernicious, the marriage-bond done away with, and children declared to be the property of the State.[1] That will be the best Constitution in which individual interests will be promoted, sensual gratification enhanced, and the interests of the many made identical with those of the few by means of a wisely-ordered code of laws. Such is the system of morality which humanistic teaching proposes to us.

By doctrines like these, which, far from having been disavowed by the Craft, procured for their author a solemn tribute of respect some time after his death, Helvetius cuts at the root of all morality, and proves that apostasy in a Christian people is infinitely more terrible than ancient Paganism, notwithstanding its attendant train of evils. And a creature such as he dared, in his hate of God and eagerness to serve the devil, to overwhelm the Christian Church with blasphemous accusations, charging her with excusing crimes to serve her own ends, and with making saints of those who have done most for her interests ; accusing her of requiring self-denial on the part of her followers, and thus doing violence to human nature ; of enjoining humility, and by this means encouraging meanness and idleness (for does not pride alone give energy and courage ?) ; of extolling chastity as the highest perfection, and, finally, insisting on the indis-

---

[1] Here we have the terrible doctrines of the Paris Commune of 1871, long ago prepared by the Craft, and publicly proclaimed by the apostles of its principles.

solubility of marriage; an intolerable burden though this be, to which is far preferable either marriage as in Africa, where a couple may live together for three years before making a final decision, or the other alternative of liberty to exchange wives, which furnishes a means of rewarding men who have deserved well of their country, of inciting magistrates to the exercise of justice, and soldiers to the exhibition of valour. Our author further states that the religions of Paganism were not only less pernicious in their influence than was Christianity, but that they did far more than the latter system to promote intellectual advancement and moral courage; that the saints were ignorant, whimsical, good-for-nothing beings, enjoying in their convents a monopoly of wealth; finally, that the Jesuits have ever been the most terrible scourge inflicted upon the nations of the earth.[1]   On this account it is indispensable to deprive the Church of all power, and this can only be effected by means of obstinate resistance to her encroachments, and by legislative and educational reform.

In these theories, which, unfortunately, have not been allowed to remain simple *theories*, we find the paradise awaiting the worshippers of humanity already pointed out: man's highest reward is to consist in sensual gratification; that is to say, in transgressions of the sixth commandment.   All the

---

[1] These blasphemous sentiments are found in " De l'Homme," vol. iv. pp. 38, 233, vol. ii. p 247, and in other parts of the Paris edition, from which we are quoting.

religious ceremonies of Freemasonry tend in this
same direction. The Festival of St John the Evangelist which falls in the winter, corresponds to that of
Isis and Astarte; the Feast of St John the Baptist,
kept in the summer, replaces that of Adonis and Osiris.
In the Vienna *Freemasons' Journal* (3d year, No. 4,
p. 78 *seq.*), we find the following amongst other
things :—"The name of Adonis is too sacred to be
handled by the ignorant critic; it is the link which,
if it does not immediately connect the Samothracian
mysteries with our occult rites, at least brings the two
into close proximity. To recognise in the principal
deity of classic antiquity, especially of the Samothracian mysteries, the Adon-Hiram whose death Freemasons can never sufficiently bewail, appears to me
no far-fetched idea, but one which bears a strong
stamp of truth, one which my Brethren will hail with
satisfaction, one in support of which strong proofs are
not lacking. I do not hesitate to assert that the
history of Busiris-Bacchus, including all the attendant
incidents, may be justly laid before Freemasons as a
counterpart to the sad career of our adored Adon-
Hiram; and I rejoice to be able to show you the
classic work I have discovered under that figurative
representation which was in ancient mythology an
emblem of fertility. I need not remind you that our
false ideas of modesty must all be set aside. The
desire to find truth is a noble impulse, the search after
it a sacred avocation, and ample field for this is offered
by both the mysterious rites peculiar to the Craft,

and those of the Goddess Isis, adored in our temples
as the wisest and fairest of deities. Is it not from
this that the name of Ision, applied to our temple, is
derived ? "

If we recall the feasts of Isis as celebrated in
Egypt, and the hideous orgies held in her name at
the time of Julius Cæsar and other Roman Emperors,
orgies which even at that period excited such disgust
that it was thought fit to suppress them ; if we remember the conduct of Claudius on one of those
Isis' nights, we feel that our acquaintance with these
mysteries need be carried no further.

The *Astræa*, an organ of Freemasonry (year
1848, p. 50), reports the following passage from a
festive speech delivered by a high dignitary of the
Craft, Councillor Bechstein, before an assembly of
the Brethren and Sisters on this Feast of Roses [1] (St
John Baptist's day). "To-day we meet adorned with
roses in the halls of our sacred temples " (the Lodge) ;
"adorned with roses we stand around its altar. We
wear an emblem common to all Masons, which decks
every breast and gladdens every eye, and is fraught
with a deep and hidden meaning. This is the queen
of flowers ; the rose, the emblem of beauty and of
virginal charms ; the flower of love, springing from the

[1] " The Feast of St John is the Feast of Roses of Freemasonry, the
festival of loving union " (in a sensual sense). These words are taken
from an oration delivered at Leipzic.   See *Leipzic Freemasons' Journal* for private circulation, 1855, p 227.   The *Astræa* also terms
the Festival of St John " a festival of light, love, and strength."—
Busiris' Fest.

bosom of the earth, as the goddess of beauty sprang from the foam of the sea." At the distribution of roses to the Brethren and Sisters (*Astræa*, 1842-43, p. 108), the following verses were sung, in which the word *love* is certainly used in no Christian sense :—

> " Masons, take these fragrant roses,
>   Take and bind them to your breast ;
> To some, not nearly all, is known
>   The meaning by those flowers exprest.
>
> Winning grace and fragrance sweet
>   Lie within their half-closed form,
> But the full-blown chalice offers
>   Draughts that take our hearts by storm.
>
> Innocence her modest crown,
>   Love the heart-shaped leaves declare ;
> To the sons of earth proclaiming
>   Praise of Him who made her fair.
>
> John [1] learnt of love the secret love,
>   Whilst seated at his Master's side ;
> Learnt the tender lambs to cherish,
>   Teacher wise and faithful guide.
>
> He of love the living image
>   Looks on all with kindly pleasure ;
> Speaks to all with words of mildness,
>   Wishing all to share His treasure.
>   \

---

[1] St John the Evangelist is here Isis under a Christian mask, and therefore must be taken to represent the feminine sex See Eckert, " Die Frage," &c That the Holy Redeemer should be found in such company is, we suppose, a source of edification to the simple minded Mason ; the initiated see the blasphemy, and are edified too in their way.

Brethren, if throughout creation
  Love is life and life is love ;
If to love alone is given,
  Earth below and heaven above ;

If made by love and made for love,
  Man begins his life on earth,
Following out its sacred impulse,
  Thus he learns his truest worth.

When love, the sacred spark divine,
  Brightly burns in every heart ;
When mankind wakes up rejoicing,
  And illusions all depart ;

Then the Mason's course will prove
  A track of light o'er moor and fen ;
Then is love's most glorious triumph ;
  Love shall hold high festival then."

On the opening of the Lodge for women at
Weimar, on St John's Day 1843, the Master of the
Lodge thus addressed his fair audience :—" Yes, my
dear Sisters, we are indeed your Brethren. We cherish
towards you feelings of the sincerest devotion, re-
membering, as each one of the Brothers here present
to-day cannot fail to do, the words of warning which
the Most Worshipful Master pronounces each time
that he hands the white gloves to a candidate who
seeks admission into the Craft.   Moreover, every
Mason knows the meaning of the second pair of
gloves, which the Master is bound to present ; a
meaning that principally refers to you, beloved
sisters."

Similar expressions of an erotic nature are constantly recurring at the festive gatherings of the Brethren, sometimes in the form of innuendoes, sometimes without any such disguise.

We give a literal translation of a poetic toast, taken from the Almanac for Dutch Freemasons 1872, p. 228, of which frequent mention has been made :—

> " Come, Brethren, remember your lessons of yore !
>   Up, Brothers, and shoulder your muskets once more !
>   For Wisdom first fire, whose time-honoured name
>   Is a beacon, enlightening the world with its flame !
>   Then again, fire again, salute masculine might,
>   The mainstay of life that makes all hardships light ;
>   But let the last volley surpass all the rest,
>   In honour of Beauty, that gives life its true zest."

From all this it may easily be gathered that even the motto of the three lowest grades, Wisdom, Strength, and Beauty, conceals beneath the surface a meaning which inculcates immorality.

The paragraphs we have quoted will suffice to show that the heaven of humanistic Freemasonry is a very carnal one. From first to last the Craft is true to its character of an open enemy to God and to His kingdom. Who, therefore, can wonder that the most heroic efforts of Christianity scarcely suffice to keep down the rising flood of moral depravity in education and in literature, in the theatre and the press, in public and private life ? At the same time, we see verified the apostle's words, when he says that God delivers up to shameful affections those who give themselves over to heathenism (Rom. i. 26). When man in the pride of his heart endeavours to seat himself on the throne of God, he loses by the fact of doing so the last remnants of his native nobility, and having become " like to horse and mule, which have no understanding," sinks into the quagmire of vice and degradation.

The father of lies has frequently been compared by the early theologians to an ape, who imitates the actions of God. He has, in fact, erected a temple of his own, in opposition to the divinely-founded Church, and gathered together a band of unhappy dupes as worshippers in his sanctuary. He rules with an iron sceptre, and strikes in pieces all who dare to profess allegiance to the God of love. But the work of the spirit of darkness cannot last, and this consoling conviction gives us the joyful hope that the temples of the Craft will ere long crumble, and that mankind will return to the one true and holy Church, who alone can make her children happy.

But should God in His Providence permit the schemes of darkness to triumph for awhile, and the age of martyrs to return once more, then the Church —at least if we interpret aright the signs of the times—will not fail to exhibit the same heroic courage of obedience unto death which was displayed in the first three centuries of her struggle with Paganism, a courage never equalled by warriors fighting for earthly glory alone. Those who fall in the unequal strife will, in very deed, be so many conquerors; their

blood will be a pledge of the final triumph of the
Cross. It may be that the kings of the earth will
perhaps ask, in the trouble of their heart, "Shall
our people give their money and offer their sons for
nothing better than that the will of the Craft may
be done?" In this case the day of reckoning would
not be far off. But this solution, however, is not one
which we would wish to see; rather do we send up
earnest supplications to heaven that it may please
God to open eyes that are blinded, and soften hearts
that are hardened, so that the troublous times of confusion and rebellion may cease at last, and Christ be
all in all. Then shall the words of Charlemagne be
inscribed once more in letters of gold upon our
senate-houses and churches, "Christ lives; Christ
reigns; Christ triumphs!"

CHAPTER IX.

POLITICAL AND ANTIRELIGIOUS AGITATION.

I. SPEECH of the Belgian Brother and Grand Master
VERHAEGEN, at the Festival of the Summer
Solstice, in the Grand Orient of Brussels.—
(Tracé des travaux de la grande fête solsticiale
nationale, célébrée par le Gr. Or. de Belgique ; le
24 J. du 4 M , l'an de la V. L.—vraie lumière—
5854. Bruxelles, établissement typographique
du F. Henri Samuel, 1854, pp. 13–19.)

THE following speech affords evidence of how eminently political and anti-religious are all the efforts of
the Secret Society. It is one of many delivered by
Verhaegen, who afterwards came to such an unhappy
end, and it was printed by the unanimous request of
all the Masons present, as a magnificent rhetorical
"construction." We omit the introduction as unimportant :—

". . . . Events have recently occurred in the profane
world claiming our careful attention, and our newly-
elected Grand Commander has expressed the opinion

that they are not without a special significance for
Freemasons. It cannot be that numbers of devoted,
enlightened, and patriotic men, friends of progress
and of liberty, should meet in so many places all
over the country" (in the Lodges) "without having any
definite aim, or producing any definite results. It
would indeed be no small disgrace to Freemasonry,
did it content itself with barren efforts, while the
enemy is everywhere organising his forces, while the
sinister league" (Catholic) "of ignorance and oppression spreads its nets abroad in the darkness, and adds
daily to its ominous and ever-increasing power by a
system of terrorism and selfishness. I am well aware
that on entering upon such a topic as this I shall
awaken the fears and scruples of the timid. It will
be alleged that this is perilous ground, of special
danger for Freemasons, since our statutes" (that is,
those intended for the lower grades, and for the eyes
of the outside world) "forbid us to take part in any
religious or political discussion. My Brethren, this
subject must be thoroughly sifted once for all; and
in presence of the unwelcome dilemma of either remaining completely silent, or violating its own laws,
Freemasonry must at length speak out boldly as to
the principles it means to adopt, and the course of
conduct it intends to pursue.

"First of all, we feel no hesitation in stating that
on many occasions Freemasons have overstept this
barrier, and have taken an active part in political
struggles. And since the triumph of our cause has

been joyfully hailed by the whole nation, proving
how many are found throughout the length and
breadth of the land to sympathise with the League,
who will dare to blame our conduct?[1]   To do so
would be to take a false view of history, and deny
the greatness of the service we have rendered to
the country.

"In addition to this, we are justified in saying
that Freemasonry, on the occasion referred to,
obeyed a plain call of duty, and that under similar
circumstances it would do well to pursue a like
course of action in the future.

"One remark I must be allowed to make, namely,
that the prohibition in question (concerning political
and religious agitation) is not to be gathered from
the general statutes of the Order, where not the
slightest mention of it is to be found.   If the original authors of those constitutions had intended
to make the aforesaid prohibition absolutely binding,
they would have inserted it amongst the statutes
as a positive law.   But as this restriction is only
indicated in the special rule of the Grand Orient,
it is merely to be taken as having a relative importance.   Besides, it can be at any time altered or set
aside at the request of five deputies.

"This, then, is the only obstacle which stands in
our way.   If the Grand Commander and the Grand

---

[1] Verhaegen seems here to refer particularly to the separation of
Belgium from Holland, which was planned by the Craft, and finally
carried out under its auspices.

Orient concur as to the advisability of setting aside this restriction, it would be childish on our part to attach any value to it. Thus we find ourselves at liberty, theoretically and practically, to regard this law as virtually a dead letter.

" Were Freemasonry compelled to confine its action to the limits of the narrow circle which some would prescribe for it, I ask further, Of what use would its vast organisation then be, and the extensive development to which it has attained ? If its life is to be cramped in this manner, we had better close our temples at once; outside we shall find ample means of accomplishing the miserable remnant of our task. What I say here has been repeated a hundred times over by the most enlightened, the most devoted, the most valued of our Masons. I am only their echo; I merely state aloud what each man thinks in his secret heart. Any one, therefore, who is of opinion that it is an infringement of Masonic law thus to explain away the rule in question, may, hearing this, take heart again.

" If I interrogate the past history of our Order, I cannot shut my eyes to the fact that Freemasonry has ever been a heedful watchman, guarding the Vessel of the State as it struggles in the surging sea of politics. Does it not, amid the storm and darkness, kindle the friendly beacon to show that rocks are nigh ? Does it not, when danger threatens, run up the signal of alarm ? Does not its whole history bear

the same testimony ?   Has not the Craft, in the hour
of need, ever proved a fortress and bulwark against
the encroachments of error and deceit " (*i.e.*, the
Christian Church and Christian State) "from whatever
quarter the attack may come ?   And what she has
done in the past may she not do, under like circumstances, in the future ?

" It appears to me that there can be no doubt on the
subject, and the Grand Commander and the Grand
Orient think as I do.   Brethren, the hour of danger
has now come, the enemy threatens, let us be up and
doing.   The call to arms has sounded ; do you not feel
that there is something menacing in the very air ?
The voice of conscience seems to be stifled, treachery
shows itself with unblushing effrontery, and in broad
daylight incense is burnt on the altars of those false
gods, shameful egoism and craven timidity " (the
Christian religion).   " Enemies destitute of all sense of
honour, devoured by a vulgar and insatiable ambition,
dare to dream of political omnipotence, of consciences
enslaved, of the overthrow of all our cherished rights.
Everywhere our foes are organising their forces,
everywhere they proclaim aloud that to take a part
in the politics of the day is their bounden duty, their
indisputable right.[1]   Under cover of works of bene-

---

[1] Here we have again the random cry about " political interference,"
an " endangered State," and " necessary action on the part of the
Legislation and of the police," which is raised whenever a Christian
nation asserts its constitutional rights, demands liberty of conscience
and the independence of the Church, refusing to bow beneath the
yoke which Freemasonry would lay upon it.

volence, they are arraying their hosts in order for
battle; they fight under the ægis of our own
principles, the words liberty, toleration, charity, and
all other virtues are ever on their lips. The Society
of St Vincent of Paul inscribes on its banners the
noble motto 'Humanity,' but in the mouths of its
members this word is a mockery. And in face of
these continual advances" (of the Christians), "on the
eve of a decisive struggle, are Freemasons to hide
themselves like cowards in their temples, and say,
'Let us keep quiet; we must not have anything to do
with politics?'

"No, my Brethren! let us no longer compel Freemasonry to foul her own nest, and voluntarily acqui-
esce in this unjust forfeiture of her rights.

"In consequence of this suicidal policy, which I
do not know how severely enough to condemn, we
are rushing to our own destruction, we repudiate
our whole past. Let us not bequeath to our children
the disgrace of an apostasy such as this! Let
not futurity have to blush for this our shameful
present time. Let us at any rate be assured of one
truth, that if our Order lays upon us a most
sacred and lofty mission, it cannot at the same
time deprive us of the means which are necessary
for the fulfilment of that mission. It would indeed
appear paradoxical if, while entertaining so high an
opinion of us on the one hand, it should, on the other,
show such degrading mistrust of us.

"It is now high time, my Brethren, to call out

all our resources. If you cast your eyes around,
you will see that whilst fools and knaves of every
description are hastening to make friends with the
party of reaction, the party of opposition is altogether lacking in unity. Nowhere can a central
point be found powerful enough to draw together
the men of the future, nowhere a banner under
which they can all meet, although, in spite of varying shades of opinion, they in the main love and
desire but one thing, and that thing is—progress "
(*i e.*, revolution). "Therefore, by some means or
other, let those whose intentions are good form themselves into a united body; for they are the friends
of truth, the apostles of what is good and beautiful,
they form the brilliant twin-constellation which en-
lightens the moral and material world in its twofold aspiration after knowledge and happiness.[1]

"But what more is needed than what we have at
hand ? It exists already, and you know it well. It is
this phalanx of upright and enlightened men, who are
preparing the way for the future, or who give reality to
the present, men who open a free arena where all that
is good in the opinions of diverse parties may meet on
common ground. And who is she, the noble mother
of so numerous and widespread a family—who, after
the example of Christ, says to all pure and honest

---

[1] "The Good and Beautiful," "Progress," "The Twin-Constellation ;"—to the initiated all these mean liberty and equality in a political,
social, and religious sense, *i e*, a thorough revolution in the existing
state of things.

souls, 'Peace to men of good will!'—who, in a word, is that parent alone able to solve the great problem of the present, and quell the storms which may, perhaps, be in store for ourselves in the womb of the future? You guess who she is, Brethren; you recognise her in the loftiness of her nature and the omnipotence of her strength. Freemasonry is her name!!!! . . . .[1]

"But we must go to the root of the matter. It is not enough to exclaim in a moment of enthusiasm, 'We are strong, we are all-powerful, we cannot fail to conquer!' Let us take good heed as to what we are about. We shall be strong if we are united, powerful if the object we have in view is clearly defined, victorious if the principles that actuate us are fixed and enlightened.

"We must *know*, and I emphasise the word, what it is we really want; and, above all, we must know both what the needs of society are—a knowledge of which can only be obtained by conscientious study of those needs—and what the laws of social economy ought to be — a discovery only to be made by patient and intelligent research. *We must know what we really want!* and, knowing it, our wills must be united, firm, and fearless. Essential to us above all is unity of purpose, a unity that cannot be shaken; for this alone will entitle us to conquer, will ensure us the victory.

[1] The notes of exclamation are to be found in the original document.

"I will sum up all in a word. The motto, I say, which it is incumbent on Freemasons to adopt in the present exigency—one, too, which they would do well to adhere to and follow out in future times, is this—*Know what you want, and want what you know.*

"A few more words in explanation, and I have done. *Know what it is you want.* . . . . This is the indispensable preliminary for the work ; every Mason must undertake it for himself, every Lodge must propose it as the object of its labours.   If we are once set free from the restrictions imposed by Article 135, every Mason will feel that he has a right to take an interest in everything, that it is his duty to inquire into everything, and form a definite opinion, both as a member of the Craft and as a citizen of the State, on all the questions of the day, whether moral or material, social or philosophical " (*i.e.*, political or religious). " In a word, let Freemasonry boldly announce the divine prin-ciple—which is not only a sacred right but a bounden duty, the charter of our public and most cherished prerogatives, sealed with the blood of martyrs " (revolutionary ones)—" I mean liberty of research.   This gives the Mason an infallible guide for the direction of his conduct : *he knows what he wants.*

"And then, in the co-operation of his Brethren, in the mighty organisation of the Craft, in the true and solid unity prevailing there, the Mason will find that strength which concord imparts, whereby alone great things can be achieved. And since he not only hopes, but knows for certain, that he may reckon upon the triumph of those views to which he clings with invincible tenacity, nothing that he can do will be left undone to bring about their speedy realisation. *He will want what he knows.*

"Then let all those come on who hurl anathemas against the Craft" (*i.e.*, the Pope and the Bishops), "let them make ready for the battle; with these deadly foes of man's true welfare" (atheist social-democracy), "who have ever striven to keep the human intelligence in swaddling-bands, the sons of true light will know how to grapple; they will cast them for ever into outer darkness."

Notwithstanding the omission of several passages in the report, we think the speech before us is sufficiently intelligible. It was greeted with immense applause, and the proposal it contains was passed as a resolution; that is, it was resolved to extend to the members of the lower grades a liberty long exercised to a great extent by those of the eighteenth and thirty-eighth grades — liberty to agitate on behalf of religious, social, and political revolution.

II. SPEECH delivered by the Grand ‘Orator, Brother
JULIUS BOURLARD, in the Grand Orient of
Brussels, on occasion of the same festivities.—
(Tracé, &c., pp. 30–38.)

" . . . . My Brethren of the Grand Orient, and
you, my Brethren, who have come hither from all
the Lodges of the country, in order to be present at
the imposing ceremony of to-day, I can readily
imagine how anxious you all are to hear more in
detail the future plan of operations for the Grand
Orient, and I doubt not you will receive full and
satisfactory information respecting the manner in
which every dignitary proposes to co-operate in
carrying out the great task of Freemasonry.

"I will expound to you without reserve the principles by which I am actuated, and the desires I
have most at heart ; laying before you my deepest
convictions with the greatest candour and openness.
My Brethren, who can shut his eyes to the fact that
it is of absolute importance for Freemasonry at this
time to take the field, and put forth all her activity ?
(*qu'il faut que la Maçonnerie soit active, qu'elle soit
militante*). Have not we, a body of thoughtful and
enlightened men,[1] been for years obliged to remain
passive, unable to make practical use of the ideas
which inspire us, unable to carry them out into

---

[1] This disgusting self-laudation is perpetually recurring in the
speeches of Freemasons.

action? compelled to witness the indefinite post-
ponement of those results which both heart and mind
eagerly anticipated? Now the very same day which
sees the question proposed must see it solved; all
must unite with heart and soul in order that Freemasonry may act, that it may execute its designs,
that it may achieve its triumphs. Brethren, I desire
progress in the widest and most comprehensive
sense of the word. I desire intellectual cultivation,
moral perfection. I desire improvement in the
material condition of so many millions of mankind
who are all our brethren, of so many unhappy
beings who dwell with us under the same heaven,
and cultivate with us the same earth. Yes, since
every being upon the earth is a part of the same
universal matter as myself, and contains besides
within him a spark of the great and all-pervading
Spirit, I desire that this divine spark may in each
and all grow and kindle into a vivid flame, that
every created intelligence, from the highest to the
lowest in the social scale, may be elevated and
enlightened, that every heart may throb with a glad
sense of existence; in a word, that man may become
God. (Applause.)

"This is what I understand by intellectual and

---

¹ Who can fail to recognise here that atheistic social-democracy
which is the Mason's ideal? But in order to avert suspicion from
itself, the Craft was cunning enough, in accordance with its habitual
tactics, to accuse the clergy of socialistic schemes, and shameless
enough to speak to a credulous public of a *black* International League.

moral progress. I desire the whole world to know
and confess that there is a moral law which governs
the universe, which is the same in all lands, amongst
all peoples, and that this moral law forms the true
religion of nations. (Renewed applause.)[1]   I desire
that all should learn to pay due respect to the just
man, and that the upright should everywhere attain
to the position of dignity which he deserves to fill.[2]
This is my idea of progress, of moral improvement.
How easily might all this be carried into effect, if
only the opinions, the plans, the institutions of Freemasonry were entrusted with the guidance of national
education.   (Prolonged cheering.)[3]

"Let us pause here, and philosophise for a moment.
Here we will take our rest until we have formed our
judgment and fixed on our resolutions, in order to
be ready for prompt and decisive action when the
fitting moment shall arrive.

"And I would appeal to you, Brethren, and ask
whether, if we are thoroughly penetrated with these
opinions, if they are dear to us as our own lives, we
can for a single moment allow an article in the rules

---

[1] Thus, according to the Craft, all positive and dogmatic religions,
especially Christianity, are altogether false.

[2] Does not this point to a republican form of government as the
only fitting one?

[3] This enables us to comprehend the efforts everywhere made for
the introduction of undenominational instruction, for school inspection as
exclusively confined to the State, for the elimination of any religious
element from teaching, the general secularisation of education, and
the consequent tyranny exercised over parents and children.

of the Grand Orient to stand in our way, or regard
it as an insuperable obstacle to the accomplishment
of those holy and noble desires which inflame our
heart. Can we honestly see in Article 135 a regulation prohibiting, under any circumstances whatever, the introduction of religious or political topics
in our Lodges? Would not this be tantamount to
condemning us to a life of inactivity, subsisting on
theories alone? In such a case our wisest course
would be to shut up our Temples without delay.
What is the meaning of a prohibition to occupy
ourselves with any religious or political problems?
What are these problems? They are the realisation
of our ideal, the carrying into operation and putting
into practice the views and designs of the Craft.
But as soon as we leave theory, and come to facts
and realities, a clause of our rule is thrown in our
teeth; we are indeed free to form opinions on these
subjects, but must on no account presume to act on
our opinions. (Applause.)

" The earnestness of our purpose and the purity of
our intentions are, it is true, admitted on all sides;
but we are told to remain behind the screen, and not
seek to extend the results of our studies and observations beyond it. From the mere statement of a
false position such as this we must inevitably draw
the unalterable conclusion that it is not simply the
right, but also the duty of Freemasonry to occupy
itself with political and religious questions, since by

this means alone can we succeed in putting our theories into practice. (Great applause.)

"And I ask you further, my Brethren, the right of free inquiry being conceded to us, under what conditions is this concession made?

"Liberty of research is permitted us in theory, but at every step they tell us we are interfering in affairs of State, in politics, and in religion; that is to say, in the process of self-aggrandisement, which some people pursue in the name of God, and dignify with the title of religion. And this is termed free inquiry! For my part, I would briefly say to all who would deny me liberty to range at will throughout the whole realm of thought, 'I am a man; everything that concerns humanity concerns me, and is full of interest to me.'

"But, my Brethren, let there be no mistake as to what is, in my opinion, to be understood by this active and continual intervention of Freemasonry in politics and religion. I am far from wishing the Grand Orient to imagine that the quota I shall contribute in my character of Speaker will be to converse daily upon the politics of the hour, and certain current religious topics. On the contrary, we must be most careful to steer clear of everything that is petty or personal. Exciting discussions about the conduct of this man or the other would only bring about that state of things which, of all others, it is our duty most strenuously to endeavour to avoid — dissension and mutual dislikes.

But all the great fundamental principles of politics —everything which refers to the organisation, formation, and life of a State, these are what most prominently concern ourselves ; these come into our special sphere ; these must be duly tested in the crucible of reason and intelligence. (Applause.)

" But if the Ministry should propose to the country a new scheme of popular education, then I would cry out, ' That is a matter for us Freemasons ! The question of education belongs to me ; it is for me to investigate it, for me to discover the solution ! ' (Fresh applause.)

" Were the Ministry to bring before Parliament a bill for the reorganisation of benevolent institutions, I should raise my voice again, and say, ' That is my business as a Freemason ! It is my business to control public charities ! This branch of the administration must not be allowed to pass into unworthy hands, which will abuse it, to the injury of the cause we have constantly at heart. Leave, therefore, the question of organising charity to me ; it must be well weighed, worked out, and put in practice, according to our convictions and the spirit of our Order.' (Prolonged cheers.)

" Furthermore, we are bound to make our voice heard if any Minister puts a false construction on the rules of international hospitality.[1] Should

---

[1] Much more ruthlessly would they desire to see the hospitality of the Belgian soil outraged in the event of its affording a shelter to the members of any of the Religious Orders. In such a case, even an ostensibly Catholic Ministry dares not insist on the maintenance of the territorial rights of his country.

the great principle of fraternity be overstrained, and the hospitality of the Belgian soil be abused, on the plea of considerations which the rights of nations neither warrant nor admit, then rally round me, O Masons! (Universal expressions of assent.)

"And if at last the day comes—a day perhaps not far distant—when the nation itself has to adopt decisions of the most important nature;[1] if, on the eve of a great and momentous crisis—one perhaps already imminent—Belgium is called upon finally to determine what position she will take up, what part she will play, then away with you, all you Masons who would tell me that I am to have nothing to do with politics! I shall myself summon to my side all those who are faithful and devoted to their Order. I shall call on them to cast aside all anxious fears, and proceed with me first to search out, and afterwards publish abroad, what it behoves our dear and glorious country to do, in order to maintain her position at the head of European progress. (Here the speaker was interrupted by prolonged and stormy applause.)

"I must apologise to you, my Brethren, for having allowed myself to be thus carried away by my feelings; but I think this expression of our sentiments must have been a relief to the minds of all. You will forgive me, I am sure, for having perhaps trespassed too long on your kind attention. (No, no.)

[1] It appears that in this passage the speaker reckons on the eventual accession of Belgium to the universal social and democratic republic prophesied for the future.

"With regard to religion, my Brethren, do not imagine that I shall ever bring forward for debate in the Grand Orient, or within the narrower limits of our Temples, either dogmatic questions or scholastic propositions; such, for instance, as the weighty question of Transubstantiation. (Laughter.) Nor shall I take into my own hand the dissecting-knife to investigate these obscure points, to which the severe rule of former times, forbidding interference in religious matters, probably had reference. But if my Lords the Bishops issue pastorals, ostensibly containing Lenten regulations, but really inculcating a deep and cunning policy; if establishments professedly of a religious nature, but in my opinion nothing else than schools of idleness—(expressions of assent)—settle themselves all over the country; if crowds of healthy, vigorous adults take the bread out of the mouths of our poor and consume it in indolence, bread which should be the reward of honest toil ; if these things are so, then, I say, it is high time for us all, and for me especially, to occupy ourselves with religious matters, and with the conventual question ; to grapple with them boldly, and subject them to a careful scrutiny. And the country must take the law into its own hands, employing force if necessary, in order to cleanse itself from this hateful leprosy.[1] Let Freemasonry, therefore, exert untir-

---

[1] This vulgar appeal to the standing army of the Craft, the dregs of the populace. democrats kept in the pay of Freemasons, and stirred up by them at their will, speaks for itself. It is a plan which has, unfor-

ing activity to get rid of these useless converts, these homes of idlers." (Bravo !)

"Even in the middle of the nineteenth century, in the year 1854, we hear of new miracles being noised abroad ; we learn that the Belgian people have a new saint held up to them for venera- tion, a certain St Babola (*sic*), who rises from his grave, and calls on the Belgian nation to pro- cure his canonisation. Is not one tempted in such a case to disbelieve the testimony of one's senses ? However, it is really true, and took place quite recently in my native town of Mons, where the Lodge of Parfaite Union holds its sittings. Yes, new saints do indeed make their appearance day by day, and are, at the very time I speak, receiving from the Jesuits exaggerated honours ; at the same time the nation at large is told to seek the cure of its maladies in the waters of La Salette. Now, then, answer me, ' Is Freemasonry to take part in religious matters, or is she not ? Must we not all unite to sup- press abuses such as these ? '

". . . . And now a word respecting the manner in which we must really desire what we know we have need of. Above all things, we must manifest our desires by conscientious labour within our Lodges, by united study, and by the subsequent employment of legitimate means for the realisation of those principles

tunately, been put into execution only too often. Freemasonry is, how- ever, not afraid of the *idleness*, but of the *activity*, of the Religious Orders ; this is why it hates the Jesuits, whom no one ever accused of idleness.

which are established by common consent. And
I hope the press will not fail to fulfil a part at
least of its mission, by diffusing in a popular form
the truths of Freemasonry. When I see how the
Jesuits invariably erect a printing-press close to
their houses, and set up an office, whence they issue
some mischievous periodical, I say, let us do
likewise. Let us establish side by side with our
Temples this powerful organ—alike legitimate and
constitutional—the press, and make it speak in the
cause of truth, as it has already often spoken in defence of falsehood and deceit. (Boisterous cheering.)

"Finally, how are we to accomplish what we
desire? By means of *action*, namely, by being
under all circumstances ever at our post, ready to
wrestle with our adversaries. Wherever there is
good" (*i.e.*, evil) "to be done, whenever opportunity
for usefulness presents itself, at all times and in
all places, whether in his private or public capacity,
each one of us must ever be the *Freemason.* The
Craft must be represented in all official posts, in
all committees for public charity or poor relief,
everywhere keeping watch, and, if need be, fighting
for the truth."

The conclusion of this speech is unimportant,
and can therefore be omitted.[1] Now it is useless to

---

[1] We would only remark that one of the toasts proposed was
the following —"To the reign of Liberty, Fraternity, and Equality."
See Tracé, &c , p. 42.

allege that it is only in Belgium that the Craft makes such rapid advances.   This opinion is quite an erroneous one.   Its principles are the same everywhere, only in some countries it is necessary to preserve a stricter disguise and closer secresy, leaving all action to the select class which constitutes the core of the Order.   But since in Belgium such circumspection can be dispensed with, on account of the nature of the Constitution, and for another reason we prefer not to mention, Freemasonry may speak out boldly.   The publications of the Belgian Lodges are therefore, of all others, the most important and the most trustworthy.

SUPPORT GIVEN BY FREEMASONRY TO THE INTERNATIONAL LEAGUE.

I. Proposal for a Masonic Workman's Congress.[1] (*Le Monde Maçonnique*, tome viii. p. 9, Mai 1865. *La Patrie de Bruges*, 27 Juin 1865.)

THIS Congress was to have been held at Brussels in August 1865, and was to have consisted of workmen from England, France, Germany, Italy, Belgium, &c.

The Paris Lodge, Temple des Familles, under the direction of Brother Gamier, accepted the following proposal made by Brother Fribourg (a Jew), a member of the Lodge Avenir, and the Paris correspondent of the International Working-Men's Union :—

"Since Freemasonry is an association universal

---

[1] The evident object of this proposal was the extension of the International League, founded in 1864 in London. The first general Congress did not meet until 1866, when it was convened at Geneva, and sat from September 3d to 8th.

in its range, wise and humane in its influences, it
must for the aforesaid reasons encourage, protect,
and endeavour to extend all those praiseworthy
efforts which have for their object the amelioration
of the condition of the working-classes. For this
end, respected Brethren, I have the honour of requesting you kindly to lend me your assistance,
both moral and pecuniary, in furthering the great
work to be carried out ere long in Belgium, namely,
the emancipation of working-men. It is proposed
to hold a Workman's Congress in this town, and
our contributions in money will be needed to defray the expenses unavoidable at such a gathering
as this. The workmen are poor, and it is our duty
to assist them.

" The transactions of this Congress, and the
documents which will then be drawn up, will
doubtless serve in no small measure to increase
that light" (Masonic) " which is to illuminate the
path of social progress. The recent international
treaties have done much to bring nations together
by means of industrial emulation; it remains to
effect their closer union through the noble bond
of a common Fraternity, and the means to accomplish this is by holding vast assemblies of men
from all lands."

This appeal of the Jewish Brother Fribourg was
well received by the Lodges; amongst others, by
those belonging to the Scotch rite, La Ligne Droite,
Les Hospitaliers de St Ouen, Lodge No. 133; and

also by those belonging to the French rite, La Rose du parfait silence, L'Avenir, La Renaissance.

In this way we learn whence the funds at the disposal of the International are supplied, at least in part, and particularly who was expected to defray the expenses of the General Congress, expenses which must necessarily be considerable. At all events, it is curious to observe with what absolute liberty social democracy is allowed to avail itself of the privileges of holding meetings, and of forming Unions, although its efforts are known to be directed to the complete subversion of the existing order of. things. Were a religious body to claim a hundredth part of such liberty, it would most assuredly be proscribed over and over again within the course of a few days.

II. DEMONSTRATION OF FREEMASONRY IN FAVOUR OF THE PARIS COMMUNE. (An article by SAINT-GENEST, which appeared in the *Figaro*, and was copied in *Gautrelet, La Franc-maçonnerie et la Révolution*, Lyon, 1872, p. 618).

IT was on April 26th, 1871, that the leading Lodge of Paris held an extraordinary sitting in the Temple N., in order to make known publicly its espousal of the Communist cause. On the following day a deputation was sent to the members of the Communal Government, when the leader,

Brother Thirifoque, spoke thus :—"Every hope of a peaceful accommodation being now at an end, the Freemasons have consequently determined to plant their banner on the city walls, and if the army does not cease firing, the Grand Orient is prepared to declare war against the Versailles Government." " Citizens ! " he exclaimed, " the Commune is the grandest sight which has ever been presented to the world. It is the modern Temple of Solomon, all Freemasons are pledged to defend it."

At these words Citizen Jules Vallès took off his red sash and handed it to Brother Thirifoque, who wound it round the flagstaff of the colours they were carrying, and the Deputation withdrew after having fired three volleys (of cheers) according to the Scotch and French rite. Two days after, on April 29th, a day ever memorable in the annals of Freemasonry, a procession of Freemasons paraded through the streets of Paris in the following order :—

First, the Rosicrucian Knights (eighteenth grade),
    wearing the azure collar round their necks.
Next the Knights Kadosch (thirtieth grade), who
    wore their scarves, fringed with silver, crossed
    in the form of a cross of St Andrew.
The members of the Royal Arch (thirteenth
    grade).
The Frère Terrible (Novice Master of the Order).
The Princes of Lebanon (twenty-sixth grade).

The Knights of the Brazen Serpent (twenty-fifth grade).

The Venerable Master of the Shining Circle.

The Scotch Grand Master of the Sacred Arch of James VI.

Lastly, the Brothers Felix Pyat, Lefrançais Franckel, Clement Potier.

With theatrical gravity, and an air of assumed importance, they marched to Avenue Friedland, No. 59, where the Grand Orient held another sitting, and dispatched messengers to the Government of Versailles, with the intimation that the firing must immediately be stopped.

Thereupon the procession was again set in motion, with colours flying and drums beating, being followed by an immense rabble, shouting at their heels, "Vive la Commune! Vive le Grand Orient!"

Having arrived at the city walls, the two "Guards"[1] went forward, followed by the members of the Lodges Neuf Sœurs, and the Knights of the Iris; the Almoner of the Lodge, attended by his two acolytes, turns the square towards the East; the Princes of the Tabernacle take up the prescribed positions; before long the azure standards are seen to wave upon the bastions amongst the red flags of the Commune.

Was it possible that the army of Versailles had heard nothing of this would-be imposing demon-

[1] Or *Tilers* (*Thuileurs*); their office is to see that all who enter the Lodge appear as true Masons, and that Candidates come duly prepared.

stration? At least the Brother Almoner had already turned his square towards the East three times, and yet the artillery continued to thunder.

Then the Worshipful Master spoke:—" Since things are thus, let the whole tribe of Mizraim advance, and let the high command be executed without delay!" Amidst universal admiration, the chosen tribe slowly approaches the walls; its leader turns towards the West; Brother Thirifoque grasps his flashing sword with his left hand, and exclaims three times, " I call upon the army of Versailles to lay down its arms immediately! For should a single one of our banners˙be struck, we swear, by the great Architect of the Universe" —— Whilst this unfinished sentence was still hovering on his lips, his square was dashed out of his hand by a mischievous ball; this spread consternation in the ranks of the Freemasons, and the crowd, dumb with terror, hastened back to the Avenue de la Grande Armée.

" Do they still resist?" cries the Worshipful Master. " Then let the Brethren of Kadosch advance."

On seeing the Grade of Kadosch approach the walls, solemn and terrible to behold, the people firmly believed the disastrous war to be at an end, and broke out into enthusiastic shouts; balloons bearing the emblems of Freemasonry were already seen to ascend into the air, in order to announce to the provinces the termination of the struggle, when a perfect shower of bullets drove back the crowd once more.

"Monstrous!" exclaimed the Worshipful Master. "But no matter. If the reactionary party will not give way, the Knights of the Sacred Arch of James VI. shall unfurl their banner in face of the sacrilegious army."

This news spreads the greatest excitement throughout Paris. A reverential silence generally prevails; every one feels that at last a power is approaching which no human force is able to withstand.

The column of the Knights of St James advances slowly towards the bastions, with the great banner of Useda flying. On the summit of the wall they put the points of their swords together on high, and in this way form the great Arch of Steel, while their bands play a triumphal march, and the Brothers Thirifoque and Fabreguette, together with Felix Pyat and Jules Vallès, begin to form the "Chain of Union."[1]

The Brethren of the Grade of Kadosch shout "Hurrah, hurrah!" "Mirra," respond the Knights. Meanwhile murmurs of "Vive la Commune," "Vive le Grand Orient," are heard from the populace.

At the very moment when the Worshipful Master is waving his staff three times as a sign that peace is concluded, behold a shell comes flying down, bursts in the midst of the Steel Arch,

---

[1] The explanation of this expression will be found later on.

and scatters the "Chain of Union" in the wildest disorder.[1]

The *frère terrible*, seized with panic terror, drops his flashing sword, retreats towards the East, drawing with him in his headlong flight the Knights of the Brazen Serpent as well as the Princes of Lebanon, the Brethren of the Shining Circle and of the Kadosch. The consternation is so great, that the Knights of the Sacred Arch of James VI. spring hastily from the rampart, and solemnly declare that the time has come to hold a new sitting. After an hour's deliberation, the announcement is made that a most weighty determination has been arrived at.

In consideration, namely, of the highly perilous position in which France is at present, the Worshipful Master has resolved that the Supreme Grand Councillor of the Sovereign, and absolute Grand Master of the thirty-third grade (according to other reckoning the ninetieth grade), should, in his own most exalted person, ascend the wall; and if *this time* a ball should come near the banner, the Grand-Orient would forthwith condemn M. Thiers to death, as it had done King William six months previously.

Now the people of Paris were to see a sight such as they had never witnessed before. "O spectacle ever to be remembered!" exclaimed a Masonic periodical of that day in grandiloquent bombast.

[1] This is not to be wondered at, as the majority of the members of the Grand Orient of Paris are of Oriental descent.

" O spectacle deserving of eternal admiration ! "
The whole column of the highest grade advanced
in solemn silence through the astonished crowd,
headed by its illustrious and chosen Knight. Having arrived at the foot of the wall, the Worshipful
Master himself kindled the three stars (lights) on
the great gold candlestick, grasped the candlestick
of the East and turned it towards the West. The
column of harmony (band) struck up the Noachite's
march, while envoys were dispatched at full gallop
to announce to the troops of the vanguard that the
banners seen upon the walls were those of the
Supreme Councillor of the Sovereign Grand
Master.

But in the most solemn moment of all, just as
the exalted and chosen Knight took up the golden
hammer and attached it to his blue ribbon, behold a
procession of Religious, who had just been expelled
from their convent hard by, was seen wending its way.
This caused a slight confusion in the ranks of the illustrious children of light. The sight of these followers
of the Christian superstition produced a feeling of
the greatest contempt in the minds of all present.
Many of the Religious even held in their hands a
Crucifix, the very symbol of their superstition and
idolatry ; and to every one who had but a moment
before witnessed the pompous and imposing ceremonies of social democracy, this could not but
appear a challenge on the part of those black robes
who dared thus to promenade past the Brethren of

Kadosch and the Scotch Knights of the Sacred
Arch of James VI.

However, it was feared that serious consequences
might ensue from the justifiable indignation felt by
all lookers-on.   In order to calm the excited crowds,
they were informed that a suitable number of hos-
tages had been selected from the members of this
hateful class of men, and that they should certainly
be put to death the moment the troops of Versailles
dared to set foot in Paris.   "All right, let them go
then!" cried the sovereign people. "Away with you,
birds of night, your day is over for ever!   People
nowadays know too much and see too much for
you!   We want no more of your mysterious doings
and absurd ceremonies!"

While the priests who had been thus loaded with
abuse were forced to pursue their way amid the
curses of the mob, the Column of the Grand Councillor of the thirty-third grade set forth once more
on its triumphal march, preceded by the drummers.
Seven crossed swords formed the Steel Arch.
Brother Thirifoque turned his compasses three times
towards the East, crying, "Absa, Absa, Absa!" the
column of harmony meanwhile playing "The Great
Architect of Nature."   At last the news got wind
that the army of Versailles had declared itself con-
quered, and that a Brother of the Craft, an officer
in the Versailles vanguard, demanded an immediate
parley with the members of the Grand Orient.

The details of what passed in this interview were

not made public, but one thing is certain, that the populace were profoundly moved, and the soldiers greatly astonished to see their officer all at once take up the solemn (Masonic) position while the envoy approached, extending one arm towards the East, and holding in the other the brazen staff. On finding that the members of the Supreme Council of the *Ne plus ultra* degree had set up their standards, a truce was forthwith agreed upon, and "a deputation sent to the President of the Republic."

What went on between the "Brethren" and the sceptical President Thiers? Who can tell? Thus much, however, we know for certain, that all negotiations were fruitless. In vain did the *frère terrible* thrice successively strike his white wand upon the ground; in vain did the Knights Kadosch, looking to the East, form the great Steel Arch above Thiers' head; in vain did the Knights of the Brazen Serpent offer him the golden mallet amid threefold huzzas. After twenty-four hours the fighting recommenced with more fury than ever.

Some may now wonder that common cause was made between the Grand Orient and such men as Jules Vallès and Felix Pyat. Others may feel indignant that, immediately after the murder of two French generals, and on the eve of the burning of the capital, ten thousand Freemasons should declare in Paris that the Commune was the modern Temple of Solomon. To the initiated it has long been no secret that the relationship existing between Free-

S

masonry and social democracy, is as close as that
between a mother and her child. But when posterity
shall be informed that in the middle of the nineteenth century, in the midst of an unbelieving generation, which openly denied God and His Christ,
under the very guns of an enemy in possession of all
the French fortresses, hostilities were all at once
suspended, and the course of a portentous and
calamitous civil war interrupted, because, forsooth,
Brother Thirifoque, accompanied by two Knights
Kadosch, went to offer to M. Thiers' acceptance the
golden mallet of supreme command (in the Craft);
when, I say, this story is told to those who come
after us, it will sound in their ears as a nursery tale,
utterly unworthy of credence.—*Figaro.*

MASONIC FESTIVALS.

(*These accounts will also serve to explain some technical
expressions.*[1])

I. A MASONIC BANQUET AT PROVINS (Dep. Seine-
et-Marne) 1845.—(From the *Franc-maçon*, 1st
Series, p. 121.)

THE banqueting-hall had been recently painted; thus
all was in perfect order, fresh, and attractive, presenting a pleasing and festive appearance. The

[1] It is, however, necessary to remark that the technical terms are
not the same in all grades, nor even in all Lodges.

waiters were active, noiseless, attentive, and well-drilled ; they moved silently and busily around the long plank (table), which had been arranged in the form of a horse-shoe. The net (table-cloth) and the banners (dinner-napkins) were of dazzling whiteness, the unhewn stone (bread) was of the purest wheat, the white sand (salt) and the yellow mortar (pepper) were ground as fine as possible. The shovels (ladles), pickaxes (forks), and trowels (spoons), shone with the brilliancy of the purest silver. The transparent cannons (glasses), which had been cast expressly in a triangular form, and the barrels (bottles) stood in line (were placed) upon a blue ribbon laid in a curve along the whole length of the net (table-cloth), on both sides of the workshop (dining-table). A hundred small candelabra were on the table, each with a star (taper), one being placed opposite to every cover. The swords (knives), tridents (large forks), tiles (plates), and squares (dishes), made a clatter by no means unpleasant. Every guest pushed his bench (chair) and cannon (glass) somewhat nearer to that of his neighbour, in order to enjoy a friendly chat. The red and white powder (wine) gleamed in the hands of the joyous Brethren ; the less powerful powder (water) in those of the officials of the Lodge, whose duty it was to keep a watchful eye on all, to direct the works, to hew the blocks of stone (cut the bread), to hand the other materials (dishes), to see that nothing is wanting at the table, to superintend the distribution of the strong powder (wine), the detonating powder (liqueur), and the white stone (sugar), and finally, to order the customary cannonades or batteries (toasts). Nothing could give a better idea of the arrangements of Freemasonry than this splendid banquet at Provins. The Worshipful Master[1] sat in the midst of the workshop, the two Wardens at the two ends, the Orator at the head of the South Column (the row of guests on the southern side). . . . .

II. MASONIC BANQUETS AND TOASTS. (Clavel[2] " Histoire pittoresque de la Fr. M.," Paris, 1843, p. 38.)

Two festivals are annually kept in the Order, one on Midsummer-day (St John Baptist), and the other on December 27 (St John Evangelist). Both of these festive gatherings are closed by a banquet,

[1] This Worshipful Master was, the same journal informs us (July 1851), the son of Mocquard, formerly private secretary to Napoleon III. Epicurean banquets such as this are intended to serve as baits to the profane (those not yet initiated), and to satisfy such as see in Freemasonry an institution designed to promote conviviality and the enjoyment of life, but are never meant to see its real secrets. To the "liberal" Mason they are, however, wearisome, on account of their elaborate ceremonial.

[2] This author was expelled for ever from the Craft, by command of the Grand Orient of Paris, for having to a certain extent divulged the secrets of the Order in his history. See *Gautrelet, la Fr. M.*, Lyon, 1872, p. 6.

at which all Freemasons, without exception, are expected to be present.

The banqueting-hall must be so roofed in (only accessible to Freemasons) that the rain may not penetrate (none but Masons be present). It is generally decorated with festoons of flowers, on the walls hang the banner of the Lodge, and those of such workshops (Lodges) as have sent deputations to it. The table is arranged in the form of a horse-shoe; the Worshipful (Master of the Lodge) occupies the place of honour in the middle, the Wardens sit at the two ends. All the things on the table are arranged in four parallel lines; in the first, counting from outside, are the plates, in the second the glasses, in the third the bottles, in the fourth the dishes.

The Masonic table has its own phraseology: to chew or spread mortar—to eat; to fire a cannonade— to drink; a battery—toast. Every one is forced to make use of these technical expressions, each *lapsus linguæ* being punished with a discharge of weak powder (a glass of water). The same punishment is inflicted for every fault committed at table; it is the place of the Master of Ceremonies to hand the instrument of punishment to the culprit.

During the feast it is the rule to propose seven toasts. While the healths are being fired (drunk), the masonry (eating) ceases. By command of the Worshipful Master the cannon are loaded (the glasses are filled); obedient to orders, the Brethren rise, and throw their banners (napkins) over the left shoulder. Then the Worshipful Master begins thus—" My Brethren, let us drink the health of our dearly-loved N   . Let us fire a volley, a good volley, a sharp, quick volley. Now, Brethren, your right hand on your sword (knife)! Swords on high! Salute with the sword! Pass the sword to the left hand! The right on the weapon (glass)! Present arms! Take aim (hold before the lips)! Fire (every man drinks)! A good volley (they drink again)! A sharp volley (the glasses are emptied)! Shoulder arms (the glass is held to the right shoulder)! Arms in front! Present arms! One (the glass is brought to the left shoulder)! Two (to the right shoulder)! Three (before the breast)! Arms at rest! One! Two! Three! (At each word of command a movement is made with the glass in the direction of the table, until, at "three," the glasses are deposited on the table with such military precision, that only one sound is audible.[1] The sword in the left hand! Swords on high! Salute! Swords at rest (here the knives are laid down)! Follow me, Brethren (in imitation of the Worshipful Master, the Masons make the sign, fire the battery, and give the plaudits)!"

In giving toasts, it is generally the custom to speak a few words expressive of esteem and good

---

[1] Does not all this remind of little boys playing at drill? This childish ceremonial is unworthy of grown-up men. Though the ritual is simplified in some Lodges (for instance the Belgian), yet, in spite of this, it is puerile enough. And these are the men who mock at the grave and dignified ritual of the Church!

wishes for the Brother whose health is drunk.
Thanks are returned after all toasts, the Master of
the Ceremonies answering for absent or newly-re-
ceived Members. When the health of the reigning
monarch is drunk, the Master of Ceremonies takes
his place between the two Wardens, asks permission
to speak, and returns thanks in the name of his
Sovereign.[1] His speech being ended, he discharges
a battery in the manner described above, and at the
conclusion dashes his glass on the ground, as a sign
that it is never to be made use of on any less solemn
occasion.[2]

The seventh toast marks the close of the banquet.
The arms having been loaded and placed on the
line, the Brethren rise and form a circle; each one
gives to his neighbour on the right and on the left a

[1] At the extraordinary meeting of Masons convened at Mons, in
Belgium, in 1839, the Master of the Ceremonies, in responding to the
health of the King, spoke as follows :—"Your good wishes and
acclamations have reached the throne, and touched the heart of your
Mason-King By his own free will and desire he became a-member
of the Craft, and Masons ever find in him a sympathising friend. He
knows that your principles are those of law and order, and that the
children of light have ever proved the firmest supporters of constitutional monarchy. Be assured, therefore, that the Prince's Lowtons
(or Louvetons, whelps = the sons of Freemasons) will be trained from
their childhood in these principles, and will devote their life to
promote the happiness and prosperity of their country." In sober
truth, do expressions such as these show due respect to the dignity of
the crown ? Do they proceed from hearts devoted to the cause of
monarchy ? See "Tracé de la tenue extraordinaire du 12 j. du 3
mois, 5839," Mons, p 57.

[2] This symbol of a loyalty soon to become extinct may perhaps
bear a directly opposite signification for the fully initiated.

corner of his banner (napkin), and in his turn lays
hold of theirs; thus the "chain of union" is formed
(symbolic of unity).

III. BANQUET IN A LODGE OF WOMEN. (Clavel,
"Histoire Pittoresque," Introduction, p. 33.)

THE banqueting-hall is divided into four climes
(the walls). The East is called Asia; the West,
Europe; the South, Africa; and the North, America.
The table is in the form of a horse-shoe; all other
arrangements are similar to those in the Lodges
of men. The Lady-President or Grand Mistress
is supported by a Grand Master, and sits in the
clime of Asia. The Sister Inspectress, supported
by the Brother Inspector, and the Sister Trea-
suress, supported by the Brother ∴ Treasurer, occupy
severally the two ends of the table; the former
sitting in the clime of America, the latter in that
of Africa. The ladies are not without a phraseology peculiar to themselves. The Temple (Lodge)
is called Eden; the doors, barriers; the register,
ladder; the glasses, lamps; the wine, red oil; the
water, white oil; the bottles and decanters are
termed pitchers. To put oil in the lamps is to fill
the glasses; to extinguish the lamp is to drink the
wine; to hold on high in the five fingers is to carry
the glass to the lips; to "fire!" is to drink.

The sign is to place the hands on the breast

so that the right lies on the left, and the **two** thumbs joining, form a triangle. The word is " Eve," repeated five times.

Healths are drunk much in the same way as in the Lodges of men. The Grand Mistress is presented with the hammer, with which she strikes before giving the words of command.[1] These are immediately communicated to the groups at the different tables by the male and female officials of the Lodge. When the lamps are prepared and placed in a line, and all is made ready, the Grand Mistress speaks in the following terms : — " My Brethren and Sisters! The health I am about to propose to you is that of N . To honour so welcome a toast, let us extinguish our lamps in five blasts! The lamp in the right hand! Extinguish the lamps! The lamp in front! Set the lamp down! One, two, three, four, five!" From " one" to " four" the Grand Mistress and all the assembled guests hold the "lamps" before their breast, at " five" they simultaneously set them down upon the table with considerable noise.

We prefer not to enter upon the consequences which in olden times resulted from the repeated " extinction of lamps" by uncontrolled women in the company of masculine libertines. Catholics will readily understand why many " Children of the Widow " (members of the Craft) can refuse to

[1] To wield the hammer is synonymous with governing the Lodge in the capacity of Master.

believe in the existence of purity in the hearts of
their fellow-men as a thing possible.

IV. OBSEQUIES CELEBRATED BY THE GRAND
   ORIENT OF BRUSSELS ON THE DEATH OF
   BROTHER LEOPOLD OF SAXE-COBURG, KING
   OF THE BELGIANS, 1866.

THE hall is draped with black. In the background
the tapestries are adorned with festoons of white,
with tears and silver fringes.   On the side-walls
are hung shields inscribed with funeral mottoes in
letters of silver.   In the midst stands the catafalque raised on three steps, and guarded on the
right and left by four high dignitaries with their
swords drawn, and the black riband of the *Maitre
élu des Neuf* around their necks. A funeral lamp
is suspended from the ceiling.

   The whole nave of the Temple is dimly lighted ;
the altar, draped with black, stands in the left
corner at the side of the tomb; in the right corner
is a statue of the deceased veiled with black crape.
Before the tomb stands an antique tripod, on
which a lamp is burning; to the right and left
are brasiers, from which clouds of incense and perfumes arise ; on a table are placed a basket filled
with leaves of flowers, a vessel containing wine,
another containing milk, and a third containing
purifying water (in imitation of holy water).

The Grand Master, Brother Van Schon, advances to the altar, where the sacred fire is burning, and speaks as follows:—

"Listen to my words, honoured shade of our distinguished Brother! In the name of all Masons here present, I offer thee water, by means of which Nature is perpetually renewed, and which, in the course of its various transformations, casts off all defilement, thus becoming a fit emblem of purity. I offer thee wine, which the labours of man win from the vine. It is the emblem of strength. I offer thee milk, the first food of mankind. It is the emblem of simplicity.

"Death, like a devouring flame, consuming all things, has caused thee to disappear from our midst; but to destroy thy memory is not within his power. This memory, like these sweet perfumes diffusing themselves in the air, will serve to animate our courage, kindle our zeal, and guide us in the performance of the duties incumbent upon us."

After this a speech from the Grand Orator followed, on the conclusion of which the Grand Master approached the altar, threw incense on it three times, with these words—"As the smoke of this incense rises to heaven, so may the soul of our Brother ascend to its celestial source."[1]

---

[1] It is to be observed that the whole ceremony hinges on the immortality of the Pantheists (the being absorbed into space, and surviving only in the remembrance of posterity). The idea of *personal* immortality is left entirely out of the question.

Returning to the throne, the Grand Master begins
afresh—" My Brethren of the Orient, unite with me
in scattering flowers upon the tomb of our honoured
Brother, as a token of our friendship and an emblem of our grief." The Grand Master and the
Brethren, sitting on the East side, then advance to
the catafalque, and thrice cast upon it a handful of
flower-leaves. The Brother Wardens at the head of
their columns do the same in their turn.

After this offering to the dead, the Most Serene
Grand Master invites all present to stand up in order
of rank, while he pronounces the last farewell to
the departed. He then calls upon the two Wardens
to assist him in closing the tomb. Arrived at the
foot of the catafalque, he strikes with the hammer
three times on the edge of the tomb, saying,
" Farewell! farewell! farewell!"

Then returning to his throne, he thus speaks:—
"My Brethren, stand up all of you in your ranks.
Our venerated Brother Leopold of Saxe-Coburg is
no more! We shall never again behold that distinguished Freemason; but the soul of our beloved
Brother has returned to its celestial source. So let
us hope; let us hope!"

For the closing scene the decorations are changed,
the Lodge being transformed into a temple of immortality, radiant with light. In the centre is a
bust of Leopold of Saxe-Coburg, brilliantly illumi-
nated; around it are allegorical figures holding
out to him crowns and palms of immortality. `In

the background are some scenes, painted by Brother Welbrandt, representing Elysium. Music is heard ; as the last chords die away, the Grand Master exclaims, " Brethren, our hopes are fulfilled ! Our Brother has taken his place amongst the benefactors of humanity; he will eternally shine in the temple of immortality ! "

OATH TAKEN BY THE PAPAL ZOUAVES, PLEDGING THEMSELVES NEVER TO JOIN THE SECRET SOCIETIES.—(Taken in the presence of General Lamoricière, in the Church of St John Lateran).

" I SWEAR to Almighty God, to our Chief Pastor and Holy Father Pope Pius IX., and to his lawful successors, fidelity and obedience. I swear to serve him honourably and faithfully, and even to sacrifice my life in the defence of his illustrious and sacred person, for the maintenance of his sovereignty and his rights. I swear never to belong to any civil or religious sect ; to any secret league or association which directly or indirectly attacks the Roman Catholic religion, and aims at the overthrow of social order. I swear never to join any sect or society which has been condemned by decrees of the Popes of Rome. So help me God and His Holy Gospel, through Jesus Christ our Lord. Amen."

EXTRACT FROM A SPEECH OF THE HOLY FATHER
PIUS IX. (Delivered in the Church called
Delle Stimmate, 1867).

NOTHING in the Papal Allocution of September
25, 1866, aroused the angry hostility of members of
the Craft so strongly as did the following passage,
in which the Holy Father warns the faithful against
the snares of secret societies. But, unmoved by the
war of words, the Supreme Pastor of Christendom
reverted to the same subject in an address delivered
the year after in the Church *Delle Stimmate*, in
Rome. In this speech the following most interesting passage occurs, which we copy from the *Osser-
vatore Romano* :—" O my sons !" said the Pope,
addressing the young men assembled before him,
" consider the dangers which surround you, and cling
closely to the precious treasure of the faith. Evil-
minded men will hold out to you worldly advan-
tages. These you must reject. They will offer you
counsel. Flee from it. They will seek to draw you
after them. Escape out of their hands. How many
there are, who, when in the first bloom of youth, as
you are now, held the faith and practised it, but of
whom, later on, we learn with sorrow that they have
been seduced by evil men, and have fallen into error
and vice ! I myself was personally acquainted with
one who in these days has attained a melancholy
celebrity ; one who, as a young man twenty years
ago, used to talk with me about the state of Chris-

tian perfection and holiness, and seriously thought
of entering a Religious Order. Later on I heard,
to my grief, that he had been led astray by bad
companions, and had been dragged from one abyss
to another, until at length he gained for himself a
European, indeed a world-wide notoriety, and finally
laid his head on the block in expiation of his crimes.
I bid you therefore beware, and keep this warning
ever before your eyes. Pray God to grant you perseverance in all that is good!"

The victim of bad companions and secret societies
to whom the Pope here alludes was the Freemason
Felix Orsini, the originator of the infamous attack
on the life of Napoleon III.

FREEMASONRY AND THE OCCUPATION OF ROME,
SEPT. 20, 1870.

To all acquainted with the real state of affairs,
it has long been no secret that Freemasonry was
closely concerned in the late occupation of Rome
(Sept. 20th). Let us hear more particulars on the
subject. The *Journal de Florence* (*Univers*, Jan.
31, 1873), says—"After the battle of Sedan, our
(Italian) Ministers were for some time undecided
with regard to the occupation of Rome. Most
probably this event would never have taken place
but for a deputation of Freemasons, who obtained
an audience of the Minister Lanza. They handed

him a small slip of paper, on which was written this truly laconic message—*If the Government does not immediately give orders to march on Rome, the revolution will break out in every town of Italy.* Lanza read the paper and examined the signatures; he saw that they were exclusively those of heads of Lodges, and at once he gave General Cadorna orders to march.   The petition was made public, as well as the signatures attached to it, and any one desirous of knowing who the persons were need only consult the *Annuario della Frammas- soneria Italiana.*   From the foregoing, it appears evident to us, and we think all editors of newspapers must share our opinion, that the members of the Craft occupy themselves with something very different to harmless banquets and grotesque ceremonies."

THE END.

PRINTED BY BALLANTYNE AND COMPANY
EDINBURGH AND LONDON

www.ingramcontent.com/pod-product-compliance
Lightning Source LLC
Chambersburg PA
CBHW020603270326
41927CB00005B/159